AN INTRODUCTION TO CHRISTIAN ETHICS

ROGER H. CROOK

Meredith College

PRENTICE HALL, Englewood Cliffs, New Jersey 07632

Library of Congress Cataloging-in-Publication Data

Crook, Roger H.
   An introduction to Christian ethics / Roger H. Crook.
     p. cm.
   Includes bibliograpihcal references.
   ISBN 0-13-479023-5
   1. Christian ethics. I. Title.
BJ1251.C79 1990   89-28746
241--dc20   CIP

Dedicated

to

Mary Ruth Crook

Editorial/production supervision and interior design: Virginia Rubens
Cover design: Wanda Lubelska
Manufacturing buyer: Carol Bystrom

© 1990 by Prentice Hall, Inc.
A Division of Simon & Schuster
Englewood Cliffs, New Jersey 07632

Printed in the United States of America

10 9 8 7 6 5 4 3

ISBN 0-13-479023-5   01

Prentice-Hall International (UK) Limited, *London*
Prentice-Hall of Australia Pty. Limited, *Sydney*
Prentice-Hall Canada Inc., *Toronto*
Prentice-Hall Hispanoamericana, S.A., *Mexico*
Prentice-Hall of India Private Limited, *New Delhi*
Prentice-Hall of Japan, Inc., *Tokyo*
Simon & Schuster Asia Pte. Ltd., *Singapore*
Editora Prentice-Hall do Brasil, Ltda., *Rio de Janeiro*

CONTENTS

iii

PREFACE

This book is designed to be a college level introductory textbook in Christian ethics. This statement indicates three important facts about the work. *First*, it is based upon the Christian faith and is written for people who stand within that faith. The book recognizes as viable options a number of other systems, and indeed because of their significance describes some of them briefly without attempting to assess their strengths and weaknesses. Yet this book is an effort to state a Christian ethic—a Christian method of making moral decisions. It makes certain assumptions which are a proper subject of debate in Christian theological discussion. Those assumptions reflect the theology of Protestant Christianity. While in the field of ethics there is significant mutual influence between Protestant and Catholic thinkers, there are significant differences. At many points, therefore, my own Protestantism is clearly revealed. *Second*, it is an introductory textbook. It is intended to acquaint beginning students both with the field of ethics in general and with varieties of Christian ethical systems, and to assist them in the formulation of an approach which they will find valid for themselves. It is further intended to help them consider from a Christian perspective a wide variety of ethical issues, both personal and social, with which modern men and women must deal. *Third*, it is written for college students, most of whom are between the ages of eighteen and twenty-two, and is designed to help them develop a method of dealing with the thorny moral issues which they face not only while they are students but also for the rest of their lives. It does not therefore assume either the experience or the preparation of graduate students.

The plan of the book is clearly indicated in the chapter titles. The first three chapters introduce the student to the field of ethics and to the variety of approaches to the study of ethics. The next three chapters describe my own method for making ethical decisions. The remainder of the book, chapters seven through fourteen, deal with some of the issues which demand attention today. No attempt is made to draw a line between "personal" and "social" issues because most issues have both personal and social implications. Rather, both the personal and the social elements are considered in the discussion of each issue.

I am deeply indebted to two longtime colleagues at Meredith College, B. H. Cochran and Allen Page, and to a junior colleague, Bob Vance, for continuing discussion and debate on issues, the fruits of which are reflected in much of what I have written. I am further indebted to the students who have taken my course in Christian ethics, and particularly those of the past five years, who have criticized this work in both oral and written form. Finally, I am grateful to Meredith College for having provided the sabbatical during which time the major portion of the actual writing of this book was done.

INTRODUCTION:
TO THE STUDENT

No one can avoid making decisions on ethical issues. Even routine, day by day choices often involve judgments about good and bad, right and wrong. Sometimes the issues are clear and one simply has to decide whether to do the right thing. More often, however, it is not quite so apparent what "the right thing" is and one has to weigh the options, examine the implications, and choose "the better way." The more one's choices affect other people, the more urgent the moral problem becomes. For example:

Students live and work in a setting in which their conduct is regulated by "the rules of the game." Certain expectations about preparation for class, about participation in class, about the writing of papers, and about the taking of tests and examinations demand a self-discipline of them and involve them in a relationship with the subject matter, with their fellow students, and with their instructors. Most students, sometimes for reasons beyond their control and sometimes because of their own neglect, occasionally find themselves in situations where a violation of the rules seems a viable alternative. Will they or will they not try to pass off someone else's work as their own?

Not all teachers curve the grades in a class. Yet in every class the students who do the best work are likely to be given an *A*, most students will receive a *C*, and students whose work is significantly inferior to that of others in the class will get a *D* or an *F*. Whether they like it or not, students are competing with each other. What should one do who becomes aware that a classmate is getting good grades by plagiarizing or by turning in work done by another student or by cheating on tests?

Every student makes decisions about sexual activity. One who believes that intercourse is to be reserved for marriage faces challenges to that conviction over and over again. One who does not insist that intercourse take place exclusively within a marital relationship nevertheless has to make choices about persons and circumstances. Many people, married and single, have to make up their minds what to do about unplanned pregnancies. Many persons have to deal with the unfaithfulness of marital partners. Many persons discover that they are homosexual and have to decide how they will deal with that fact.

The marketplace demands decisions that are surprising not because of their frequency but because of their variety. What should an employer do, for example, when a worker who is paid the minimum wage requests payment in cash rather than by check? The salary is not enough to meet the needs of the employee's family. Payment in cash would make it easy for the employee to get by without reporting the income, and perhaps to get help from welfare. What is the responsibility of the employer for seeing that the needy employee abides by the letter of the law?

Consider another marketplace situation. A department store advertises a low-priced lawn mower. The clerks, however, are instructed that they are not to sell the mower that was advertised but to pressure customers to buy a more expensive one. Can a clerk appropriately urge all prospective customers to buy a more expensive mower, no matter what their needs and no matter whether they can actually afford to pay more?

Students often ask their professors to write recommendations for them as they seek employment or as they try to get into a graduate or professional school. Should the professor be completely honest in the recommendations? If a student did not take seriously the responsibilities of the academic life, should the teacher say so? If a student has been guilty of academic dishonesty, should the teacher report that fact? If the teacher thinks that the student is really not qualified, should the teacher say so?

As knowledge of the natural order increases and as our ability to manipulate that order grows, new moral issues are raised. How can we balance our increasing need for energy with our need for a clean and safe atmosphere? How can we deal with the fact that we now know how to keep people physically alive far beyond the point when life can hold meaning for them? What are the moral implications of genetic screening and *in vitro* conception and surrogate motherhood? What are the moral implications of organ transplants and of the use of artificial organs? What are the bases on which we can decide about the best use of our scanty resources?

These matters are not moral issues only. They are scientific and political and religious and economic issues as well. They are sociological and psychological and philosophical. They are theoretical and practical. They are emotional and rational and volitional. They are, in short, matters in which the whole person is involved. They require value judgments in personal life, in vocations, in social relationships, in politics. Precisely because they involve the whole person, the fundamental issue is that of morality. Morality is not concerned with a limited number of specific matters; it is concerned with every course of action that involves human beings. In this book you are invited to examine this wide range of issues from the perspective of Christian ethics—to ask: In light of my Christian faith and commitment, what is the *right* thing for me to do in the circumstances in which I live?

ONE

THE FIELD OF ETHICS

Modern people tend to think of the natural order as characterized by a high degree of certainty. The very term *order* implies regularity, dependability, and predictability. We assume that there are certain laws of nature which are immutable and to which there are no exceptions. We talk of cause and effect, of predictability, of doing certain things so that we can obtain certain results. We believe that once we have discovered the cause of a disease we can treat it, perhaps cure it, possibly even prevent it. The more we know about genetics the more we can improve plants, animals, and human beings. The more we discover about energy the greater the possibilities of harnessing energy to suit our own purposes.

When we think about the social order, however, we are much less likely to think in terms of certainties. While the disciplines of psychology and sociology, for example, require the use of scientific methods, those methods are necessarily different from those of the physical sciences. Social scientists cannot experiment in the same way that the physical scientists do. The accuracy of their predictions is much more open to question. There are more variables than they know what to do with. Social scientists are acutely aware that dealing with people is radically different from dealing with things.

The natural sciences and the social sciences, however, share a concern for an accurate description of what exists. Both deal with an objective reality. They observe how specific entities act and react, and try to find ways to deal with those actions and reactions. They can describe those entities, compare notes with one another, evaluate the work of their colleagues, and debate conclusions. They create images and discuss the reality represented by them. They describe processes and speculate on why things operate as they do.

We move out of the realm of science when we speak of good and right, of value and duty. Science does not know what to do with value and duty because it can neither describe them nor experiment with them. As a person, the scientist has values and feels obligations. Those values and obligations, however, cannot be subjected to the kind of empirical examination that is employed in the study of physics, chemistry, psychology, or sociology. Much less can the scientist examine the values and the sense of obligation which a fellow scientist has.

Although the methods are different, however, the study of value and duty is no less rigorous a discipline than is the study of the natural or the social sciences. To do good work in the study of ethics one must be well informed, must think carefully, and must be open to additional information and insight. Unfortunately, it is deceptively easy to do poor work in this realm. Because the ethicist does not have the same tools with which to work that the scientist does, and because the work of the ethicist is not subject to the same type of objective verification, one can appear to be thinking logically and critically when in fact such is not the case. A conscientious student learns that there are no quick and easy solutions to the difficult problems of moral judgment.

Most, if not all, studies are oriented to the future. We analyze what has been and what is in order to attain some desired goal. We study the cause of a disease in order to find a cure and ultimately to find a means of prevention. We study soils, seeds, and chemistry in order to provide more adequate food and fiber. We study history to understand how we got to where we are so that we can move into a better future. Certainly some study is not immediately practical; much research is abstract rather than utilitarian. Because human beings care about the future, however, the utilitarian issue is ever present.

The study of ethics is entirely at home with this utilitarian approach. Ethics is not fundamentally concerned with evaluating past actions, assessing guilt or innocence, or attaching blame or credit. It is primarily interested in guidance for decision making. It is concerned with helping people answer the question, "What is the good or right thing for me to do?"

Many different types of questions can and must be asked about any proposed course of action. During the mid-1980s, for example, there was worldwide discussion of the plans of the United States to deploy equipment in outer space which would detect, intercept, and destroy nuclear missiles launched from any place in the world and aimed at this country. Can such a safety net that is 100 percent effective be created? That is a scientific question. Can the United States finance the project? That is an economic question. What would the undertaking of that project do to our relationships with other nations? That is a political question. Would that be the best way to defend our country? That is a military question. Should we do it? That is an ethical question. The answer to the ethical question will take the other questions into account but will go beyond them.

Another development widely debated in the mid-1980s was experimentation with heart transplants using animal hearts instead of human hearts, hearts of brain-dead persons, and mechanical hearts. Many of the same questions were pertinent: Can it be done? At what risk to the patient and anxiety to the family? At what cost in terms of money, personnel, and facilities? With what emotional impact upon the patient and upon the patient's family? What factors are to be considered in deciding who will be the subject of the experiments? Once perfected, can the procedure be made available to everyone who needs one? And finally, the ethical question: Should it be done?

DEFINITIONS

Ethics is a systematic, critical study concerned with the evaluation of human conduct. That evaluation, as has been noted, is oriented toward the future. That is to say, it is concerned with the making of decisions. Its basic question is not, Did I do right? Was my conduct good or bad? To raise the ethical question, of course, is to take the past into account. The valuation of past conduct, however, is not for the purpose of creating a sense of guilt. It is for the purpose of helping make decisions about the future. Its concern is, What am I to do now? Such evaluation requires some standard, some canon by which to measure. The beginning point in the study of ethics, therefore, must be the choice of some worldview, some philosophy of life. Ethics does not stand on its own feet, but rather is based upon a philosophy. The person who decides that something is good must be prepared to answer the question, Why? What makes this good and that bad? Why is this value superior to that one? The answer to the question Why? is determined by one's basic view of life.

Christian ethics is the critical evaluation of human conduct from a Christian perspective. The Christian ethicist stands within the Christian faith and makes Christian assumptions about human nature, about the relationship of human beings to one another, and about their relationship to God. The Christian shares some beliefs with adherents of other religions, and some with nonreligious ethicists. Whether they agree with those ethicists on a particular idea, or whether they reach the same conclusions, is not the issue. The starting point is the issue. The Christian faith defines the motives from which the Christian ethicists act, the generalizations which they may make about value and duty, and the conclusions which they reach about a proposed course of action.

The word *morality* is used freely in discussions of ethics. Indeed, in popular discussion *ethics* and *morals* are often used interchangeably.

There is a distinction, however, that should be maintained. Properly understood, *ethics* has to do with theory, while *morality* has to do with specific actions. The person who accepts Christian ethics as the standard attempts to use that standard to make moral decisions. This distinction, however, is not always maintained either in popular usage or in academic discussion.

SUBJECT MATTER

In the study of ethics, one is concerned with making value judgments. *Value* literally means "worth, importance." We are accustomed to evaluating almost everything in terms of money. We understand that the cost of many things besides materials, labor, and distribution enter into a decision about the price to be placed upon an object. One such factor is the desirability of the object, or the willingness of the public to pay a high price. For many things this factor appears to be the major one. Put in simple terms, the question is, Would you rather have this than money? The issue is therefore one of establishing priorities. If one thing must be sacrificed (or paid) for another, what will you hold on to? In the study of ethics we do not think primarily in terms of money. Yet we are dealing with the question, What is the value of this proposed course of action? The way of answering that question is the subject matter of the study of ethics.

Some thinkers insist that the proper approach to the making of ethical decisions is to begin by determining what is the highest good in life. If that be true, we must look for the one thing for which we would sacrifice everything else. Discovering that, we can understand what will determine our lesser decisions. Everything else will have value in relationship to our movement toward that highest good. In simple terms, the question is, What do you want out of life? Happiness? Power? The approval of someone else? A sense of accomplishment? A sense of being true to yourself? Once we have answered that question we can evaluate things in terms of whether they help us attain our objective or whether they interfere with that attainment. This approach is *teleological;* that is, it is concerned with movement toward an ultimate objective. Duty is derived from value; we ought to do what helps attain the goal.

Other thinkers, however, make duty primary and say that value is derived from duty. The word *duty* refers to an obligation that is based on a relationship or that results from one's station in life. It is closely related to the word *responsibility*, which implies an action prompted by a sense of loyalty to something outside the self. The person who acts from duty acts not in order to attain a goal but because of an inner commitment. The focus is on the motive rather than on the objective. Satisfaction comes from doing one's duty; the good life is the life of response to this inner sense of compulsion. In that sense, value is derived from duty. Such theories are *deontological*; that is, they are concerned with movement from a basic obligation.

Whether Christian ethics is teleological or deontological can be debated. In either event, however, it is concerned with norms or standards. It is not interested simply in describing the patterns of actions of people, or in analyzing their moral beliefs, customs, and practices. That is a function of the social sciences. Those sciences, however, try to avoid making value judgments. They are not in the business of saying that this way of acting is good and that way is bad. The most that they will say is that this way of acting achieves certain results and that way of acting achieves other results. The essence of ethics, however, is the making of value judgments. The nature of ethics is to be prescriptive rather than descriptive. It is to recommend a way of acting either for the achievement of certain desirable goals (teleological) or as a response to certain fundamental relationships (deontological). Like the natural and the social sciences, ethics recognizes the fact that we are not merely individuals; we are individuals in society. The ethicist does not try to impose standards upon an individual or upon a group; rather the ethicist tries to find and to recommend to individuals in society a valid way to make sound decisions about moral issues.

ASSUMPTIONS

In every discipline students are required to make certain assumptions. Whether the discipline be history, biology, mathematics, economics, music, or physics, the study does not proceed in a vacuum. The assumptions of one discipline may well be a proper field of investigation in another. Indeed, within the same discipline there may be debate as to what assumptions are necessary. Agreed upon or not, however, no work proceeds without them.

It has been observed that the study of ethics is based upon a world view and that the world view upon which Christian ethics is based is the Christian faith. This, then, is the first assumption that underlies this particular study of ethics. In every religion there is a distinctive understanding of value and duty, of right and wrong, of good and bad. At many points Christian ethics and the ethics of other religions overlap, and at many points they differ. Nonreligious philosophies have their own understanding of value and duty, of right and wrong, of good and bad. In their conclusions they too have much in common with Christian ethics as well as having much at variance. Within Christianity there are differences both in theology and in ethics. Recognizing all of that, however, the Christian ethicist stands within the Christian faith and draws conclusions from it.

A second assumption underlying this approach to the study of ethics is that there is an orderliness within the universe that is independent of our knowledge of it. This assumption, in fact, is made in all scientific investigation. Patterns are observed and on that basis predictions are made with a high degree of accuracy. The more we know those patterns the more we can use them to our own ends. In this study of Christian ethics the assumption is made that there is a pattern, an orderliness that underlies human relationships. In those relationships, therefore, we can talk about cause and effect, about consistency, and thus about norms. We can make predictions with a reasonable degree of accuracy.

A third assumption is that human beings can know something about that orderliness. We cannot know everything; that is no more possible in the realm of ethical concerns than it is in scientific investigation. An honest scholar in any discipline maintains a spirit of tentativeness about discoveries and about conclusions. Information may be incomplete, data may be misinterpreted, and later discoveries may alter thinking about what is now believed to be true. That tentativeness keeps the scholar going: there is more to be learned. To learn, one must proceed on the basis of what is now known or believed. That is exactly the way that the Christian ethicist is invited to proceed. The quest is for truth which will be the basis for moral decisions. The ethicist can act confidently on the basis of present insight and at the same time be open to new understanding that is yet to come.

A fourth assumption is the freedom of the will. Human beings do in fact make choices and act upon them of their own volition. No one assumes that people are totally free. We live under the restrictions of the natural order and of the social order, some obvious and some not so readily apparent. Within those restrictions, however, we make choices. While we cannot violate the law of gravity, for example, we can use it in a wide variety of ways to accomplish our purposes. While we cannot choose our parents, we can make decisions about how we deal with them. While we cannot choose whether to be sexual beings, we can decide how to deal with our sexuality. We recognize therefore that certain conditions and influences restrict our choices even though they do not determine them. We can talk about why a person is a criminal, for example, and recognize that a poor family setting, bad companions, and personality problems, influence that person. At the same time we recognize those matters as influences, not determinants, and know that the individual makes independent decisions.

The final assumption is the responsibility of the individual. In one sense this responsibility means that having made a decision a person must live with it. The consequences of an action are the logical result of the choice. One is not free to choose an action and to refuse its consequences. Nor can one attribute the results of a choice to some other person or to some other set of circumstances. This responsibility means that a person who chooses is held accountable. One's choices and actions often come under judgment by some external authority. That authority may be as informal as group pressure or it may be as formal as community law. From a Christian perspective, the final authority to which we are accountable is God. At this point the concept of duty becomes involved in Christian ethics. One has a duty to oneself and to the communities of which one is a part. That duty, however, is contingent. The Christian's ultimate duty is to God and moral choices are made in response to God.

ETHICS AND OTHER DISCIPLINES

In the academic disciplines, ethics is one branch of philosophy. Historically, philosophy concerns itself with several major issues: *metaphysics* deals with the ultimate nature of reality; *epistemology* deals with the nature and limits of human knowledge; *logic* deals with the nature and problems of clear and accurate thinking; *aesthetics* deals with the nature of the beautiful and with judgments concerning beauty; and *ethics* deals with value and duty. Most study and writing in the field of ethics, therefore, has been done by philosophers.

While theology and philosophy are different disciplines, there is considerable overlap in their subject matter. One of the more important areas of overlap is that of moral conduct. Christian ethicists are not necessarily philosophers; yet most of them are at least aware of the work of the philosophers, and some of them draw heavily upon that work. By the same token, philosophers are not necessarily Christian. Many stand in other religious traditions and many claim no religious faith. Yet many are aware of the work of Christian ethicists and in one way or another are affected by it.

The social sciences provide a great deal of information which the ethicists use. The focus of ethical thinking is the making of value judgments about human conduct. No human conduct is exclusively private. Whatever is done or even thought in private both reflects social contact and influences future contacts. If valid judgments are to be made about conduct, they cannot be made in the abstract. They cannot be made without an understanding of what happens and of the context within which things happen. Both a personal decision about whether to have an abortion, for example, and a public decision about legislation dealing with abortion require a great deal of information. The judgment is not simply a reporting of information; it is not based upon that information alone; but without information a valid judgment cannot be made.

Like ethics, law is a normative discipline. It speaks of what is required and what is prohibited. In that sense, allegiance to the law is good conduct and violation of the law is bad conduct. The law therefore sets standards and prescribes behavior. The person who obeys the law is good and the one who breaks the law is a criminal. While ethics is not best approached in a legalistic manner, it shares with law the effort to evaluate behavior. And, like law, its basic purpose is not to find someone—either oneself or another person—guilty of violating the standard but to direct individuals toward the living of a good life.

Because law and ethics are both concerned with norms, people sometimes confuse the two. At one time, for example, the law in this country prohibited all abortions except those necessary to the physical health of the mother. A major argument against seeking an abortion, therefore, was the fact that it was illegal. Some physicians affirmed that the only reason they did not perform abortions was that they were against the law. At present that is no longer the case and there are few legal restrictions regulating what is now regarded as a medical procedure. Now that the law has been changed has the moral issue been resolved? Many people believe that abortions are immoral and are seeking new legislation which will again make them illegal. If they have their way and the legislation is passed, will the moral issue be resolved?

PURPOSE

In order to maintain a careful objectivity, and in order to maintain the integrity of their study as an academic discipline, many ethicists stress the fact that they aim at knowledge and not at behavior. John Hospers, for example, says that "ethics is concerned to find the truth about these moral questions, not to try to make us act upon them." Hospers is not indifferent to behavior, and hopes that people who find the truth will act upon it. But, he insists, ethics "is concerned not directly with practice but with finding true statements about what our practices ought to be" (*Human Conduct*, p. 9). Such ethicists may overstate the case. It is probably true of all disciplines, and it is certainly true of ethics, that knowledge is not sought for its own sake; it is sought so that it can be used. No knowledge of goodness, of course, can make one good. To know the good is not necessarily to do the good. Armed with the best information available, one may nevertheless make bad decisions. Knowledge, however, provides one with a necessary tool for action. One learns an approach to decision making in order to make good decisions.

In the pursuit of this objective of learning a method for making right decisions the student encounters serious problems. For one thing, there is no consensus on the nature of good and bad, of right and wrong, of value and duty. At the starting point is the question of whether there are indeed any absolutes. Is it possible to say "always" or "never" about anything? This is, of course, the whole question of objectivity. Is truth simply within the human mind or does it exist independently of human thought and knowledge? Neither philosophers nor theologians agree among themselves as to whether there is objective truth in the moral realm. Those who believe that there is objective truth do not agree among themselves as to its content. They do not agree, therefore, as to whether there are any reliable universal criteria of judgment and they do not agree on what makes something good or right.

Many views that once were generally accepted are now being challenged. No longer is there a consensus on matters of sex morality, including premarital and extramarital relationships, abortion, and homosexuality. Although there was never a time when the standards were universally followed, those who ignored them knew that they were violating the standard. Now the question is not so much whether to violate the standard as whether the standards are valid. The same thing is true on the matter of the use of violence in the achievement of good ends. Until quite recently it was generally agreed that only the state had the right to use violence in that way, and that it was wrong for individuals to do so. Individuals were expected to work within the system to correct what they considered to be unjust. Increasingly, however, people are insisting that violence may be a correct way to bring about change. Thus the mob violence in American cities in the 1960s, it is sometimes suggested, was a regrettable but necessary step in the quest for racial justice. Thus bombings in London and in Belfast are necessary tools in the struggle to drive the British out of Northern Ireland. And thus a private citizen may be morally right in carrying a concealed weapon for self-protection, and in firing it when threatened.

Another difficulty one encounters in the effort to develop a pattern of right conduct is the fact that few problems are simple, clear-cut choices between right and wrong. Most problems which people face are highly complex and one is aware that any decision will bring certain undesirable consequences. The pressure to establish a racial balance in the public schools in the South, for example, was an effort to prevent certain injustices of the past from being perpetuated and to prepare young people for life in an integrated society. At the same time it placed many people in emotionally stressful situations, it created problems of discipline in the schools, and it undermined the neighborhood concept which many people found meaningful. The bussing of children was the most effective way to achieve the goal of desegregation in the schools, but it required many children to take an unduly long ride to reach their school. The quota system in the employment of teachers guaranteed a racial balance but worked a hardship on many individuals and brought emotional stress to children and teachers of both races.

The same difficulty troubles people in the making of certain intensely personal decisions. Suppose that by doing honest work on a test you made a C, while your friend cheated and made an A. Your knowledge of the cheating inevitably will affect your relationship with your friend, even if you say nothing. By the same token, the relationship will be affected if you confront your friend with the fact. Furthermore, your friend's action has a bearing upon the teacher's curve. If it were true that your friend's cheating hurt no one else in the immediate situation, what about the long run? Decisions about conduct, whether on a social issue or on a personal matter, are rarely simple choices between right and wrong.

Convinced about what is an appropriate thing to do in a given situation, we may find ourselves frustrated as we try to do it. Consider for example the efforts of a middle-class family to help some poverty-stricken neighbors. An elderly widow lives in a two-room shack with four grandchildren, the illegitimate sons and daughters of her own daughter. The daughter lives in another city. The widow's only source of income is public welfare. She is too old to work and if she did work there would be no one to care for the children. The shack in which she lives is heated with a wood stove and is a fire trap. The children are ill fed, ill clothed, ill educated, and have inadequate medical care. She frequently asks for help from her middle-class neighbors, playing as much as she can upon their sympathy. In the face of such obvious need, they cannot refuse assistance. Yet by helping they contribute to the perpetuation of the pattern in which the woman is living. The problem is personal and individual: this woman and her grandchildren have immediate and urgent needs which they cannot meet. It is also social: our society has not learned how to deal with poverty. People often respond spontaneously to cries for help, particularly when they feel that the victim is worthy, but they know that such spontaneous response leaves tremendous unmet needs. They deal with the symptoms of a social problem without knowing how to cure the disease. The welfare system is an important effort to meet the needs of the people but it is subject to abuse. We believe that we must provide for the poor in our land—and in our neighborhood—but we are not satisfied with any method that we have devised.

One further difficulty complicates our efforts to make moral decisions. All of us are subject to a variety of influences and we act from mixed motives. No one has only one loyalty: all of us are members of families; we have friends; we are citizens; we belong to social clubs, churches, and political parties. We learn the news from the mass media and we are entertained by the same media. We are pressured by advertisers who want to sell us something and by exhorters who want us to do something. Bombarded on all sides by merchandizers and charities, we find it difficult to look objectively at value and duty.

In spite of all the difficulties, however, in this study we shall try to establish a pattern for making sound moral decisions. A part of our work will be theoretical: we shall try to formulate a system for dealing with the moral issues. We have already made it clear that our system will be developed within the framework of the Christian faith. We shall look briefly at certain non-Christian alternatives, without trying to evaluate them, because we need to understand the basis on which many of our contemporaries operate. But we shall move from them to a Christian approach.

Another part of our work will be practical: we shall attempt to cultivate an uneasy conscience. We shall raise questions about commonly accepted practices. While we cannot deal with all ethical issues, we shall raise questions about a wide variety of personal and social activities. As we deal with them we shall cultivate the practice of raising questions that will invade every realm of life.

TWO

ALTERNATIVES TO CHRISTIAN ETHICS

The making of decisions about relationships with other people is of central concern to Christians. Wishing to make those decisions on the basis of their faith, they look both at personal issues and at social concerns from that perspective.

Christians have no monopoly on ethical concern, however. Adherents of non-Christian religious groups face the same issues of life as do Christians, and they want to deal with them from the perspective of their faith. Many nonreligious persons, facing the same problems, have a powerful concern for issues of morality. They think just as seriously about values and obligations as do religious people and they have just as strong a sense of compulsion as do people of religious faith. We turn therefore to a discussion of some of the most viable alternatives to Christian ethics current in American society. We have not chosen classical philosophical systems, but ways of looking at life that are characteristic of people in our day. The representatives of the systems which we cite are not necessarily formative thinkers. Rather they are people who give clear statements of systems by which many people operate.

HUMANISM

Of all current alternatives to Christian ethics, one of the most important is that offered by humanism. In essence, this approach to moral issues affirms that our basic obligation is to the human race—to humanity. One form of this approach is properly called *secular humanism*. The current careless and even malicious misinterpretation of this phrase should not blind us to the credibility of this philosophy of life. Its emphasis on the centrality of persons and on the possibilities of human achievement commend it to the modern mind and provide for many people a way of making sense of an otherwise morally chaotic world.

Morris B. Storer is an excellent representative of secular humanism. He identifies as humanist those persons who

> have set aside faith in revelation and dogmatic authority (if they ever *had* it), and have settled for human experience and reason as grounds for belief and action, putting human good—the good of self and others in their life on earth—as ultimate criterion of right and wrong, with due concern for other living creatures. (*Humanistic Ethics*, p. 2)

Humanism, therefore, emphasizes the centrality of humankind in the universe. This means both that the human race can control its destiny and that human beings are of supreme value. Humanists do not find any belief in a divine power necessary to explain either the origins of the universe or its operation. They see human beings both as a part of the natural order and as unique in that order. What people do in manipulating that order should be done for the benefit of humankind. Judgments about good and bad, right and wrong, must be made in relationship to their impact upon human beings.

Another secular humanist, Paul Kurtz, characterizes humanism as (1) based primarily upon science, (2) committed to the use of critical intelligence and rational inquiry in understanding the world and solving problems, and (3) an ethical philosophy (*In Defense of Secular Humanism*, pp. 8–9). Since he stresses the scientific approach to all of life, for him the first two characteristics provide the foundation for the ethical philosophy. The humanist, he says, strives "to lead the good life on his own terms and to take destiny in his own hands." He is therefore committed to the defense of individual freedom, to "the right of the individual to make up his own mind, to develop his own conscience, and to lead his own life without undue interference from others." The moral problem—and therefore the great challenge of life—is "to actualize one's talents and satisfy one's needs, while also developing moral awareness and a sense of moral responsibility to others" (p. 9).

Not all humanism, however, is secular. Indeed, the "Humanist Manifesto" issued by leading American humanists in 1933 has a strongly religious note. A humanist understanding of religion, however, is quite different from that of traditional Christians. The seventh item in the Manifesto defines religion as "those actions, purposes, and experiences which are humanly significant." The Manifesto insists that scientific knowledge "makes unacceptable any supernatural or cosmic guarantees of human values" (Item 5). Most of the fifteen items in the Manifesto affirm faith in the scientific method and deny the affirmations of traditional religion. They insist that humankind can and must cope with life without any assistance from the supernatural.

Forty years after the publication of this Manifesto, in October, 1973, more than 275 philosophers, psychologists, and sociologists issued "Humanist Manifesto II." Like the first document, this one gives a good deal of attention to a denial of traditional religious affirmations. It differs significantly from the earlier one, however, in that it is more explicitly secular. Its first affirmation, while acknowledging that "religion may inspire dedication to the highest ethical ideals," continues, "We believe, however, that traditional dogmatic or authoritarian religions that place revelation, God, ritual, or creed above human needs and experiences do a disservice to the human species." It differs from the first also in that it focuses on morality. Its first four affirmations deal with religion; the other thirteen deal with the individual, democratic society, and the world community.

Humanism, then, is committed to a high moral ideal of respect for the person, of individual responsibility, and of the establishment of a social order that operates for the benefit of all people. It has complete faith in the ability of humankind to deal effectively with the personal and social problems which people face by using the same methods that have proved successful in dealing with the natural order.

One matter with which the humanists struggle is that of establishing an adequate basis for their moral concern. While they differ among themselves as to the process by which they reach their conclusions, and as to the proper way to implement their decisions, they seem to agree upon a kind of twentieth-century utilitarianism as the basis for making moral judgments. They think of moral imperatives as focusing on the consequences of one's action. Those moral rules are valid which will lead to the best possible life for all concerned. They do not eliminate self-interest but they recognize that all personal well-being is dependent on an orderliness which makes it possible for all human beings to achieve desired goals.

What are those goals? The humanist assumes that happiness and self-awareness are fundamental human goals and that pain and suffering are never desirable in themselves. The only way that human beings can be assured of a social climate in which they can achieve these fundamental goals is to cooperate with other human beings in their quest. The *sine qua non* for such cooperation is a community in which each person is recognized as deserving respect and in which each person's interests are given equal consideration. Max Hocutt says:

> I think we are obliged…to give consideration to the needs and interests of others—not because doing so is right according to some transcendent standard of morality laid down by some almighty deity, but because doing so cannot be avoided if we wish to pursue our own ends effectively in a world that contains people. ("Toward an Ethic of Mutual Accommodation," in Storer, p. 147)

Humanism, then, focuses upon humankind as central in the universe. Although we are a part of the natural order, it affirms, we are supreme within that order. No supernatural force is in charge of the destiny of the world, no power to which we may or must relate. All that we have to deal with is the natural order. Our most effective way of doing that is to use the scientific method. We human beings are preeminently rational creatures and the scientific method is the tool by which we cope with our environment. Our personal goals cannot be achieved in isolation. Because we exist in community, our goals can be achieved only in community. That community, furthermore, cannot be defined in terms of immediate and direct contact alone. It must include the entire human race. This fact is the ground of all moral obligation. As we deal with our environment we establish rules which move us toward our goals. Those rules are never absolute; they are always subject to change as the circumstances change. All moral values, therefore, are created rather than discovered. They are always relative, always tentative, always to be tested by usefulness.

OBJECTIVISM

A second alternative to Christian ethics is the idea that one's primary obligation is to oneself. From that perspective, the basis for decisions on moral issues is the effect of an action upon oneself. Although this attitude is probably present in all cultures, it is a major characteristic of our society. For most people it is not a carefully worked out system but rather a subconscious disposition. Its most thoughtful and eloquent literary expression is Ayn Rand's philosophy of *objectivism*. Best described in her novels *The Fountainhead* and *Atlas Shrugged*, it is more systematically elaborated in her nonfiction works, *For the New Intellectual, The Virtue of Selfishness*, and *Capitalism: The Unknown Ideal*.

Rand vigorously attacks altruism, which in one way or another is a central element in most traditional ethical systems. She considers it fundamentally evil because it is contrary to human nature. It is totally irrational, she believes, because there is no sound basis to support the sacrifice of one person for another. She calls the doctrine of altruism "moral cannibalism" and "anti-self ethics." Instead of altruism as the fundamental moral obligation, she proposes *selfishness*. She recognizes that in popular thought this word is synonymous with evil, but she stresses the basic meaning of the word: concern with one's own interests. That definition makes no moral evaluation; it merely describes. It is traditional ethics, she says, that has designated such concern as evil and has insisted that a person must renounce self-interest for the sake of other people.

Rand recognizes that her use of the word *selfishness* is unusual. She does not use it to mean immediate responses to irrational desires, emotions, or whims. She means rather a "rational self-interest" which seeks the values necessary for human survival. The ultimate value, she insists, is human life, and our final responsibility is to preserve life. She does not believe that the quest for this value will bring rational people into conflict. She claims that "there is no conflict of interests among men who do not desire the unearned, who do not make sacrifices nor accept them, who deal with one another as *traders*, giving value for value" (*Selfishness*, p. 31). Her basic idea is that "the actor must always be the beneficiary of his action and that man must act for his own *rational* self-interest" (p. x).

Rand does not believe that an action is made right merely by the fact that one chooses to act in a given way. She does not imply that "anything goes," that there is no objectivity to the concepts of right and wrong. Quite the contrary, she insists that people often make wrong choices. One's judgment is not the criterion of right and wrong; it is the means by which one determines one's actions. Rand insists that one must validate one's choices by reference to some principle. She defines ethics, therefore, as the discovery and definition of "a code of values to guide man's choices and actions" (p. x).

For Rand, a value is created whenever a person acts to gain or to keep something. In this sense, the ultimate value is life. One's senses enable one to identify the experiences that threaten life and those that enhance life. One's reason identifies and integrates the material which the senses provide. Reason, therefore, is our basic means of survival; whatever is appropriate to the life of a rational being is the good, and whatever opposes or destroys it is evil (pp. 17–25).

But what of social responsibility? The one such responsibility which Rand recognizes is to live in a way that does not interfere with the well-being of other people. She says that "every human being is an end in himself, not the means to the ends or the welfare of others.... Each person must live for his own sake, neither sacrificing himself to others nor sacrificing others to himself." One additional sentence sums up her perspective. "To live for his own sake means that *the achievement of his own happiness is man's highest moral purpose*" (*Selfishness*, p. 27).

This objectivist philosophy is popularly expressed in the affirmation that "I have to be myself." This implies that each person must be independent of all external controls. One understands one's personhood not in terms of what one has in common with other persons but in terms of one's own unique interests and abilities. The search for self-understanding is the quest for individuality. Rather than looking outward to other individuals to get in touch with them, one looks inward in order to get in touch with oneself.

Traditional society imposes certain external restraints upon people. Certain rules of the game are laid down by the great institutions:

the state, the family, the educational system, religion, business, and industry. Those rules define the good life and point the way toward its achievement. The rules are the same for all, the objectives are the same for all, and the rewards are the same for all. The person who does not play by the rules is a misfit and is subjected to a wide variety of sanctions in the effort to pressure him into conformity. The rules of the game are the major social force.

The reaction against those external restraints began to be apparent on college campuses in the 1960s, particularly in the protest against American involvement in Vietnam. By the 1970s it had spread into all segments of society and was challenging more and more of the commonly accepted values and standards in the area of sexuality, marriage and the family, personal objectives, and national loyalty. It expressed itself in new lifestyles, in liberation movements, and in protest movements. It took on big government and big business in the interest of the rights of the individual. The dominant mood was one of questioning what for so long had been taken for granted.

This reaction was more of a revolution than a reformation. A reformation deals with weaknesses within a structure and seeks to correct them, even when drastic steps must be taken to do so. It does not challenge the validity of the system; it merely seeks to make the system operate properly. A revolution, however, challenges the system itself. It assumes that the system is intrinsically evil and must be replaced by a new one. The very assumptions on which traditional institutions are based are questioned. That seems to have been what has been going on in American society for nearly three decades.

In traditional American society the concept of self-denial has been regarded as fundamental. Christians recognize it as an ideal taught by Jesus. Through the influence of Christianity it has been made an essential element in our way of relating to all social institutions. That ideal, in simple form, insists that we put the interests of other people ahead of our own.

The emphasis on individualism, however, rejects the ideal of self-denial and substitutes for it the insistence that one must do what is right for oneself. That change is based on the conviction that self-denial results in frustration, insecurity, and a wide variety of other negative and life-destroying emotions and attitudes. "I must be true to myself" is therefore the theme of this view of life. "I must be an authentic person, not governed by the attitudes of others, either other individuals or society, but by my own inner nature. I will not stand in judgment over other people, and I will not allow myself to be judged by them. I insist on my freedom to live by my own decisions, and I will not restrict the freedom of other people to do the same thing."

This view of life led to a radical challenge to such things as the traditional status of women, the mores regulating relationships between the sexes, and attitudes toward homosexuality. It led to an increasing unwillingness of people to remain in marriages which had gone sour, to remain on jobs that they did not find personally rewarding, to pursue courses of study in which they were not interested, or to participate in institutional activities which did not seem relevant to the direction their lives were taking.

Objectivism, then, along with its popular expression in individualism, involves a radically different understanding of morality. The locus of authority for one's actions is entirely internal, not any external social structure. One is obligated first of all to oneself; only secondarily is there a sense of duty to anyone else other than the duty to respect that person's freedom and individuality. One's goal is to be an authentic, self-directed person. Because this approach is so intensely personal, the social problems that once claimed the attention of a large segment of society are ignored by all but those who are the victims.

BEHAVIORISM

A third alternative is that way of thinking which conceives of human behavior not as a matter of free choice but as one of conditioning. People do what they do because of social, cultural, and economic circumstances, because of personal history, genetic factors, or some other factor over which the individual has no control. That way of thinking essentially eliminates any consideration of morality. It sees human activity as *reaction* more than *response*.

The best statement of this alternative is that offered by the behavioristic approach to the study of psychology in the work of B. F. Skinner. Skinner eloquently and effectively reaffirmed the concept developed in the early part of this century by J. B. Watson. Watson insisted that the proper study of psychologists was not mental processes but human behavior. Obviously Skinner does not merely repeat Watson; fifty years of scientific investigation cannot be ignored. Skinner, however, does agree with Watson about the basic subject matter for the study of psychology and about the proper approach to that study.

Behaviorism is an understanding of human nature, and as such it has profound implications for the study of ethics. Skinner affirms that all human behavior can be understood in strictly scientific terms. While he recognizes the existence of thoughts, feelings, and sensations, he insists that they are best understood by studying one's genetic and environmental history (*About Behaviorism*, p. 117). A person is "an organism...which has acquired a repertoire of behavior" (p. 167). Because no two persons have the same repertoire, no two will behave in precisely the same way.

Furthermore, each person's repertoire is constantly being altered by changes in the world in which that person lives. Behavior patterns are therefore constantly changing. And in the last resort one's actions are determined by that cumulative history. Skinner says, "A scientific analysis of behavior must, I believe, assume that a person's behavior is controlled by his genetic and environmental histories rather than by the person himself as an initiating, creative agent" (p. 189).

According to Skinner, then, we are not autonomous creatures but ones which respond to the total environment. We are animals—more complex than other animals, with certain abilities that other animals do not possess, with a self-awareness not characteristic of other animals—but animals nevertheless. We can manipulate our environment in a highly effective way and thus affect our way of life. That does not mean, however, that either individually or as a species we are autonomous. We are the product of the culture which humankind has devised (*Beyond Freedom and Dignity*, p. 206). Although every person is unique, each is "merely a stage in a process which began long before he came into existence and will long outlast him" (p. 209). For Skinner, therefore, there is no such thing as freedom in the sense in which most students of human nature conceive it. He insists that human beings are not autonomous; they merely react to their environment. There is no such thing as individual responsibility or achievement. Any improvement in the human situation will result not from the effort to free people from controlling forces but from an alteration of the kinds of control to which people are exposed (p. 43).

With this understanding of human nature, what then is the nature of morality? It is merely action in conformity with the patterns of conduct set by the total environment. One does not make decisions and act as an autonomous person, but merely reacts to the environment in such a way as to be comfortable within it. Society labels certain action as good and certain action as bad, reinforcing the one and punishing the other. Persons accept those labels as rules, learn to live by them, and feel good (or "rewarded") when they do so (*About Behaviorism*, p. 193).

The highest good, according to Skinner, is survival. That becomes the basis upon which moral judgments are made. Whatever promotes survival and well-being, either individually or socially, is good. Skinner does not think of the kind of blind struggle for survival that Darwin talked about, however. Rather he thinks in terms of the possibility of things being put right by explicit design. "The behavior of the individual," he says, "is easily changed by designing new contingencies of reinforcement" (*About Behaviorism*, p. 206).

Skinner does not avoid the thorny question of who is to determine the design. He sees that not as the function of any leader but rather of "the culture as a social environment." He foresees the evolution of a culture in which individuals are not concerned with themselves but with "the future of the culture." No one person, therefore, really intervenes in the process. Persons are simply a part of a slow and even erratic development of an environment in which they live with some degree of personal satisfaction (*About Behaviorism*, p. 206).

In this kind of setting, how do we make decisions on moral issues? Skinner does not discuss this question, nor should he be expected to do so. He is, after all, a psychologist rather than an ethicist. From his perspective, however, the question is a nonsense one. Moral decisions can be made only by autonomous individuals, and the autonomous individual, according to Skinner, is nonexistent. Our choices are hedged in by our personal history; we do not act, we react. As we react, of course, we affect our environment, changing it to provide greater comfort. That change, however, is not decided either by an individual or by divine purpose. "No one steps outside the causal stream. No one really intervenes," says Skinner. Humankind evolves "slowly but erratically" (*About Behaviorism*, p. 206).

Skinner sometimes talks about values and ideals. He always thinks of them, however, as socially determined. He makes free use of such words as *should, must,* and *need.* He raises questions about what is "ethical" in the treatment of people. He talks about the conditions that must be met before a person is subjected to the methods of behavior modification. All of that discussion, however, is shaped by his conviction that such values and ideals are socially determined.

SELF-REALIZATION

Among modern philosophers, except for those committed to linguistic analysis, the most popular approach to the problems of morality is that identified with self-realization. This approach conceives of the highest good in life, and therefore of *the right*, in terms of the harmonious development of the normal capacities of human nature. It is therefore much concerned with an understanding of human nature. Proponents do not identify the philosophy with any religious presuppositions; yet they do not see it as inconsistent with the ethical teachings of any of the great world religions.

Self-realizationists build their system on what they understand a *self* to be. Charles M. Patterson, for example, lists five characteristics of the self: (1) It is both mind and body, which interact with each other. (2) It desires, and that desiring quality makes progress possible. (3) It is social, needing interaction with other selves. (4) It seeks to know, and what it learns then becomes a part of the self. (5) It is moved by ideals. The good life is lived to the extent that all five of these characteristics are incorporated and integrated into a single and harmonious whole (*Moral Standards*, pp. 181–186).

In the same vein, Harold Titus and Morris Keeton list what they call "the unique and distinctive qualities of selfhood": (1) self-consciousness, (2) abstract thought or the power of reflective thinking, (3) ethical discrimination and some freedom of choice, (4) aesthetic appreciation, (5) religious aspiration and commitment, (6) transcendence of particular conditions of time and space, (7) development fulfilled through community living, and (8) unique powers of creativity (*Ethics for Today*, p. 91).

Titus and Keeton believe that in the realm of ethics "the basic moral postulate is the worth of persons." That is right or good, they say, which has value for persons. On that basis they outline certain moral guidelines: (1) Action is right if it leads to physical, intellectual and spiritual development or to a more harmonious personal and social life. (2) The right choice is the selection of the greater or greatest value. (3) The good life depends on the nature of man, as well as on the nature of the world in which man lives. Man must live in harmonious adjustment with the basic structure and processes of the universe or he will court disaster. (4) Man is a being with feelings and emotions that need to be developed and expressed if life is not to be impoverished (pp. 89, 93–95).

Titus and Keeton summarize their approach to decision making by stating four principles by which persons might choose between conflicting values: (1) Seek the greater of two alternative values. (2) Select a value that has worth in itself over one that has instrumental worth only, and a present good over a future one that has no greater intrinsic worth. (3) Choose the more productive of two otherwise equivalent values. (4) Choose the more permanent or lasting values, other things being equal. They follow that statement of principles with a tentative list of human rights which they consider fundamental: (1) health; (2) education; (3) freedom; (4) work and a living wage; (5) security; (6) love and a home; (7) recreation and leisure; (8) a share in controlling the conditions of life; (9) a share in the cultural heritage; and (10) worship (pp. 254, 258–260).

MARXISM

A large portion of the world is dominated by Marxist ideology. That is not to suggest that this ideology has persisted intact from the days of Karl Marx to the present. Marx changed his own thinking on a number of significant points, and since his time his position has been modified by many Marxist philosophers. The basic concepts of modern communism, however, are those which he developed and elaborated.

Karl Marx, born in Germany in 1818 to Jewish parents who had converted to Lutheranism, was educated in philosophy at the Universities of Bonn and Berlin. After completing his university studies, he devoted himself to socialistic journalism. He lived in a revolutionary era and was primarily concerned with economic and social issues. For a time he worked in Germany, until his journal was suppressed by the state censor and he decided to leave the country. After some years in Paris and Brussels, he returned to Germany, only to be expelled in 1849. He spent the rest of his life in London until his death in 1883.

One of the most important elements in Marx's intellectual background is G. W. F. Hegel's concept of *dialectic*. Hegel, an idealist who believed that Absolute Spirit or Mind (God) is the whole of reality, taught that history is the gradual self-realization of God. That self-realization can be known by human beings by virtue of their rational ability. Hegel taught further that in the universe all development takes place by the overcoming of contradictions through a dialectical process. All thinking, he said, is the contrasting of an idea with its opposite, and the uniting of the idea (thesis) and its opposite (antithesis) into one concept (synthesis). Underlying this approach is the assumption that all reality is self-contradictory. Every idea is only partly true, and in its opposing idea there is also some truth. Only when the two opposites are reconciled does one get a glimpse of the higher truth. But since every idea is only partly true, this higher truth itself becomes a thesis, for which there is an antithesis, and the process continues. In political, cultural, or economic terms this means that no pattern is absolute and none can remain unchallenged and unchanged. While Marx criticized Hegel's thought at many points, this concept of *dialectic* remained central in his thinking throughout his life.

With his challenge of Hegel's idealism, Ludwig Feuerbach provided the second major element in Marx's intellectual background. Feuerbach assumed that reality is *material* rather than spiritual. He said that what generated human thought, therefore, is not Spirit (God), but material circumstances. History is not God's struggle for self-realization but humankind's struggle. Concerned with action rather than merely with thought, Marx combined these two concepts into his own brand of *dialectical materialism*.

For Marx, then, philosophy was not an intellectual exercise. It was an effort to understand and to improve human existence. His interests were therefore fundamentally ethical. They reflected the political, economic, and social conditions of nineteenth-century Europe. Marx observed that the industrial revolution, which held so much promise for the improvement of human welfare, rather than freeing the masses of people from poverty had driven them into lives of drudgery, misery, and further poverty in the mines and the factories. He saw the masses of workers as being exploited by a small group of individuals who controlled the capital and the political system. He devoted himself to an effort to free the masses from that oppression.

Marx's view of this struggle can be understood only in terms of his interpretation of history. He considered history to be humankind's efforts to satisfy needs, and described those efforts in terms of four premises. First, history has a materialistic foundation: history begins with our efforts to satisfy our basic needs for food, clothing, and shelter. Second, the satisfaction of those needs gives rise to other needs: we are in a constant process of generating and satisfying needs. Third, we reproduce our lives in our children: the necessary cooperation in the rearing of children introduces the social factor into human history. Fourth, all social expansion is determined by material needs and our way of satisfying those needs.

Marx saw history as falling into five stages: First, there was a primitive communism in which all property was held in common rather than individually. Second, the development of the concept of private property resulted in the aristocratic-slave system. Third, serfs replaced slaves in the military-feudal era. Fourth, the factory system resulted in the rise of capitalism. Finally, the end of the class conflict which characterized stages two, three, and four will come and an era of freedom, equality, and abundance will be instituted when capitalism is destroyed and communism is restored.

Marx considered alienation to be the basic human problem in capitalistic society, and spoke of that alienation in three ways. First, he said that the worker is alienated from himself because he is not seen as a human being but as an instrument whose labor exists "outside himself, and alien to him." That kind of labor reduces the worker to an object. Second, capitalism alienates the worker from the product. The product is in no sense a fulfillment of the person, in no sense related to the worker's well-being, in no sense a self-expression of the worker. Rather it is negative and destructive of the person. Third, capitalism estranges human beings from their own social nature. It requires a specialization which separates them in the production of goods, which makes real cooperation impossible, and which indeed creates the competition which divides people.

This specialization which is a fundamental characteristic of capitalistic society exploits human beings, said Marx. It requires people to work not at tasks that provide an opportunity for self-expression but at tasks dictated by the production process. A person labors not to produce something that is needed, either by the worker or by someone else, but to earn wages. The product belongs not to the worker but to the person who owns the materials and the tools of production. There is no real link between labor and product, between production and consumption. The laborer has no claim upon the product and no voice in controlling the conditions of production. To that extent the worker is not a person but a tool, an instrument for making things for other people.

According to Marx, capitalistic society is dominated by a class struggle between the bourgeoisie, the owning class, and the proletariat, the working class. The bourgeoisie control all natural resources and all means of production, distribution, and exchange. They dominate the political and economic system, and they use those systems to exploit the workers. They dictate standards of conduct which will enable them to maintain themselves in their privileged position, and they resist all efforts to change the structure.

How, then, can justice be done? How can the workers be freed from these oppressive forces? Marx believed that there is no possibility of improving the present structure; the only answer is a revolution which will destroy existing social conditions and create a new order in which there will be no classes. In that new order there will be no conflict between capital and labor because all productive powers will be restored to the whole community. All persons will make their contributions to the life of the community. All persons will be assured of all that they need for the good life. The formula by which society will operate is, "From each according to his ability, to each according to his need."

Marx believed that the coming of this new order was inevitable. There are, he insisted, no stable, permanent structures of reality. History is the process of change which occurs in accordance with the inexorable laws of historical movement—with the dialectical process. Humankind may delay or accelerate the process, but there is no way to stop it. Marx thought that he had discovered the built-in laws of change by which history moves relentlessly from one era to the next. On that basis he predicted the inevitable fall of capitalism and the creation of the qualitatively different social order of communism.

While Marx did not see himself as an ethicist, and while those who have revised his thinking did not develop an ethical system, this philosophy, like all others, has significant moral implications. Those implications are summarized in the moral code adopted by the Communist party of the Soviet Union in 1961. That code included the following principles:

- devotion to the communist cause; love of the socialist motherland and of other socialist countries;
- conscientious labor for the good of society—he who does not work, neither shall he eat;
- concern on the part of everyone for the preservation and growth of public wealth;
- a high degree of public duty; intolerance of actions harmful to the public interest;
- collectivism and comradely mutual assistance; one for all and all for one;
- human relations and mutual respect between individuals—man is to man a friend, comrade and brother;
- honesty and truthfulness, moral purity, modesty, and unpretentiousness in social and private life;

- mutual respect in the family, and concern for the upbringing of children;
- an uncompromising attitude to injustice, parasitism, dishonesty, careerism and money-grubbing;
- friendship and brotherhood among all peoples of the USSR; intolerance of national and racial hatred;
- an uncompromising attitude to the enemies of communism; peace and the freedom of nations;
- fraternal solidarity with the working people of all countries, and with all peoples. (*The Road to Communism*, Documents of the 22nd Congress of the CPSU [Moscow: 1961], pp. 566–567. Cited in Titus and Keeton, p. 212.)

This code does not create a new system but rather reflects commonly accepted communist ideals. As would be expected, it is not based upon any concept of eternal values, any immutable laws, any authority beyond humanity itself. Moral judgment is based solely on human society. Thus the communist's basic moral obligation, public and private, stems from a commitment to communism. All specific judgments are to be based on that commitment. There are, of course, approved patterns of conduct, some of which are not unlike those in other political and economic systems. Yet there are no absolutes, and right conduct is conditioned by circumstances. All actions are to be judged as good or bad in terms of their consequences for the cause of communism.

In the ethic of communism, then, priority is given not to the individual but to the community. It is not individual welfare that is paramount, but the well-being of society as a whole. That is not to suggest that the welfare of the individual is ignored; it is only to say that all individual welfare is derived from group welfare, and is indeed submerged into it. In the final analysis, one's obligation is not to oneself but to the community. This commitment to the well-being of the group explains the concentration of communist ideologists on such matters as the basic living standards of people, the conditions of labor for the working class, and access to education for all people.

The communist ethic is a class ethic. In communist theory, all ethical systems reflect the interests of the ruling class. Because the communist movement is concerned with the interests of the proletariat, true morality is that which serves the cause of that class. Lenin, who founded the Communist party in Russia, who led the 1917 revolution, and who ruled Russia from 1917 until his death in 1924, stated it bluntly:

Our morality is entirely subordinated to the interests of the class struggle of the proletariat....We say: Morality is that which serves to destroy the old exploiting society and to unite all the toilers around the proletariat, which is creating a new communist society—we do not believe in an eternal morality. (Address to the Third Congress of the Russian Young Communist League, cited in Barnette, *An Introduction to Communism*, p. 51)

THREE
ALTERNATIVES WITHIN CHRISTIAN ETHICS

One cannot talk about *the* Christian ethic because there has never been unanimity among Christians on moral judgments. Christians differ on such individual questions as whether honesty is an absolute requirement and on such broad social issues as civil rights. There is no one Christian position on nuclear disarmament, reverse discrimination, abortion, health care, or any other moral issue.

One reason for the lack of unanimity is the difference among Christians on the approach to the making of decisions. On what basis does one determine values? What makes something good or bad, right or wrong? What procedures does one follow in deciding what to do? Several distinctly Christian approaches to the decision-making process can be delineated. One needs to be aware of these alternatives, not only to know that there is variety but also to know how to establish a method which will serve one's own needs. No attempt is made to evaluate or to criticize the systems which are described here. All that is attempted is a careful and accurate presentation of alternatives.

ROMAN CATHOLIC MORAL THEOLOGY

Vatican II was a major turning point for the Roman Catholic church. The significance of the deliberations and decisions of that Second Vatican Council, which met from 1962 until 1965, can hardly be overemphasized because they have brought about some radical changes in the life of the church. One area in which the impact of the Council has been most important is that of Christian ethics.

To understand current trends in Roman Catholic ethical thinking one must understand the approach which dominated the church until Vatican II and to which many Catholic moral theologians still subscribe. (Two excellent examples of the traditional approach are Edwin F. Healey's *Moral Guidance* and Robert H. Dailey's *Introduction to Moral Theology*.) That approach assumes a dualism in which the human spirit is thought of as bound up in the less important (though not evil) body. The salvation of the soul is achieved through a rigorous spiritual discipline in the pursuit of the theological, intellectual, and moral virtues. These virtues, however, can be attained only with the help of God. God's grace, which gives one the necessary strength for Christian living, is mediated by the church through the sacraments. The sacraments, therefore, are indispensable to the good life.

For the person who tries to live a moral life there are two basic sources of guidance. The first is the law, which is clear and precise. The law falls into three categories: (1) Natural law is communicated through the human reason and is available to everyone who will submit to the discipline of careful observation and logical thinking. Its implication is clouded, however, by the fact of human sin. This law, since it was written by God into the natural order, is universal and unchanging. (2) Divine positive law is recorded in sacred Scripture and is available to those who give themselves to the discipline of that revelation. Because it is the law of God, no human power can alter it. (3) Human positive law is made by human beings and includes both civil law and ecclesiastical law. Ecclesiastical law, created by the church to guide its members in making decisions, is an application of the first two types of law to the specifics of time and place. Since it is made by the church it can be changed by the church when appropriate.

The second source of guidance is the conscience. Whereas the law is general, the conscience is individual. Conscience is the judgment which one makes about the moral goodness or badness of a contemplated action. It is the conclusion which one reaches through the reason in the attempt to apply the principles of morality to specific actions. The conscience must be informed by the law, by instruction, by experience, by reason, by worship, and by the inner voice of the Holy Spirit.

In this system three principles must be taken into account in deciding about the morality of a proposed action: (1) *The action itself* must be intrinsically good and not evil. (2) *Circumstances* can change an action which is ordinarily not sinful into a sinful one. (3) *The purpose* which the actor has in mind must be good. An action is moral if all three conditions are satisfied, but immoral if any one of them is not met.

Recognizing that not all issues are clear-cut, and that one often has to make decisions in ambivalent situations, this system makes two significant provisions. The first is the principle of the *twofold effect*. Few actions have single results; most have many consequences. What if one consequence of a contemplated action will be good and another bad? In this situation an action is considered good if the good effect is directly intended, if the action itself is not intrinsically evil, and if the good effect is not produced by means of the evil effect. The second provision is the rule of *probabilism*, which approves actions which reason suggests are right, even though the conclusion is not absolutely certain.

In this traditional approach there is an objectivity in morality which makes possible the determination of whether an action is good or bad, right or wrong. The responsibility of the believer is not so much to *decide* as it is to *discover*. The route which one follows in that discovery is clearly marked and the conclusions which one reaches are, for the most part, valid not only for one making the choice but also for other persons as well. What one finds to be the right thing to do in a given circumstance would be the right thing for anyone in the same situation.

Since Vatican II a number of Catholic moral theologians have taken a new tack. Vatican II did not bring those changes into being; rather it opened the door to a new approach which had already begun to appear. Before the end of the nineteenth century certain German theologians had begun exploring a number of options, and their influence was felt throughout Europe and America in the first half of the twentieth century. In the mid twentieth century Bernard Haring's influence was critical in giving a new direction to Catholic moral theology. His most important work, *The Law of Christ*, first published in 1954, stressed the importance of Scripture for the making of moral decisions and interpreted the moral life as the believer's response to the gracious gift of God in Christ. That approach characterizes the thought of many, though by no means all, post-Vatican II moral theologians. Charles E. Curran, one of those influenced by Haring, contrasts the two approaches by saying that the older places emphasis "on specific acts, and whether or not these acts were mortally or venially sinful," while the new reflects on "the whole life of the Christian including the call to the faithfulness of love and not merely as addressing the minimum of what constitutes sin" (O'Connell, *Principles for a Catholic Morality*, p. x).

Timothy E. O'Connell's work is a good example of this new approach. O'Connell defines moral theology as the attempt to answer the question, "How ought we, who have been gifted by God, to live?" (p. 7). It deals both with the general shape of the Christian life and with questions about specific actions. It raises questions about appropriate behavior in such areas as justice, respect for life, truth telling, property rights, and sexuality. O'Connell uses the framework of the older approach, but at almost every point reaches a different conclusion. Sometimes the difference is merely one of emphasis: he gives a great deal more attention, for example, to the study of biblical teachings than do traditional moral theologians. At other times, however, the difference is more striking: he gives far more attention, for example, to "the moral person" than he does to "the moral act." Again, whereas the older approach began with a discussion of the objective authority and moved to the person, O'Connell begins with the person and discusses the law in light of what it means to be human and what it means to be Christian.

O'Connell's analysis of "the moral person" is central to his approach. While he does not reject Catholic tradition, the emphases which he draws from that tradition move him in a new direction. He discusses what it means to act humanly, emphasizing the freedom of the person. Acknowledging the reality of certain impediments, he nevertheless asserts that a human being exists "in a situation of alternatives that are really there and really available to him or her" (p. 51). Men and women, he says, "have taken charge of themselves." Beneath all their actions is a "fundamental stance" which gives their lives direction (p. 64). Even after one has assumed a basic stance for God, however, one still has to make decisions about sin and virtue. Christians are capable of sinful actions, in other words, just as sinners are capable of good actions.

O'Connell sees the conscience as central in Christian morality. For him conscience is a sense of moral compulsion, a sense of "oughtness." Rather than equating it with a sense of guilt, he identifies it with commitment to values. Although he accepts the authority of the church, he gives that authority an unusual interpretation. He says that in the past Catholics have been taught that when there is conflict between conscience and church authority, they should follow authority. He insists, however, that "this understanding is *not* the authentic tradition of the Catholic Church," and that ultimately one must follow the dictates of conscience (pp. 292–293). Thus, whereas the older approach moved from law to conscience, O'Connell moves from conscience to law. Yet he stresses the need of human beings for instruction and moral leadership from the church. Although the work of the Holy Spirit is not limited to the church, the Holy Spirit is present in it in a unique way. In its quest for truth, the Christian conscience will listen respectfully to the insights of the church (p. 95).

O'Connell believes that the objective validity of moral values is supported by natural law. He differs from the traditional theologians in his understanding of that law, however. He says that although it is knowable, our formulations of it are inadequate, partial, tentative, and therefore subject to change. Yet, as responsible, accountable human beings we must shape our lives by the knowledge that we have.

On the basis of his understanding of natural law, O'Connell tries to work out a "strategy for living," the first step of which is to consider values and norms. He assumes that in the "real world" there are certain values and disvalues that compete with each other: truth and error, knowledge and ignorance, understanding and confusion, harmony and friction, union and alienation, companionship and loneliness, health and sickness, comfort and discomfort, fertility and sterility, possession and losses, beauty and ugliness. Our moral problem lies in the manner in which we deal with them. The general objective of moral judgments is "to do what is right," to do "as much good as possible and as little evil as necessary." Doing good and avoiding evil entail the practice of certain virtues (honesty, justice, chastity, reverence for life, and so on) and the avoidance of certain vices (cruelty, lust, contempt, injustice, and the like). The virtues are usually articulated in certain "normative language": Be honest. Respect life. Give to each his due. Honor your father and mother. These norms teach the Christian way and encourage the Christian life. While they may not tell us what to do in specific crises, they describe the kind of person we ought to be (p. 164).

O'Connell therefore rejects the traditional Catholic view that certain specific actions—such as the violation of the marriage contract, the direct taking of innocent life, and extramarital sexual intercourse—are intrinsically evil. He thinks that while the traditional stand of the church is valid in most cases, no action is evil in itself without regard to circumstances. He also rejects the principle of double effect, by which an action that will have both good and bad consequences is permitted if: (1) the action itself is either good or indifferent, (2) the motive is good, (3) the bad effect is not the means of achieving the good, and (4) there is a proportionate reason for tolerating the evil effect. He says that every human action involves both good and bad effects. It is the predominance of the good that counts, he says, and often we must allow evil to function as a means of achieving the good (pp. 170–171).

According to O'Connell, human law (human positive law) is a helpful but not authoritative guide. Because we are weak and sinful we need the guidance that law gives. But that law is not ultimate in any sense. It is a tool which we use so long as it serves us. When it ceases to meet our need it is properly ignored (pp. 194–195).

O'Connell is aware that he does not make a sharp distinction between Christian ethics and non-Christian ethical systems. Indeed, he says that it is incorrect to speak of a Christian or a Catholic morality as having unique ethical obligations. He thinks of right and wrong in terms of whether an action is helpful or harmful to people. An assertion about the morality of an action, therefore, is not related to the question of whether one is a Christian; it is an assertion that the action under consideration should or should not be performed by anyone. The Bible and the traditions of the church do not offer a unique moral judgment. They simply "reaffirm facts of human experience which have been, or can be, discerned and validated independently." They are accepted by the Christian as a presentation of "the sort of person a Christian should be." The Christian does not approach any moral issue with "any unique and dependable sources." Rather he is encouraged by his Christian resources to make his decisions "with the hope of achieving some reasonable, relative degree of certainty." In the last resort, therefore, "Christian ethics is human ethics, no less and certainly no more" (pp. 201–202).

In one sense, however, says O'Connell, we do have a distinctive Christian ethic. The fact that we are followers of Christ gives us a distinctive view of the meaning of the world. Within the context of this worldview we make concrete moral judgments. What we have, therefore, is a humanistic ethic with Christian foundations. It reflects the intermingling of the divine and the human in the lives we lead. It is "human in its content and its source" and "Christian in its essential meaning-conviction and its existential motivation." Ultimately, according to O'Connell, "the natural law and the law of Christ are one and the same thing" (p. 206).

THE ETHICAL CENTER OF PROTESTANTISM

First published in 1950, Paul Ramsey's *Basic Christian Ethics* defined an approach to Christian ethics which many people consider to be more helpful than any other option. In the introduction to this book Ramsey states his thesis: "The central ethical notion or 'category' in Christian ethics is 'obedient love'—the sort of love the gospels describe as 'love fulfilling the law' and St. Paul designates as 'faith working through love' " (p. xi). This love, according to Ramsey, is not a universal quality known and understood by persons everywhere, like "blueness or fatherhood." It is known only as Christ is known. Ramsey is therefore thoroughly Christocentric. For him, "Analyzing ethical problems from the viewpoint of Christian love simply means that Jesus Christ is the center" (p. xvii).

According to Ramsey, Christian love is rooted in two things. The first is the righteousness of God, by which Ramsey means God's way of dealing with people. In biblical terms, the righteousness of God is essentially the same as *justice*. It is rooted in God's nature and God's activity, not in human nature. It is not what human beings deserve because they are human but what God does for humankind because God is God. The covenant which God has established with humankind is the standard by which human justice is measured. God's righteousness is seen essentially in Jesus' work of redemption. The human response to this redemptive work is called "grateful obedience or obedient gratitude." The meaning of Christian love can therefore be understood only "by decisive reference to the controlling love of Christ" (pp. 5, 21).

The second source of Christian love is the Kingdom of God. Ramsey acknowledges that Jesus' teachings about the Kingdom must be understood in eschatological terms. He observed that Jesus expected that soon God would suddenly and catastrophically bring an end to this present age and inaugurate a new kingdom of righteousness. Jesus' belief in the imminence of that eschatological event gave added urgency to all of his teachings.

The bearing of the eschatological hope on the content of Jesus' ethical teachings varies, says Ramsey. Some maxims are obviously universally valid: "Be not angry, avoid inward lust, decide once and for all time, with singleness of purpose, for some cause allegiance to which will be superior to all other duties and all other goods." Some others, however, such as nonresistance and returning good for evil, seem to suit only an apocalyptic perspective. Regardless of that eschatological factor, however, the ethical teachings remain valid. They are valid in the sense that they work, or in the sense that they solve human problems, or in the sense that they will bring about the Kingdom. Indeed, Jesus did not suggest that these things would result from following his teachings. Rather, he taught a way of life which was the vocation of his disciples. The fact that he assumed the imminence of the Kingdom does not minimize the import of his teachings. Those teachings should be considered on their own merits or demerits alone, and not by reference to the conditions out of which they arose (p. 41).

Ramsey calls the Christian ethic "an ethic without rules." He summarizes Jesus' attitude toward the Law by saying: "A faithful Jew stayed as close as possible to observance of the law even when he had to depart from it. Jesus stayed as close as possible to the fulfillment of human need, no matter how wide of the sabbath law this led him" (p. 56). Ramsey focuses on Jesus' love and respect for persons, particularly for those in need; on the essential inwardness of morality, with an emphasis on motive rather than overt action; on Jesus' summary of the requirements of the Law in the commands to love God supremely and to love one's neighbor as one's self; and on Jesus' "ethic of perfection which transcends any possible legal formulation." He considers Paul to be a sound interpreter of the ethical teachings of Jesus. In a chapter entitled "What the Christian Does Without a Code" he summarizes Paul's view with the statement, "Everything is lawful, everything is permitted which Christian love permits" and "everything is demanded which Christian love requires" (p. 79).

Ramsey sees the Christian life as one of faith rather than one of cultivating virtue. Christian goodness, therefore, is not self-conscious and not an end in itself. It is not even the consequence of the life of faith; it is one of the ways in which the life of faith invariably expresses itself. He sums up the implications of love by saying that it creates and preserves community, that it teaches us to attribute value to persons, and that it works through power systems for justice (pp. 234–248).

The last of those three works of love is the basis for applying the ethic of love to social problems. Ramsey believes that the fact of sin must be taken into account in any effort to deal with social institutions just as it is taken into account in dealing with individual matters. Every social institution is affected by it and no plans for any institution can ignore it. Yet "obedient love" on the one hand and realism about human nature on the other can guide us on what to do in government, in education, and in business and industry. They can help us formulate social policy. The Christian operates within the social structure on the basis of love and tries to bend social policy in the direction that love requires.

SITUATION ETHICS

In the 1960s and the early 1970s, discussion of Christian ethics was dominated by debate on situation ethics. The most eloquent spokesperson for that approach was Joseph Fletcher. In his early writings Fletcher had operated from that perspective, even though he had not defined it in any precise manner. In 1966, however, he described and defended his position in a book entitled *Situation Ethics*. The central affirmation in his "nonsystem," as he called it (p. 11), is that the only ethical absolute is love. "There is only one thing that is always good and right, intrinsically good regardless of context," says Fletcher, "and that one thing is love" (p. 60). "When we say that love is always good," he adds, "what we mean is that whatever is loving in any *particular* situation is good" (p. 61).

Fletcher devotes a great deal of attention to an argument against the legalistic approach which he thinks dominates Christian ethics. The situationism which he espouses finds solutions to specific problems based not on prefabricated rules but on doing the loving thing. He says that the situationist fully respects the traditional ethical maxims and uses them to illuminate his problems. Yet he is always prepared to compromise those maxims or to set them aside in any situation in which love seems better served by doing so (pp. 18, 26).

Fletcher states his presuppositions in terms of four working principles. The first is pragmatism, by which he means that the criterion by which an action is to be judged as right or wrong is love. The second is relativism, by which he means that one cannot use words like *never, perfect, always, complete,* and *absolute.* The third is positivism, by which he means that Christian ethics reasons out what obedience to God's commandment to love requires. The fourth is personalism which, Fletcher says, thinks of people rather than of things. On the basis of these working principles he concludes that the only universal requirement is the commandment to love. All other so-called commandments are at most only *maxims,* never infallible rules. He insists that "for the situationist there are no rules—none at all" (p. 55).

Because love alone is always good, whatever is loving in any situation is good and whatever is unloving is bad. No action is intrinsically good or evil; all actions are good or evil in terms of whether they help or hurt persons. Not even the Ten Commandments can be taken as absolutes; any prohibited action might, in given circumstances, be the right thing to do because it would be helpful to a person. While laws are necessary for community living and are helpful in personal relations, they are always to be ignored when human welfare is better served by ignoring them than by obeying them.

Fletcher believes that one cannot decide in advance of a situation what is the right thing to do. "Love decides then and there," he says (Chapter 8). Every decision-demanding situation is unique, and one cannot know all the facts of any situation until that situation has arrived. One always has the benefit of experience and of the accumulated wisdom of the past. At the same time, however, there is no precedent for any situation. One must decide *in the situation* what is the loving thing to do.

Paul Lehmann, whose *Ethics in a Christian Context* was published in 1963, is very much at home with Fletcher's approach. His book does not have the popular style that Fletcher's does, and it is more carefully reasoned and more detached. Lehmann includes one element which if not missing from Fletcher's thought at least does not play a prominent role in it. He talks about faith in Jesus Christ and about involvement in the Christian community. He defines Christian ethics as "disciplined reflection upon the question and its answer: *What am I, as a believer in Jesus Christ and as a member of his church, to do?*" He says: "Christian ethics is not concerned with *the good*, but with what I, as a believer in Jesus Christ and as a member of his church, am to do. *Christian ethics, in other words, is oriented toward revelation and not toward morality*" (p. 45).

For Lehmann, the concept of koinonia (community) is fundamental. He stresses the idea of the church as the body of Christ and calls the church "the *fellowship-creating* reality of Christ's presence in the world." The fellowship of the church cuts across all barriers and creates a new race of people. The goal of the individual who is a part of this new Christian community is *mature manhood*. "Christian ethics," says Lehmann, "aims, not at morality, but at maturity" (p. 54). It is within the church that one strives for Christian maturity. While the *koinonia* is not the same as the visible church, it is intimately related to it. Thus one makes decisions on the issues of life within the context of the Christian community. In the decision-making process, the Christian is guided by the question, what is God doing in the world? Within that fellowship we learn that what God is doing is relating people to each other.

Lehmann agrees with Fletcher that love is the only absolute. Beyond that, he says, one cannot generalize about Christian behavior. Decisions about conduct must be made within the situation. One major element in that situation, however—even the dominating factor—is one's response to what one perceives to be God's work in the world. For the Christian the basic context of any moral decision is the fact of life within the Christian community. The formative factor for the Christian community is the fact that God is incarnated in it and through it is at work in the world.

EVANGELICAL ETHICS   *Smedes*

A large segment of American Christianity identifies itself as *Evangelical*. Ethicists within that tradition are aware of the impact of situationism and indeed are not totally unaffected by it. For the most part, however, they do not argue with situationism; they simply reject it as an effort to operate without principles and as therefore offering little help to the Christian trying to make moral decisions. They do not regard themselves as legalists, and they do not fit Fletcher's definition of a legalist as one who "enters into every decision-making situation encumbered with a whole apparatus of prefabricated rules and regulations." They see the Christian life as the response of the believer to God. God is therefore the final authority. God does not leave humankind to make decisions without any guidance. The Scripture is the unique and authoritative record of God's self-disclosure, Christians are God's covenant people, and the Holy Spirit guides that people in their effort to live in the world as God's children. On the basis of the truth which God has made known, Christians decide what to do in moral situations.

The work of Lewis B. Smedes is an excellent example of the Evangelical approach. In the introduction to his book, *Mere Morality*, Smedes states the proposition that morality is a basic component of human life. All people have a sense of morality, he says, and there is in fact a consensus on certain fundamental moral judgments. Morality is not to be identified with Christian devotion, or even with religious devotion. It is a matter of universal concern. Yet Smedes states his position in terms that are distinctly Christian—and thus in terms that would not be accepted by all people. He says that morality "has to do with what God expects of all people, regardless of whether they believe in him." One is not exempt from God's moral demands, he says, simply because one does not believe in God. Those demands can be understood by any reasonable person who will try to understand them. Morality, therefore, is not sectarian; it is human and ecumenical. It is obligatory, not just upon Christians, but upon all persons (p. vii).

Smedes begins with the assumption that the Bible is authoritative on matters of morality. He focuses on the Decalogue as capsuling the substance of the moral duty of all people. He says that the Law which Jesus fulfilled was the Law of the Ten Commandments, and that the modern

Christian is under obligation to find out what those commandments say about the will of God for today (pp. 4–5). While he does not think that God's moral will is spoken only through the commandments, he does think that there it is spoken "most urgently and clearly" (p. 50).

Smedes makes a distinction between "direct commands" and "abiding laws." Direct commands were given to specific individuals in specific circumstances and did not incorporate universal truth. God's command to Abraham to sacrifice Isaac, for example, he says, certainly cannot be translated into a general obligation. Abiding laws, however, although given to specific people at specific times, are properly translated into universals. The "Thou shalts" of the Decalogue clearly can be translated into "Everyone ought." But how do we know which command falls into which category? Smedes says that the abiding laws "fit life's design," or are appropriate to human life as God has planned it, that they embody an abiding law of human life, that they tell us to do what we already know we should do, and that they are indicators of the kind of life that the Christian lives (pp. 7–10).

Smedes stresses the importance of both justice and love. He defines justice as respect for the rights of another, and love as caring for what one needs in order to function as a member of the community. He does not identify the two, speaking as if they were simply two terms for the same thing. Neither does he separate them, speaking as if the one could exist without the other. Rather he speaks of them as inseparably connected. Assuming that the Decalogue is an authentic, abiding commandment from God, he concentrates on the question of how people today can obey them. He does not try to assess whether a person who has violated a law has sinned, but rather tries to show how the commandment can guide one in making decisions about what to do. Rarely does he take an absolutist stand and say, It is *never* right to do so and so. But he does say that there must be compelling reasons to make an exception to any rule. On the question of abortion, for example, he acknowledges the difficulty of determining just when a fetus becomes a person, and he acknowledges that the mother as well as the fetus must be considered in any abortion decision (p. 144). He concludes, therefore, somewhat reluctantly, that laws forbidding abortions are not good laws (pp. 144–145).

Smedes takes this approach to each commandment. He sees all of them as speaking authoritatively to modern people, as giving sound guidance for the good life. He concedes that for any commandment there can be exceptions. He focuses not on the exception, however, but on the directive. He believes that the requirements of the Commandments are fundamental, not merely for Christian living but for a meaningful life for all people. They are valid because they tell us how God has ordered human existence.

The first word in the title of each of Smedes's chapters on the Commandments is *respect*. In Smedes's approach this concept of respect is vital. While he does not define the term, he uses it to convey the idea that in each commandment there is an assumption which people must acknowledge and to which, indeed, they must be true. It is not to be debated; it is to be understood. Once understood, it is to be lived out. It does not give specific directions for all problems; it does provide the framework within which one can make decisions on those problems. Individual decisions within that framework may vary; the individual, however, is not free to abandon the framework. One's freedom must be exercised within the guidelines of the commandment. While the Commandments do not tell us everything we need to know in making decisions, they tell us the most important kinds of things we ought to do. While we can get help from reason and from intuition, we are to test everything by the teachings of the Scripture (pp. 239–240).

THEOCENTRIC ETHICS   *Gustafson*

A final alternative within Christian ethics which we shall discuss is the concept of theocentric ethics. James Gustafson, perhaps the most influential thinker in the field of Christian ethics during the past decade, has produced a number of volumes in which he has developed this approach. His most comprehensive statement is his two-volume work, *Ethics from a Theocentric Perspective*, published in 1981 (Volume I) and 1984 (Volume II).

Gustafson believes that both Christian and philosophical ethicists base their work upon an unacceptable assumption: the idea that everything that happens in the universe takes place for the sake of humankind, that humankind is the central reference point for all that exists. He finds that assumption both in the Roman Catholic natural law concept and in the Protestant idea of Providential intervention. Beginning at an entirely different point, he draws a radically different conclusion about the basis upon which moral judgments should be made. He asserts that God's concern extends beyond humankind to the whole of creation, and that "we are to conduct life so as to relate to all things in a manner appropriate to their relations to God." Rather than being sovereign over the created order, humankind is an integral part of that order. Our purposes and our conduct must be evaluated not simply on the basis of what is good for humankind but on the basis of God's purposes for the whole of creation (Vol. I, p. 113).

No one, of course, can claim a final and comprehensive knowledge of God's will. Gustafson recognizes that all claims about God's purposes are both tentative and risky. He acknowledges the priority of human experience in decision making, and he recognizes the deeply social character of such experience. He asserts, however, that the experience of "the Other," which for him is the context of moral decision making, has certain characteristics common to all the historic religious communities and traditions. He designates three such elements as: (1) a sense of a powerful Other, (2) piety, or "an attitude of reverence, awe, and respect which implies a sense of devotion and of duties and responsibilities as well," and (3) a belief that all human activity must be ordered properly in relation to the purposes of God (p. 340).

Discussing the relationship of humankind to God and to the world, Gustafson deals with the traditional theological concepts of human nature, the fall, and redemption. On that theological foundation he describes his theocentric ethic. He attempts to establish a perspective in which "we come to some certitude (but not always certainty) about what God is enabling and requiring, and about the appropriate relations of ourselves and all things to God." Such discernment, he says, begins with an awareness of the facts, a judgment as to which facts are morally relevant, and an understanding of what the possibilities are. Although such discernment is reflective and rational, it is more than that; it is "an informed intuition." After the exercise of human reason there comes a "final moment of perception that sees the parts in relation to a whole, expresses sensibilities as well as reasoning, and is made in the conditions of human finitude" (p. 339).

In what sense is this approach theocentric? Where is the element of divine governance? Gustafson does not believe that the will of God is revealed in moral details in the Scripture, because what the Scripture teaches is historically conditioned. What one discerns through it are the fundamental requirements for individual, interpersonal, and social life. General and formal in character, these requirements provide the basis for individual moral decision.

If moral decision is individual, however, is not ethics completely relativistic? Gustafson insists that this is not the case. Certain actions and certain relationships are always wrong, he says. Certain absolute prohibitions set the outer limits of moral conduct, and leave to the individual the resolution of specific issues. Gustafson illustrates by saying that slavery and murder are always wrong because they violate respect for persons. Yet we have to grapple with the question of how to deal with political and economic systems which dictate the conditions of life for masses of people (pp. 163–164). Within this context we are responsible for avoiding moral evil insofar as possible. We cannot do so totally, however, for many of the "good" choices we make will involve evil. A war may be just, for example, but the suffering and death it brings is no less evil. Although an abortion may be justified, a potential human being is destroyed. Economic stringencies may be necessary to a nation, but that does not ease the deprivation and suffering of the poor. The persistence of evil does not lessen our responsibility to strive for the good (pp. 340–342).

A theocentric perspective requires a reordering of values and ethical concepts. The basic moral question is, "What is God enabling and requiring us to be and to do?" To ask this question is to recognize that our ultimate responsibility is "to relate ourselves and all things in a manner (or in ways) appropriate to their relations to God" (Vol. II, p. 2). The chief emphases of theocentric ethics, therefore, are: (1) Humankind is not central in creation. (2) Human life and the rest of creation are interdependent. (3) Rather than standing in judgment over natural impulses and desires, moral thinking directs them. (4) Piety is the natural response to the experience of the ultimate power. (5) Everything must be described within the context of the larger whole. (6) A concern for the common good is essential. (7) Theocentric ethics requires an awareness of the moral ambiguity in life, and consequently an awareness of the deeply tragic character of particular choices. (8) A strong emphasis is placed on self-denial and sometimes even self-sacrifice (Vol. II, 4–29). Gustafson argues that the basic point for moral thinking is "the interpretation of God and God's relations to the world, including human beings." He develops his own thought around the central idea that human beings are not spectators of the life process and not proprietors of it, but participants in it. Humankind is a part of the larger whole (Vol. II, p. 144).

FOUR

SOURCES OF GUIDANCE

The choice between right and wrong sometimes seems so clear-cut that no decision appears necessary. No one would say, for example, that cheating on a test is morally right. In desperation, some people cheat, knowing that it is wrong but saying to themselves, "There's nothing else I can do." Others do it as a matter of course, with no concern for the moral issue at all. Knowing that they can get by with it, they simply do what they can to raise their grades. Yet they do not regard cheating as morally right; they simply ignore moral considerations. The same sort of thing might be said about murder, theft, or adultery. In extreme circumstances even a person with strong convictions might succumb to temptation and resort to any one of them. One without such convictions might kill or steal or commit adultery much more casually. In any case the performing of such actions does not mean that one thinks that they are right, but that other factors override moral judgments.

From a moral perspective, therefore, some judgments are easily made, because the right action is quite apparent. One simply has to choose whether to act morally or immorally. Having chosen and acted, one lives with the consequences. In the aftermath of an immoral action one may be repentant, defiant, scornful, sorry for having been caught, embarrassed, or relieved that the offense has not been detected. In the aftermath of a moral action one may be happy, self-satisfied, pleased with social approval, or assured of God's approval. In either event, one's thinking about right and wrong has not been challenged.

Most decision making, however, is much more complicated. *Cheating,* for example, is not a clearly defined term. What one student—or one instructor—considers plagiarism another student or instructor might consider the proper use of source material. *Murder* is defined as one person deliberately taking the life of another. Does that include euthanasia? Abortion? Capital punishment? Warfare? To *steal* is to take someone else's property without that person's consent. Does that include charging a high price for a scarce object? Does it suggest anything about how much one may pay for a meal on an expense account? Does it have anything to do with taking credit for ideas learned from someone else? The difficult task of decision making is found in areas where choices are not clearly indicated, where lines are not sharply drawn, where both choices are bad or where both choices are good, or where all alternatives have a mixture of good and bad in them.

In such difficult situations, how is the Christian to decide? It is not enough to say that one must decide for oneself. That is a truism that simply reaffirms the idea that a choice must be made. Of course if I face a problem I am the one who must act. Of course, therefore, I have to decide what to do. But can I prepare for making decisions? Is there a basis upon which I can operate? Is there help for me as I struggle with the decision? Are there guidelines by which I can make moral judgments?

As we have seen, there is no consensus either among philosophers or among theologians on how one goes about making decisions, on whether there are guidelines, and if there are, what those guidelines are. Some Christian ethical systems, as we have seen, structure an approach around the goal to be attained, assuming that certain desirable objectives dictate actions. In one way or another, these systems suggest that if we act in a given way we move in the direction of our objective, usually spoken of in such terms as the Kingdom of God, or universal peace, or the growth of the church, or the welfare of humankind. Other systems, as we have seen, structure an approach around a sense of duty or of obligation, assuming that there are general principles of conduct which are rooted in the character of God and in the nature of God's creation. These systems focus more on motive than on result. Still other Christian systems focus on Christian morality as the response of an individual to God in Christ. While there has been no disposition to argue the merits and demerits of any particular system which we have described, the reader should know that the latter approach is the one taken in this book. Although there is influence from ethicists who take other approaches, the basic stance of this writer is that Christian morality is decision and action within the context of a faith relationship with Christ.

That faith relationship is not amorphous. It does not ask that one make decisions without any wisdom from the past, without any teachings, without any reference to other circumstances. No human experience is a *de novo* matter. No choice is made without a precedent; no one is cut off from the broader human communities, including the community of faith. While each person is unique, each also has a history, an environment, and a future. For this reason, the basic doctrines of the Christian faith, and our own interpretation of those doctrines, shape our thinking on moral issues. At this point, therefore, we turn our attention to those sources of guidance available to us for the making of moral decisions.

THE BIBLE

Because the Bible is basic to the life of the church it is also basic to a Christian approach to the making of decisions on moral issues. A fundamental principle of Protestant Christianity, as a matter of fact, is the authority of the Scripture in matters of faith and practice. Many Christians agree with the affirmation in the Westminster Confession of Faith that the Scripture is "given by inspiration of God, to be the rule of faith and life," and that its authority "dependeth not upon the testimony of any man or church, but wholly upon God (who is truth itself), the author thereof."

Christians are not agreed, however, on what is meant by "given by inspiration of God." Some believe that the very words of the Bible were given by God to the writers, and that the words of the Bible are therefore the words of God. Others say that the ideas came from God but that the people wrote them in their own way. Still others think that the Bible reports humankind's best thinking about God. Although the idea of _infallibility_ is debated in some circles, most people who take the Bible seriously do not use that term. They accept the authority of the Bible because they believe that in some way the people who wrote it were acting under the inspiration of God. Yet they think of God, not the Bible, as the final authority. How we understand the Bible to have been inspired determines how we interpret it and how we attempt to apply its teachings to daily life. While this is not the place to debate the theories of inspiration and of biblical authority, the understanding of the Bible which forms the background of this study needs to be stated.

An important tenet of the Christian faith is the conviction that God works in history and that God's character and purpose are revealed in that working. God is known by what God does. Although there are problems with such particularity, the doctrine affirms that in a unique way God chose the Hebrew people and worked through them, that the history of that people is therefore God's self-disclosure, and that this self-disclosure reached its climax in the person of Jesus. As the only record of that history, the Bible is a unique source for the knowledge of God. The Old Testament was written by people who participated in the unique encounter of the Hebrew people with God. The New Testament was written by people whose encounter with God was shaped by the person of Jesus Christ. Through what those people wrote God continues to speak.

This encounter with God in history is a dynamic reality, not a static one. God is not an object to be seen and described, as one might describe a building or another human being. God acts; God takes the initiative to reach out to people; God moves upon individuals and upon communities of people. God speaks not in words but in action.

How then is the Bible related to what God says? In what sense is it "the Word of God"? There are two important ways in which the Bible is understood to be the word of God. First, a word is a message which conveys a specific idea. The Bible is the word of God in the sense that it catches up the insight of those persons who participated in the encounter with God in those historical events. What they wrote conveys definite ideas to the reader. Those ideas have to do with what God has done in the world, with God's purposes for people, and with God's will for the manner in which people relate to one another. Thus we have in the Bible more than a report of what certain individuals have thought and written. We have a report of God's self-disclosure. We have something that transcends the time and circumstance in which it was written. That does not absolutize the words of the Bible, nor the historical statements of fact, nor the specific formulation of laws. It recognizes the cultural conditioning of the documents. It acknowledges the tendency of people to invoke divine sanction upon what is merely social custom. Behind these recognitions of cultural conditioning, however, is the conviction that God spoke, that God was made known to people in a disclosure of truth and meaning that transcends time. What the Bible teaches, therefore, is taken seriously as a guide for life in the modern world.

Second, a word is a means of effecting an encounter between persons. To say that the Bible is the word of God is thus to say that it is a means by which people are confronted by God. A common term for this idea is that the Living Word comes through the written word. Through the Scripture one meets God and is required to decide how to respond. The truth of the Bible is not so much in the accuracy of its statements as in the reality of the encounter with God which it produces. Revelation is not something that long ago was made known to the writers of the Bible but that today is made known to persons who read the Bible.

What use, then, does Christian ethics make of the Bible? How are biblical teachings applied to contemporary issues? A negative statement must be made at the outset. We cannot go to the Bible to look up answers to all ethical questions. If we could do that there would be no need for decision making; the decisions would be already specified and we would have only to follow the outlined procedures. As a matter of fact, however, the manner in which the Bible treats some issues (warfare, the status of women, the attitude toward people of other ethnic groups) creates rather than solves moral problems for us. In addition, the Bible does not discuss many ethical issues which modern people face: abortion, organ transplants, nuclear energy, environmental pollution, genetic engineering, behavior modification, and so on. We cannot there-fore find in the Bible predetermined, clear-cut directives for all problems of contemporary living.

The abandonment of this simplistic approach, however, does not mean the abandonment of the Bible. Rather it means that the proper use of the Bible is a demanding undertaking. It requires the careful and honest use of the best methods of biblical interpretation. It requires the best of critical thinking about the circumstances of our life. And it requires imagination and intuition to apply ancient truths to present issues.

Thus far we have avoided the use of the word *authority* in relation to the Bible because in popular usage it has a legalistic connotation. It conveys the impression that something is commanded, and that what is commanded is obligatory upon people. It is closely related to the idea of "the will of God" which is right for people to follow and wrong for people to ignore. Authority suggests that there is a power which com-pels, with which there is no give and take, from which there is no escape. It suggests that the actions of people are regulated and regimented. The God of such authority is feared but not loved, obeyed but not trusted. The subject of such authority is neither free nor responsive, but subser-vient. The best that such a person can hope for is to escape the notice of such immutable Power.

That description, of course, is a caricature. The root meaning of the word *authority* is "one who is an author" or "an originator" or "a source." It is derived from a Greek term which means "from one's own being." An authoritative declaration, therefore, comes from one who is the source, one with the power to originate. In this sense, authority is characteristic only of God, and it is not appropriate to speak of the Bible as authoritative. Whatever else may be said about the place of the Bible in Christian life and thought, it cannot be a substitute for God.

In practical terms, however, most Christians accept the authority of the Bible because they believe that God in some way inspired the writers. That acceptance is a personal decision. The Bible is authoritative only for those who acknowledge its authority. It is authoritative for them to the extent that they see it as a means of encountering the living God. It is authoritative for them to the extent that they believe that God speaks to them through it. For them it is not enough to say "the Bible says," as if that were the last word. For them the authority is in the God who speaks through the Bible *to those who will hear*.

THE CHRISTIAN COMMUNITY

Because Christians do not exist in isolation from other Christians, the church plays a vital role in their making of moral decisions. The commu-nity of faith is the context within which one comes to know Christ and to live as his disciple. As members of the church, Christians face moral issues and the church helps to shape their moral judgments. That fact does not negate individual responsibility or imply that within the church there is a consensus on all moral issues. It does mean that the church provides invaluable resources which we may use in the making of sound moral decisions.

The Nature of the Church

The word *church* is derived from the Greek *kuriakon* which means "of or belonging to the Lord." That name, therefore implies that the reality with which we are dealing does not belong to the persons who are a part of it. It is of divine origin, not human, and ultimately its destiny is not in the hands of people but of God. Whatever form of government a particular church might take, that church is ultimately responsible to God. Its obligation is to learn what is right and good, and to make decisions on the basis of what it learns. The church is the instrument of God's continuing self-revelation and of redemption for the world.

For this reason, Paul's picture of the church as the body of Christ (1 Corinthians 12:4–31, Ephesians 4:11–16) is significant. The term suggests that the church is a continuation of the incarnation. It is through a body that one acts—relates, accomplishes, and expresses oneself. It is difficult, if not impossible, for us to conceive of a person without a body. The body is how one lives in the world. When Paul called the church the body of Christ he was saying that through the church Christ lives in the world.

Another term which Paul used for the church was *the temple of God.* When he wrote to the Corinthian Christians about their divisiveness he asked, "Do you not know that you are God's temple, and that God's Spirit dwells in you?" (1 Corinthians 3:16). A temple, for the Hebrew people as well as for others in the ancient world, was the place where God dwelt. Although the Hebrews believed that God was everywhere present, they believed that in a special and unique sense God resided in the Holy of Holies. Paul was therefore saying to the Corinthians that they, the church in Corinth, were where God lived.

The idea of a covenant community was part of Paul's spiritual heritage. Having been reared Jewish, and having been educated as a rabbi, he had believed that God had chosen the Hebrew people, and that through Abraham God had established a covenant relationship with them. The covenant phrase, "I shall be your God and you shall be my people," was engraved on the minds and hearts of the Hebrews. According to their faith, they lived in that relationship by the grace of God. In his letter to the Galatians and in his letter to the Romans, Paul insisted that the covenant relationship was continued with the disciples of Jesus. Those disciples, said Paul, were the new Israel, the new people of God. To be a

Christian was to be a part of that new covenant community, to learn from it, to be sustained by it, and to be faithful to it.

A term often used to refer to the church is *koinonia*. This Greek word stresses the idea of community, of fellowship, of unity, and of belonging together. Early in the book of Acts that idea is emphasized in the description of the life of the disciples, when it is said that they "had all things in common" (Acts 2:42, 4:32–34). Paul often spoke of the body needing all its parts, and his strongest criticisms of the Corinthian Christians were for their actions which divided and disrupted the fellowship. His strongest praise for them was for their actions which demonstrated their love and care for one another. This unity of the church is not something which exists for its own sake and it is not something which people create. Rather it is created by the common commitment of believers to Christ. It is the unity into which they enter when they become disciples. Individuals may violate it or respect it, disrupt it or maintain it, ignore it or treasure it. But it does not draw its reality from them; it draws its reality from God in Christ.

The reality of this *koinonia* overrides the differences between the churches. There are historic reasons for the origins of the denominations, and there are both organizational and theological concerns that sustain them. Because of these differences some Christians have difficulty in worshipping with other Christians, in communicating with them, and in cooperating with them in the mission of the church. Yet most Christians have a feel for the *koinonia* which cuts across differences, and they do not allow denominational divisions to stand as barriers to fellowship. They share a common Scripture, their heritages overlap with each other, their worship influences each other, and they recognize a common concern for what is happening in the world.

The Function of the Church

Religion is basically the response of people to the God who created and sustains the universe and who is the source of life. The appropriate response is a spirit of awe, reverence, praise, and gratitude. All else in a person's religious experience grows out of that. The basic function of the church, therefore, is to worship. When the community gathers for that purpose it provides some structure through which the believers may express this spirit. The structure itself is not of major significance but the reverent encounter of the worshipers with God is. From a Christian perspective, to separate moral responsibility from this experience is to deprive morality of its foundations.

A second function of the church is to teach. The relationship of this function to morality is obvious. At the heart of the teaching work of the church is the Scripture. The early church produced the New Testament as a means of sharing the faith with people who were not Christian and of instructing Christians in the content and the implications of their faith. The books of the New Testament were written to specific groups in specific circumstances, and the content of the books was determined in part by the needs of the groups to which they were addressed. The truth of the Gospel and its application to the fundamental issues of life which are reported in the New Testament have been used by the church from the beginning to the present. Although the church has taken many forms, although there has always been theological ferment, and although the problems of human existence have been expressed in many different ways, the church has used the Bible in the instruction of the faithful because it has found that it speaks to the human condition.

The teaching of the church, however, is not limited to instruction in the content of the Scripture. The church looks at the world in light of the Scripture. It makes judgments about the life of the world in both personal and social matters. It speaks what it understands to be the purposes of God for the world. In some groups the teaching takes the form of authoritarian pronouncements; in others it takes the form of recommendations. In some judgments the church is quite traditional and supportive of accepted ways of life; in others it challenges the commonly accepted stance of society and of government. Some judgments have been verified by history and some have been shown to have been incorrect. But always the church has taken seriously its responsibility to instruct its followers on matters of morality.

A third function of the church is to prompt the believer into action. No other agency is committed in quite the same way to making us ask questions about accepted practices. No other agency elicits quite the same fervor for righting wrongs, for building good relationships, for accepting personal responsibility. No other agency is quite so concerned about what is *good* except in a selfish sense, about what is *right* except in a legal sense. While much of the teaching of the church is indoctrination, much also is stimulation. The believer is made to examine moral issues and is helped to make moral judgments. Even when the moral judgment reaffirms a traditional view it does so on the basis of a sensitive conscience, and when it challenges a traditional view it does so within the commitment of the community of faith.

The Christian in the Church

Everything that we have said about the nature and the function of the church is related to the concept of community. As community, the church is a major part of the total context within which the individual makes decisions on moral issues. Because the church helps to define our environment, it plays a major role in establishing the conditions under which we think, feel, and act. This means that we make decisions both with careful attention to the teaching of the church and with careful attention to the impact of the decision upon the life of the church.

All of this presupposes that we share in the life of the church. That sharing is not simply an organizational matter, although it is difficult to understand how one can share without some such involvement. Elton Trueblood once said, "You cannot be a member of *the Church* unless you are sharing actively in the life of *a church*" (*Foundations for Reconstruction*, p. 53). We are not talking about the church in organizational terms; as a fellowship of believers, the church existed before it was organized. Jesus said, "Where two or three are gathered in my name, there am I in the midst of them" (Matthew 8:20). Community with one another and with Christ is the reality of the church. Organization is merely the means of achieving certain results, of doing certain things effectively. It is necessary but it is not the essence of the church. With that understanding, we may reaffirm the idea that Christian moral decisions are made within the context of involvement in the life of the church. That involvement is actual rather than formal. It is a matter of relationships—of feeling, of attitude, of personal identity. It is the acceptance of the reality that what happens to one happens to all, that what one does affects all. It is what is conveyed by Paul's exhortation to the Roman Christians, "Rejoice with those who rejoice, weep with those who weep" (Romans 12:15).

To come to God in Christ, then, is to enter into a fellowship with all other people who have had the same experience. There is no option, no possibility of doing the one but not the other. As there can be no such thing as a string with only one end or a coin with only one side, so there can be no such thing as relating to God without relating to God's other children. In practical terms, this means that we cannot be Christian in isolation. We learn from one another, we discern the will of God together, we make decisions in relationship with one another, we act together. This does not mean that within the church there is no room for differences. It does not mean that the majority rules, that whatever conclusion the group reaches is right. Indeed, some of the most profound insights have come from persons who rejected the judgment of the group. It does mean, however, that the individual believer lives within the fellowship, is taught by the fellowship, is prompted into action by the fellowship, and acts with concern for the fellowship.

PERSONAL JUDGMENT

When we speak of the Scripture and of the church, we deal with things external to the individual. Although they are open to discussion and interpretation, both are objective realities. Personal judgment, however, is subjective and thus is more difficult to deal with. Here we are concerned with something that cannot be argued. Just as beauty is in the eye of the beholder, so judgment is in the mind of the judge. That is not to say that there is no objective reality to a judgment, no good or bad, no right or wrong. It is only to say that no one can argue with me when I say, "This is what I think." They can question whether my thinking is sound; they cannot question whether I think it. Here the responsibility falls ultimately upon the individual. We shall here consider three factors involved in the making of personal judgments: the sense of the leadership of the Holy Spirit, the use of the human reason, and the prompting of the conscience.

The Leadership of the Spirit

The New Testament is full of references to the working of the Holy Spirit, and for Christians that work is vital to the process of decision making. The chief function of the Spirit, reflected both in the New Testament and in the continuing experience of the church, is that of teaching. That means not the imparting of information but the prompting of a person or of a group of believers to move in a specific direction. Such teaching is the development of the conviction that "We ought to do this," or "We ought not to do that." It is the giving of insight, the creating of a sense of concern, the renewing of hope, the providing of inner resources for doing what needs to be done. It is the assurance of God's presence with the person or with the church and the evoking of a sense of reverence and awe.

Some Christians accept the idea of the leadership of the Spirit as the final authority. Many people who have difficult decisions to make pray for such leadership and often have a sense of assurance that their prayer is answered. For some the idea of the leadership of the Spirit is so closely related to daily activities that it is commonplace for them to speak of "being led" in the routine decisions of daily life. Historically, the Quakers have given primacy to the *inner Light* as God's word to them. While most Christians do not speak quite so freely of divine leadership, however, the idea is implicit in the concept of prayer. Prayer is communion with God in such a way that our spirits are opened up before God so that God can speak to us through the Bible, through the church, through other people, and through the workings of our own mind. This openness enables us to receive insight from God, a perspective on life, an understanding of what has happened and is happening, so that we say, "God has done this," or "God is moving me in this direction." While we do not attribute to God's purposes everything that happens, we recognize God's working in our lives in all circumstances and we avail ourselves of God's grace as we deal with the issues of life.

The leadership of the Spirit, then, does not usually come in the form of clear and explicit instructions for dealing with a specific problem. It comes more often in an encounter of a person with Person. By such an encounter one can move beyond preoccupation with self and into concern for neighbor. One's character and personality may be changed by a continuing encounter with the Divine Presence. That change will be reflected in deliberation on difficult decisions and in action in difficult circumstances.

The leadership of the Spirit, therefore, is not an occasional matter, a "first aid" experience to which we resort when we are in trouble. It is a cumulative matter, one incorporated in all of our worship, both private and corporate. Certainly there are times when we are uncertain about the best course of action, and when we are therefore more aware of our need for help. In such times we are most likely to ask for guidance and may be more responsive to God's presence. Yet unless we are always sensitive to God's presence, we are not likely to recognize divine leadership in emergency situations. As we store up our understandings of the will of God, our feelings of *oughtness*, our experiences in which we feel good about what has happened—as we operate with an awareness of God's presence,—we are responding to the leadership of the Spirit.

Many Christians think of the leadership of the Spirit in purely personal and individualistic terms. They think of God dealing with one person, so that what that one person is led to do might be quite different from what another might be led to do. While it is true that God speaks to individuals, and that individuals respond to God, no one exists in isolation from a community. Our experience with the Spirit of God comes therefore within the context of the community of faith. We come to faith through the church, read the Scripture as a part of the church, and worship as a part of it. By the same token the Spirit leads us within the context of the church. Under the influence of the Spirit we may speak to that community of faith, but by the same token we will listen to it. The Spirit may work through us to change the direction that the church is taking; the Spirit may also work through the church to change the direction that we are taking. To be led by the Spirit, in other words, is to share in the life of the community of faith.

To stress this community aspect of the leadership of the Spirit is not to minimize individual responsibility. Of course every person has to decide for himself or herself, because there is no such thing as a group mind or a group will. The identity of a group depends, in part at least, upon the individuals who make it up. But stress on the community aspect of the leadership of the Spirit does mean that God's work in the world is not spasmodic or chaotic and that God does not lead people to ignore each other. Life in the Spirit is a life of an awareness of the presence of God, a life of fellowship with other believers, and a life of common commitment to the truth that unites people under the presence of God.

Human Reason

A second factor in the making of personal judgments is the use of the ability to reason. In most discussions of human nature it is assumed that this ability is the most distinctive human characteristic. Philosophical speculation, at least, always assumes that reason has the final word. The Christian ethical systems which we have discussed assume the possibility of the mind getting in touch with reality. Even when they talk about humankind being created in the image of God, they approach the subject in rational as well as mystical terms.

Faith and reason are not incompatible. It is not correct to assume that philosophical systems are based on logic and religious systems on faith. Philosophers make assumptions, accepting the validity of certain concepts which they have not demonstrated to be true. Theologians attempt to state their faith in a logical, intelligible fashion. Both philosophers and theologians, therefore, operate on the basis of a faith and employ the best logic they can command. Both faith and reason are functions essential to our coming to grips with life.

Neither are faith and reason two supplementary ways of arriving at truth. A popular approach is to suggest that we go as far as we can through the rational method and then allow faith to take up where reason leaves off. As neat as that package is, it does no justice either to faith or to reason. It implies that the two ask the same kinds of questions, that both seek factual information. It implies further that as the knowledge gained by the scientific method increases, the realm of the unknown diminishes and therefore the realm of faith diminishes. If this were true, we could expect that someday the need for faith would disappear completely. The fact of the matter is that a person who tries to come to grips with reality operates at the same time on the basis of both faith and reason. It is not a matter of using now the one and now the other; it is a matter of using the two at the same time. Just as the organs of one's body all function at the same time while the individual lives and works, so faith and reason function at the same time while the individual deals with meaning in life.

Thus it is not correct to say that we learn one thing by reason and another by faith. It is not correct to say that we accept by faith what we cannot understand. It is not correct to say that one thing is subject to rational examination but another is not. It is not correct to say that by faith we accept without question a divine edict, nor is it correct to say that by reason we have the right to say no to God. In Christian ethics faith and reason combine in our effort to understand our place in the universe, to understand human obligation, and to respond to the Divine in the making of decisions.

Reason is therefore a necessary faculty for the making of moral decisions. The reason is finite and limited; it is corrupted by sin; it is not the sole criterion for truth; it is not God. Yet like other human faculties it is a gift of God, a part of human nature, and therefore a vital part of the decision-making process. It serves as a critic of our attitudes, a restraint upon our emotions, an evaluator of our mystical experiences. It analyzes and reflects upon our personal encounters and our religious experiences and helps us relate them to the rest of life. As a sound theology uses reason to give coherence to religious experience and conviction, so a sound ethic uses reason to give coherent expression to a sense of value and duty.

To put this in more simple terms, reason is not the ultimate criterion of value and duty. That is the place of God. But reason is a God-given tool which is necessary to the making of sound decisions. Reason operates at its best when it is illuminated by faith; faith gives reason the impetus to search for meaning. Faith needs reason for its quest for truth. Reason functions as the instrument of faith.

The Conscience

The conscience is a third factor involved in the process of making personal judgments. The nature of conscience, and therefore its reliability as a guide, is an open question. The root of the word, *science*, means "knowledge." The prefix *con-* means "together" or "jointly" or "thoroughly." In this word the prefix intensifies the basic meaning. *Conscience*, therefore, literally means "a thorough knowledge." The term refers either to a sense of the moral goodness or blameworthiness of one's actions, or to a feeling of compulsion to do what one judges to be good or right. It is a powerful feeling that "I should have done this" or "I should not have done that," or "I ought to do this" or "I ought not to do that."

The fact of conscience seems to be universal. All people have feelings of guilt about certain actions and feelings of rightness about others, feelings of compulsion to act in a given way and feelings of aversion to acting in another way. There is, of course, no universal agreement on the content of the conscience. There is no action that all people agree is right and no action that all people agree is wrong. The content of conscience varies from one culture to another and, within a given culture, from one individual to another. The disagreement, however, is not on whether one ought to act morally but on what that moral way is. The sense of compulsion is there and the sense of aversion is there. The only difference lies in what is compelled and what is prohibited.

The force of conscience is extremely powerful. Not always is it recognized, for it may operate through the subconscious. Not always is it rational, for one's mental processes often lead to different conclusions from the ones dictated by conscience. Yet it speaks in an authoritative voice, its dictates seem final, and the person who violates its demands suffers remorse.

The content of the conscience is learned in the same way that other attitudes are learned. The formal institutions of the home, the school, and the church are major factors in the moral education of children and young people. The peer group is more important in the process than most of us are willing to admit. The experiences we have in all of our social contacts make their impact. Two important facts about the content of the conscience emerge from this understanding of where it comes from. First, the consciences of individuals vary because their cultural settings vary. And second, a person's conscience is never permanently fixed but is constantly changing.

If the conscience is so unreliable, then does it have any significance in the process of decision making for the Christian? The conscience is like any other human faculty: it can be used or abused. It can be given direction or it can be allowed to take its content from all sources without discrimination. Conscience can best be understood as a call to wholeness. In terms of morality this means that conscience is the pull of the right and the good, and an aversion to the wrong and the bad. It will be a valuable guide for the Christian to the extent that it matures through faith. The Christian can evaluate the conscience through the gathering of information, the study of the Scripture, the sharing of the life of the *koinonia*, and the worship of God.

In *Conscience and Caring* (68–75), Geoffrey Peterson has discussed six characteristics of a mature Christian conscience. First, he says, the Christian conscience is liberated by God's acceptance and forgiveness which has been made humanly visible and tangible in Jesus Christ. No longer is the Christian devastated by a sense of guilt and fear of rejection. Second, the conscience is shaped and developed by sharing in the Christian community of faith, the chief social influence in the life of the believer. Although that community is the *koinonia* rather than the institution, the two are in fact closely related to each other. Third, the Christian conscience is continually growing. New experiences within the *koinonia* and within society at large bring new information, new insight, and new sensitivity. Fourth, conscience is an integration of all of the various levels and facets of one's being. Rational and emotional factors are integrated with each other, and judgments about the past are integrated with decisions for the future. Fifth, the mature conscience calls us to care about our neighbor. Although caring can be interpreted simply as liking, or having sympathy for, or wanting to help, it means more than that here. It means the actual acceptance of another person into a warm personal relationship. And sixth, a mature Christian conscience accepts social responsibility. It works through organizations and institutions without surrendering responsibility to them.

In the last resort, the Christian must follow the dictates of conscience. The conscience is the sense of compulsion to seek the good and the right.

The Christian feels an obligation to enlighten his or her conscience with the best information available, to bring to it all of the resources of the community of faith, and to listen for the voice of God rather than the voice of the social structures. The prompting of the conscience then is understood to be the Christian's response to God's gracious action in Jesus Christ and to God's continuing activity in the world around us. Although at times we will make errors of judgment about the best course of action, we will be responding to the divine imperative when we follow the leading of a conscience so directed.

FIVE
BIBLICAL ETHICS

Because the Bible is a historical record of God's self-disclosure, one cannot understand the thought and work of the church without at least some knowledge of its teachings. Because God continues to speak through the Scripture, one who approaches contemporary issues from a Christian perspective must attempt to understand what God is saying through it. While Biblical ethics and Christian ethics are not identical, the one requires the other. The study of biblical ethics is an attempt to understand what the Scripture teaches on moral issues. The study of Christian ethics is an attempt to look at the world in light of the Christian faith. Informed by biblical teachings, it examines specific issues and tries to determine the best course of action.

THE OLD TESTAMENT

One cannot understand Jesus' moral teachings without understanding the context within which they were expressed. Jesus was a Jew, a member of a covenant community, an heir of a great tradition, and a student of a vital religious literature which he treasured and revered. That literature was produced over a long period of time by many different people living in widely varying circumstances. The writers vary widely in their viewpoints, they reflect differing values, express differing attitudes, and recommend differing procedures. The documents reflect significant development in thought from the earliest stage of Hebrew history to the latest.

General Characteristics
of Old Testament Morality

We begin with a number of general observations about the morality taught in the Hebrew Scriptures. First, in the Old Testament, morality and piety are mixed in such a way that they cannot be separated. Devotion to God involves morality; morality is obedience to the will of God. No distinction is made between the sacred and the secular; all of life is lived in the presence of God; everything is sacred and thus subject to God's direction. Laws governing rituals of worship and laws regulating neighborly relations appear side by side with each other. Hymns of praise to God stand next to songs urging people to righteous conduct. The prophets denounce people who try to separate piety from morality and assume that one can please God by the proper observance of rituals.

Second, Hebrew moral obligation is a part of the covenant relationship. The traditional covenant phrase is, "I shall be your God, and you shall be my people." In historical terms that relationship was established by God's deliverance of the Hebrew people from bondage in Egypt. God broke the power of the Pharaoh, delivered the people at the Red Sea, gave them the Law at Mount Sinai, and established them in the Promised Land. In their national festivals they celebrate the mighty works of God. In their worship they commit themselves to obedience to God. In times of national strength and prosperity they give thanks to God, and in times of danger and disaster they anticipate that God will once again save them. For them, righteousness consists of grateful obedience to the will of God.

Third, the Hebrew sense of moral obligation results from the understanding that God is the absolute sovereign. God is the King beyond whom there is no other authority. God is responsible to no one or no thing, but all persons are under the governance of God. Whatever God wills is right; whatever God forbids is wrong. One can never question God's decisions; one can never speculate as to whether an action of God is just or unjust. God's doing it makes it just and right. God's commands, therefore, are to be obeyed not because they are inherently just or good but because God commands them.

Fourth, Old Testament morality is legalistic. What God requires and what God prohibits are specified in the Law. The Law, however, is not arbitrary regulation but teaching. Its purpose is to instruct people about the way of life that is right and good. It states in clear and precise terms what God expects, giving careful direction both for the rituals of worship and for moral obligations.

Fifth, Hebrew morality has a distinctive concept of justice. It does not begin with a concept of human nature but with the character of God. The central issue is not what people deserve because they are human but how God acts because God is God. Whatever God does is right or just. For people to be just is to deal with other people in the way God deals with them. If justice were rooted in a concept of human nature, it would be rooted in something that is badly flawed. Human beings are sometimes good and sometimes bad, sometimes just and sometimes unjust. It is erroneous to assume that they are true to their nature when they are good and just, but untrue to their nature when they are bad and unjust. Because God alone is constant, only God's character can be the standard of justice.

A final general characteristic of Old Testament morality is the centrality of the community. God deals not with individual Hebrews but with the Hebrew people. Of course, persons make up the community, and certain individuals appear either as leaders or as representatives of the group. Yet it is the nation with whom God has established the covenant, not the individuals. It is the nation that is seen as obedient or disobedient, that worships God or that turns to other gods, that sins and is punished. This sense of corporate identity is a helpful way to deal with social evils. The problems of war, for example, were not merely the problems of David or of Hezekiah; they were the problems of a nation trying to survive in a world of turmoil. The conditions of the poor were not merely the problems of individuals whose lands were unfertile, and the sins of the rich were not merely the problems of individuals who inherited large estates. There were problems in the economic system itself. Apostasy was not merely the turning of some individuals to other gods; it was the nation yielding to social pressures favoring the worship of other gods. The judgment of God, therefore, fell not upon individuals but upon the nation.

The Requirements of the Law

The Law (the first five books of the Old Testament) is a mixture of narrative and legislation. Because these books are not a single work produced in a short time, but rather are the product of a long and complicated process of writing and editing covering several centuries, the laws reported in them come from various periods in Hebrew history. The several codes found in the Law, therefore, reflect changing circumstances and reveal developing concepts.

The Covenant Code (Exodus 20:22–23:33) dates from the establishment at Mount Sinai of the covenant between God and the Hebrew people. It is notable for the high value it places on human life and for the absence of any distinction between classes of people. It reflects a concern for people and an interest in protecting their rights to life, to well-being, and to the ownership of property. Attention is given to the protection of persons often victimized in society: slaves, women, the poor, the orphans.

The best known set of laws in the Old Testament is the Ten Commandments (Exodus 20:2–17, cf. Deuteronomy 5:6–21). These laws capsule the requirements of the Covenant Code, and indeed of the entire legal system of the Hebrew people. The first three commandments have to do with the human orientation to God: the first requires absolute loyalty to God, the second prohibits the use of unworthy means to worship God, and the third requires reverence and respect for the name of God. The fourth commandment sets aside the seventh day as holy to God; it provides for a basic human need, however, in setting that day aside for rest. The other six commandments have to do with fundamental human values and needs: the fifth provides for the stability of the family; the sixth protects human life; the seventh protects the sanctity of marriage and of the sex relationship within marriage; the eighth recognizes the right to private property and protects that right; the ninth protects the reputation of persons; and the tenth (which in some ways comes close to the meaning of the first) warns the individual against an attitude that disrupts relationships. The basic principles set forth in this code of laws are fundamental both to personal conduct and to national life.

A much later set of laws, the Holiness Code (Leviticus 17–26) spells out the requirements of being a "holy" people, a people "cut off" or "separated" for the service of God. Dating from a period when the Hebrews were in danger either of turning to the gods of other peoples or of allowing their faith and practice to be influenced by alien religion, the Holiness Code magnifies certain ritualistic practices that set the Hebrews apart. Yet, because holiness cannot be separated from morality, the code requires a moral purity that is dictated by the God who is pure. The central statement of the code is Leviticus 19:2: "You shall be holy; for I the Lord your God am holy." The code intermingles the ritualistic and the moral requirements, as if they were all in the same category. In Hebrew thinking, that is exactly the case; all regulations come from the one God to whom the Hebrews are bound by covenant. God is the source of that holiness which distinguishes the Hebrews from other peoples both in the way they worship and in the way they relate to one another.

The Deuteronomic Code (Deuteronomy 12–26) is entirely in keeping with the rest of the book of Deuteronomy. Its ideal is generally regarded as Hebrew religion at its best, and the morality specified in it is illustrated in the history recorded in the book. In both spirit and content it has much in common with the Code of the Covenant and the Holiness Code. It has, however, a stronger emphasis on *love* than is found in either of them. God's love for Israel is stressed, and Israel's love for God is revealed as the basic motive for obedience to God's law. In speaking of God's love for Israel, the mighty acts of God in directing Israel's history are emphasized. In speaking of Israel's love for God, the note of gratitude is emphasized. The commands of God are given as commands of mercy and grace, and the people find that obedience to them is for their own good.

The other Old Testament books presuppose the ethical content of the Torah. While the Law is not thought of as describing all moral obligations of the Hebrew people, other obligations cannot be discussed without reference to it. The Law is the starting point, the ingredient common to all Hebrew morality, the standard by which decisions can be made. Without it one cannot comprehend the ideal of the Prophets or of the Writings.

The Ethical Monotheism of the Prophets
↳ one God

Although there were precursors, the great prophetic movement among the Hebrews arose in the eighth century B.C. A prophet is one who speaks forth for God, one who declares God's judgment on historical developments. The Hebrew prophets interpreted the nation's past and spoke to contemporary issues. They dealt with the future not in terms of prediction but of guidance. Usually appearing in a time of national crisis, they spoke in an authoritarian way, claiming "Thus saith the Lord." Unlike priests, they were nontraditional and noninstitutional. They were "raised up" for a specific purpose or time. Often using radical and even inflammatory language, and sometimes using dramatic symbolism, they called upon the nation to return to God.

The message of the prophets is sometimes summed up in the phrase *ethical monotheism*. We are not sure how early the Hebrew people reached the understanding that there is only one God over the entire universe. We can be sure that they were tempted to worship other gods until long after the period of the Exile in the sixth century B.C. The prophets, however, proclaimed a faith in which monotheism was fundamental. After their work, any recognition of the existence of other gods was understood as inconsistent with Hebrew belief.

The ethical emphases of the prophets were the logical conclusion of their faith in the one God who ruled the whole earth. Proclaiming the oneness of God and functioning as the heirs of a long tradition of allegiance to the Law, they focused on those laws which regulated the relationships of people with each other. Each prophet began his work in response to some problem which he perceived in the life of the nation. In high places and in low, to persons in authority and to the ordinary people in the marketplace, the prophets announced "the word of the Lord." They dealt with economic injustice, with militarism, with sexual immorality, with domestic violence, with corruption in government and in religion. For the most part they did not attack religious institutions, but they observed the inconsistency between devotion to religious observances on the one hand and violation of the basic laws of God on the other. For them, the essence of religion was obedience to God's command that we strive for the good of our neighbors. The words of Micah (6:8) are an excellent summary of this emphasis: "He has showed you, O man, what is good; and what does the Lord require of you but to do justice, and to love kindness, and to walk humbly with your God?"

The prophets brought to the Hebrew faith an important insight into the universality and the impartiality of the moral law. As we have seen, the early Hebrews recognized a responsibility for one another but were limited in a sense of responsibility for people other than Hebrews. The prophets, however, with some exceptions, saw that the one God who rules the universe is concerned about the welfare of all people, makes the same moral demands of all people, and deals in the same way with all who fall short of those demands. This emphasis should not be overstated, for the exclusivist and nationalistic spirit of the Hebrews continued to be a problem in the time of Jesus. Some prophets, indeed, such as Nahum and Obadiah, were quite bitter in their attitude toward other nations. Yet the logical conclusion of the concept of monotheism is that God's love and concern are universal, and most prophets recognized that implication.

The prophetic stress on God's demand for righteousness is complemented by an emphasis on judgment and punishment on the one hand, and on the possibilities of divine forgiveness on the other. The prophets insisted that God would not permanently tolerate the immorality which characterized the life of the nation, and they generally saw as imminent some expression of divine wrath. At the same time, however, they saw God as gracious and forgiving, ready to receive the people when they repented. Because they thought of judgment and restoration as taking place within the historical process, they saw the fortunes of the nation as rising or falling on the basis of its response to God.

Only rarely did the prophets hint that God deals with the individual. It was almost always the nation that acted morally or immorally, the nation which God held accountable, and therefore the nation that suffered disaster or experienced restoration. Within the corporate identity there was individual responsibility, of course. Yet it was the nation to whom God spoke through the prophets, and it was the nation that reacted to the message.

The Prudential Character of the Writings

Among *the Writings*, only the Wisdom Literature contains material having to do explicitly with morality. That literature is essentially down-to-earth, practical advice for everyday living. It applies the doctrines of the faith to the experience of the individual. Often it has the flavor of good, sound, common sense, and often it seems to have no "religious" character. Although it is more like philosophy than anything else in the Old Testament, it does not engage in abstract speculation. Indeed, philosophy focuses on the asking of questions; Wisdom Literature, in contrast, focuses on giving answers. Philosophy asks, for example, "What is wisdom?" The Wisdom Literature affirms, "The fear of the Lord is the beginning of wisdom."

The assumptions underlying Wisdom Literature are those of the Hebrew faith. God is the source of all that exists. God has established the moral and social order in which humankind lives. God is wise, just, merciful; God is the defender of the poor and the helpless; God is a guide to the righteous. The proper response of people to God is trust, reverence, patience, righteousness, kindness, and generosity. God will deal kindly with those who make the proper response and punish those who do not respond in the appropriate manner. The distinctive character of the morality of Wisdom Literature is its emphasis on individual responsibility. Its prudential advice is directed to the individual for life in the contemporary social setting. The virtues recommended and the vices cautioned against are individual ones. The good fortune that comes to the virtuous and the disaster that strikes the wicked are directed toward the individual. The statement of the virtues and the vices is based upon the divine law; actions are good or bad because of divine decree. The life of virtue or the life of vice is the choice of the individual, and the chosen way determines the consequences.

JESUS AND THE GOSPELS

Contemporary biblical scholarship deals with many critical questions about the Gospel reports of the person of Jesus. Who were the authors of the Gospels? Where did they get their information? What were their purposes in writing? How are the Gospels related to each other? What can we know about the life of Jesus? To what extent do the Gospels report accurately what he said and did? To what extent are they colored by the cultural setting? By historical developments? By personal memory and oral tradition? Although this is not the place to deal with these issues, we must indicate how these records are used in this approach to Christian ethics.

Each Gospel affirms in its own way the incarnation of God in the person of Jesus. Each makes its own emphases on the nature and the meaning of the ministry of Jesus. Each reports his teachings and the events in his life in a manner consistent with its own approach, its own interests and concerns. All of them, however, talk about the same person. The synoptic Gospels often describe the same incidents and report the same teachings. Although a comparative study of the Gospels raises questions about details, a picture of one person emerges. The character of that person is shown by the way he dealt with people and by what he taught. What we learn about him is central to our approach to Christian ethics because in one way or another Christian ethics takes Jesus as the norm.

Jesus and Judaism

Jesus was thoroughly Jewish. He spent his entire life in Palestine, with only occasional ventures into surrounding Gentile territory. He lived in Galilee, a section more free of Gentile influence than the rest of the country. He knew and revered the Scripture; he participated in the rituals of worship; he accepted without challenge the fundamental doctrines of the Jewish faith. His sharp criticism of religious leaders was not directed against any basic tenet of Judaism but against the abuse of those concepts. He did not see himself as the founder of a new religion but as a devotee of the ancient faith of his fathers.

This faith undergirded Jesus' ethical teachings. Like other Jews, he made no distinction between ethical concepts and other religious teachings. He did not divide life into categories, making this theological and that ethical, this sacred and that secular, this a religious matter and that not. For him, all of life was life in the presence of God, under the direction of God, subject to the judgment of God. The idea that one could be religious without being moral would have made no sense to him, nor would the idea that one could be moral without being religious. What made sense to him was the recognition of God's presence at all times and in all the affairs of life.

Jesus, then, shared the basic assumptions of Judaism: ethical monotheism; the covenant relationship with the Hebrew people; God's involvement in and control of the historical process; God's judgment upon human sinfulness; God's mercy, loving kindness, and faithfulness which worked for the redemption of humankind. Yet he was not just another rabbi. Standing within the Jewish tradition, he criticized it as it was practiced in his day. He was critical of many religious leaders, using sharp language to point out their pride and self-righteousness, their insensitivity to human need, their "hardness of heart" which kept them from acknowledging any failure. He differed from them in his attitude toward women, in his rejection of nationalism and his openness to Gentiles, in his consideration for little children, and in his self-identification with the poor. He was different from them in his emphases: rather than focusing as they did on matters of tradition, ritual, and personal purity, he stressed the weightier matters of the Law—justice, mercy, and faith.

Was there anything new in the ethical teaching of Jesus? Some writers insist that everything he said can be paralleled either in the Old Testament or in the words of other rabbis. While the crucial point is not whether a teaching is new but whether it is true, Jesus did make distinctive *emphases*. Ideas which are found only occasionally if at all in the teachings of other rabbis are frequent in his. One of those is a stress on the worth of the individual. That emphasis is found in such teachings as the statement that "the very hairs of your head are numbered" and "you are of more value than many sparrows," as well as in the parables of the Lost Coin, the Lost Sheep, and the Lost Son. It is found also in the reports of his obvious respect for such differing persons as Nicodemus, a ruler of the Jews; Zacchaeus the tax collector; the "woman of the city, a sinner" who anointed his feet; and the "little children" whom the disciples were about to send away.

A second emphasis was God's love for all people. As we have seen, the neighborly obligations spelled out in the Jewish law were usually interpreted to refer to other Jews. Although not everyone agreed with them, the Pharisees (who indeed had great influence with the masses of people) refused to have anything to do with non-Jews, thinking that contact with such people rendered them unclean and therefore unacceptable to God. Yet Jesus moved freely and naturally through Samaria, he visited the region of Tyre and Sidon, he spent time in the area of Caesarea-Philippi, he healed the child of a Roman centurion, and he made a Samaritan the hero of a story illustrating neighborliness.

A third emphasis was a flexibility in dealing with the Law and with religious institutions. At times many people bent the Law to achieve their own purposes (cf. Mark 7:9–13). The kind of flexibility which characterized Jesus, however, was that which put human need above allegiance to institutions and to established procedures. With this kind of concern, Jesus could declare, for example, "The sabbath was made for man, and not man for the sabbath" (Mark 3:27).

Jesus' response to the eschatological element in contemporary Jewish thought is an inevitable issue in a consideration of his ethical teachings. In a broad sense eschatological thinking is found throughout the Old Testament, for the Hebrew people consistently thought of history as in the hands of God, and of the Hebrew nation as having a special place in the purposes of God. They were convinced that both their present circumstances and their final destiny were in God's hands. In a stricter sense, Old Testament eschatology was apocalyptic in character. Apocalyptic material speaks of God's sudden intervention in history to bring an end to the present order and to create something new and different. This kind of eschatology characterized those periods in Jewish history when the situation of the nation was most dangerous and there seemed little prospect of improvement. In the broad sense, therefore, eschatology deals with significant changes in the historical process in which a new and different state of affairs emerges. In the stricter sense it refers to the end of history and to the beginning of a different kind of existence for the people of God.

According to the apocalyptic literature popular in the time of Jesus, the end was close at hand. There was to be a period of distress for the faithful, a period of trials and woes in which they were to be caught up in the struggle between the cosmic forces of good and evil. In the end, however, God would triumph and there would be a final judgment in which the wicked would be destroyed and the righteous would be admitted to an ideal life in a world to come. Using elaborate and often bizarre imagery, which probably was not intended to be taken literally, the writers speculated on when the events would take place and generally concluded that the time was at hand. As signs that the end was near they often cited the distress of their present circumstances. Born out of despair, their message was one of hope for the future. It expressed the confidence that God was in control of things, that God had a purpose which ultimately would be realized, and that God's faithful people would participate in that new order.

The extent to which Jesus shared this apocalyptic vision is debated, and the extent to which it influenced his ethical teachings is not at all clear. Even if we take the apocalyptic discourse in Mark 13 at face value, ignoring the possibility of the early church reading its own ideas back into the mind of Jesus, we cannot be certain about how important this way of thinking was to him. Clearly he assumed that the end was near (Mark 1:15, Matthew 10:23). Yet he did not speculate about when it would occur, he gave little attention (outside Mark 13) to "the signs of the times," and he did not describe the glories of the New Age. Once, asked directly about the time of the coming of the Kingdom, he replied that it would not be "with signs to be observed" but that it was already present (Luke 17:20ff). Asked the same thing on another occasion, he merely cited his own actions (Matthew 11:2–6).

Jesus' vision of the future magnified rather than minimized the significance of the present. The present was not merely preparation for the future; it participated in the future. God's future for the world is salvation, and that future is being worked out in the present. God's victory is not a hope to be achieved in the future but a reality now being achieved. The appropriate response of the believer is a life of obedience. Citing Jesus' words, "Take heed, watch!", Bornkamm says: "Jesus' message demands that we reckon with the future, lay hold on the hour, do not calculate the times. Those who wait in the right way are therefore called to fulfill the will of God now with all their might" (*Jesus of Nazareth*, p. 95).

If Jesus did not give up on this world, then he intended his teachings to be significant for life in it. If he did not deal with the question of when the world would end, that question must not have been important to him. Certainty that the end was in the hands of God gave a quality of urgency to his message; disinterest in the date gave a quality of timelessness to it.

Characteristics of Jesus' Teachings

Jesus' faith in God was the basis for his ethics. He stood within a great religious system and he did not think of himself as in any sense abandoning that faith. He talked about one's relationship to God and about the expectations which God has of people. He spoke of the love of God and of the desire to please God. Even when he was at odds with the usual interpretations of the faith, he worked in response to his understanding of his relationship to God. At the heart of his teaching was his urging that people act on the basis of their sense of oneness with God.

Jesus' teaching method was quite different from that to which modern students are accustomed. He was not systematic. He did not organize discourses on a given topic and move in a progression from an introduction through carefully ordered steps to a logical conclusion. His ideas on a given topic are not concentrated in one place to which one can turn to find out what he taught about God, about human nature, about sin, about the family, about the state, and so on. Rather, his teachings were occasional, given to fit the circumstances. He answered questions. He reacted to criticism. He commented on what he saw going on around him. He dealt with problems that were brought to him. He visited synagogues and shared in the study of the Scripture. He engaged in conversation with friends. This nonsystematic approach, however, did not result in a fragmented approach to morality. Instead, there was an inner unity that resulted from Jesus' understanding of God and of God's purposes for people.

Jesus seems always to have talked in terms of the ideal pattern of human relationships. When one considers what he taught about love; about anger, lust, and greed; about divorce; and about any number of other matters, one is disposed to ask, "But what if...?" While an absolutism that prescribes actions is difficult, one that deals with emotions and attitudes seems impossible. Jesus was not insensitive to human frailty and he always dealt redemptively with people when they fell short of the ideal. Yet he regularly and consistently held up the ideal as God's will for people.

Jesus was not legalistic. He stated fundamental truths and either explained them or illustrated them. Had he legislated, his teachings would have been limited in scope and in time. They might have helped people in his day, but they would have had no more permanent value than any other legalistic system. By delineating principles for moral living, however, and leaving the application to his disciples, he offered something of permanent worth.

The fact that Jesus' teachings were based on his religion means that they were intended for his disciples. At many points Christian ethics overlaps with other religious and philosophical systems. Truth is truth, regardless of who holds it or on what ground it is held. Yet, from Jesus' point of view value and duty derive their meaning from God. One who knows and loves God holds to those values and acknowledges those duties which one sees to be derived from God. God is the believer's reason for thinking and acting in a given way. What Jesus taught was directed to those who shared his understanding of the character and purposes of God. No other appeal for moral conduct was necessary and none was valid. Jesus' ethic does not commend itself to all people; it is a way of life to be accepted by people who know God.

Basic Concepts in Jesus' Ethical Teachings

The Kingdom of God.   The idea of the Kingdom of God is central in the teaching of Jesus and basic to his ethic. Mark introduced Jesus' ministry by summarizing his message: "The time is fulfilled, and the kingdom of God is at hand; repent, and believe in the gospel" (Mark 1:15). Everything that Jesus taught about God and human beings, about the institutions of religion, about the practices of personal piety, and about morality, must be understood in light of the concept of the Kingdom.

Although the phrase *the Kingdom of God* does not occur in the Old Testament, it was readily understood by Jesus' hearers. It denoted the rule of God over the covenant people, an idea that was at the heart of the Hebrew faith. God had established a unique relationship with the Hebrew people, had given them the Law by which they were to live, and had guided their history so as to keep them close to God. Even when they were governed by a king, that king's power was not absolute: he was the agent through whom God governed. The Law, the Prophets, the Wisdom Literature, the Devotional Literature—all assumed the sovereignty of God and interpreted history as controlled by God.

With that understanding, the Hebrew people had a special way of interpreting events that other people would have regarded as disaster. They believed that such events were God's judgment, intended to rebuke the people and to bring them back to the covenant. That judgment, however, was in no sense final: God was looking beyond the immediate situation toward the redemption of the people. No matter how bad things might get, there was always a future. In that light the subjugation of the Hebrews by the Romans, beginning in the first century B.C., was viewed as a temporary situation. In due season God would expel the Romans and the nation would be free again. They would indeed be "the Kingdom of God."

But how would God free the people? Three views can be distinguished. Some people anticipated a military movement which would lead to the restoration of national independence. These people generally thought that the Messiah would lead that action. This view is associated with the Zealots, a revolutionary group active at the time of Jesus. Others also anticipated the establishment of national independence, but expected it to come as an expression of God's control of history. God would intervene not through a struggle by the people but by directing the affairs of the nations. The best thing that the people could do was to hold on to their faith by a strict observance of the Law. When the Law was perfectly kept, God would act. Still others cherished the apocalyptic hope, the expectation that God's intervention would take the form of a catastrophic end to the present order and the creation of a new one over which the Son of Man would rule.

One thing common to all forms of the expectation was the anticipation of a new order over which God would rule through the Messiah. The New Testament documents affirm that in Jesus that historic hope of the Hebrew people has in some way been fulfilled. They do not agree on how Jesus fulfilled that hope, and the effort to find in them a single, unified view of the person of Christ is doomed to failure. Yet they do come together in the proclamation that Jesus is the Christ, that his advent was the decisive event in the coming of the Kingdom, and that people are called to affirm the New Age by responding to him. In him, hope has become a reality, anticipation has become fulfillment. The claims of God upon people are made not in terms of what is yet to be but in terms of what already is. The Kingdom is *at hand;* the Scripture *has been fulfilled;* what all ages have longed to see is now here. While we must deal with the futuristic aspect of the Kingdom, it does not contradict the reality of what has happened. The early church insisted that the New Age dawned with the coming of Christ and that the disciples were already living in that New Age. They were living with new duties, new loyalties, new motivations derived from the reality of what had already transpired. A Christian sense of right and of good is rooted in this conviction that the New Age has dawned.

Yet Jesus' disciples knew that they were still living in the "old age." They worked at their trades, lived with their families, participated in traditional religious activities, dealt with neighbors, bought and sold in the market, saw Roman soldiers patrolling the land, and longed for things to be better. Many of Jesus' teachings reflect his belief that the present order would soon end (Mark 9:1; Matthew 16:28; Luke 9:27). Some interpreters insist that all of his teachings were shaped by that belief. Although that is probably too broad a generalization, his teachings were certainly affected by it. His awareness that the completion of the Kingdom was yet to come gave significance to what was happening in the old order and freed his disciples from bondage to that order. In terms of ethical responsibility, it focused allegiance beyond the social order but placed responsibility within it.

Such language may seem abstract. What is the significance of the Kingdom of God, so understood, for ethical living? At the heart of the matter is the fact that citizenship in the Kingdom imposes upon the disciples of Jesus a radical demand for obedience. Those who accept God's offer of forgiveness and become a part of the community of faith have a responsibility to obey. Right and wrong, good and bad are defined in terms of the purposes of God. Every way of acting must be evaluated not in terms of whether it is expedient or logical, but in terms of God's will. The believer's decisions about day by day activities must be based upon the sovereign will of God.

God's will is not a matter of whim or caprice. It is an expression of God's character and is therefore consistent, orderly, reliable, and predictable. In the thought of Jesus, however, there is no standard beyond God by which God's decisions can be evaluated; God is the standard by which all judgments are made. We understand right and wrong from our knowledge of God. Loyalty to God is what determines our decisions, and those decisions are good or bad, right or wrong, as they relate to God. The ethic of Jesus, then, is a radical demand for obedience to the will of God.

The Law. Against the background of Jesus' teachings about the Kingdom of God we may consider his attitude toward the Law. Because of who he was he could not have ignored the Law. He was reared in a typically pious Jewish family. His hometown was located in the heart of the most traditional section of the country. His education, like that of other Jewish boys, was based upon the Law and the Prophets. The synagogue, where the Scripture was taught, was an institution second in importance only to the home. The Pharisees, whose devotion to the Law was unmatched by any other group, had considerable influence in the area. Jesus' own teachings reflect a thorough knowledge of the Law and a deep appreciation for it. Saying that he had come to "fulfill" the Law, he regarded his teachings as fully harmonious with its fundamental truth.

Several generalizations may be made about Jesus' attitude toward the Law. First, he made a distinction between the Law of Moses and the rabbinic interpretations which had come to have the force of unwritten law. He often challenged those interpretations, pointing out how ridiculous some of them were. He always spoke with respect, however, when he dealt with the Law of Moses. Even when he rejected a specific regulation he gave what he understood to be the reason for the law and stated his reason for rejecting it (cf. Mark 10:2–4).

Second, Jesus considered some parts of the Law more important than others. In general, he was more concerned about moral laws than about those having to do with rituals. His failure to say much about rituals may signify only that he was more concerned about something else. His comments on laws having to do with morality, however, clearly indicate that for him morality was a major concern. They show also that he did not have equal regard for all moral laws. He was quite demanding in his interpretation of the laws on murder, adultery, and false swearing, for example. Yet his comments on the law of divorce essentially negated that regulation (Matthew 5:21–32)!

Third, Jesus stressed motive and intent more than overt action. His interpretations indicated that moral wrong lies in one's attitudes toward other persons (Matthew 5). That emphasis is in keeping with his statement on prayer, fasting, and almsgiving, the traditional deeds of piety (Matthew 6). It is also in keeping with his comments on the widow's gift of her "two mites" (Mark 12:41–44).

Fourth, Jesus broadened the scope of moral responsibility. While the Law specified certain duties which the Jews had in their dealings with non-Jews, its primary concern was the duty of Jews toward each other. By traditional interpretation, non-Jews were given less consideration. Jesus, however, removed such ethnic limitations.

The Central Imperative. The central imperative in Christian ethics is summed up in the term *obedient love* (cf. Ramsey, xi). The word *obedient* ties Christian morality in to the idea of the sovereignty of God which we have discussed. Related to the morality expressed in the Law and the Prophets, and to a lesser extent in the Wisdom Literature, it is tied in with Jesus' heralding of the Kingdom. It associates the concepts of justice, right, duty, value, virtue, and calling to one's relationship to God. It gives an objective reference to the Christian life by suggesting that the requirements of that life are established by God, not by human decision. It says, in short, that what is just, right, valuable, and good are discovered by human beings rather than *determined* by them. This idea does not mean that people do not make decisions about conduct; it does mean that those decisions must be made in light of the sovereignty of God. This idea is thoroughly familiar because it is completely in keeping with the Old Testament morality.

Tying obedience to love, however, is not quite so familiar. It is not correct to say that the concept of love originated with Christian morality. The idea of the love of God is presented in the Old Testament as the basis for God's dealings with the Hebrew people. Both the Law and the Prophets cite God's love, and Deutero-Isaiah forcefully and beautifully expresses the sacrificial and redemptive character of that love. At best, the obedience of God's people is their response to God's grace. Yet nowhere in the Old Testament is love so central to the human response to God as it is in the thought of Jesus. For him, love *is* that response. Although he does not always use the word, the concept is never missing. Because he considers it central in one's response to God, he considers it central also in one's response to other persons.

For us the word *love* has a variety of meanings: We love our parents and our brothers and sisters. We love our boyfriend or girlfriend. We love our roommate. We love certain kinds of music or certain kinds of food. We love our dog. We love to work. All of these uses of the word convey specific attitudes or dispositions. They describe normal and legitimate relationships. None, however, is in the same category as love for God, and none is in the same category as love for one's neighbor or love for one's enemy. No lengthy discussion of Greek terms is necessary at this point. Suffice it to say that in Greek the term *philia* is used for comradely affection, *storge* for a sense of family unity, and *eros* for desire or for response to the beautiful. *Agape,* rarely used in other Greek literature, is the distinctive New Testament word for that attitude which Jesus considered the appropriate relationship between people and God and between people and other people. Its meaning can best be explained by an examination of its use. Since here we are discussing the ethical teachings of Jesus, we shall limit our consideration to the use of the word in the Gospels.

One of the best passages to use for understanding the concept of *agape* is Matthew 5:21–48 (cf. Luke 6:27–31). After having commented on several other laws, Jesus said, "You have heard that it was said, 'You shall love your neighbor and hate your enemy' " (v. 43). Neither Leviticus 19:18, which he was citing, nor any other Old Testament law says that one should hate one's enemy. The words in Leviticus, however, stand in the context of a statement of the Israelite's obligations to fellow Israelites. One who did not wish to do so would certainly not be compelled to find there any obligation toward non-Israelites. Other Old Testament passages do permit hostility toward one's enemies. Thus the latter part of Jesus' "quotation" is an accurate summary of generally accepted attitudes. Jesus challenged that common hostility toward outsiders by saying, "But I say to you, love your enemies." In his view one has the same obligation to an enemy that one does to a neighbor.

On the basis of this passage, several things can be said about the character of love. First, love is the opposite of hatred. As hatred is divisive, love is a unity-creating force. Jesus' comments on the law against murder (Matthew 5:21–26) bring further insight into this idea. Anger and contempt fall into the same category as hatred, and therefore may also be seen as opposites of love. Second, love is active, expressing itself in some positive way. Jesus urged his disciples to "pray for" and to "greet" their enemies. In the same way, in his comments on the law against murder he spoke of actively seeking reconciliation. Third, love is an impartial concern for people, making no distinction between the good and the bad, the just and the unjust. That is the character of God's love which serves as the pattern for the disciples of Jesus. That characteristic leads to a fourth, which is that love is universal. If God loves both the just and the unjust, the evil and the good, then God loves everyone. Jesus concluded this observation by cautioning his disciples to be perfect as God is perfect. The word *perfect* means complete or mature. Jesus' disciples are therefore to be complete in their love, loving all persons.

Another brief statement in the Sermon on the Mount speaks of love in terms of service: "No one can serve two masters; for either he will hate the one and love the other, or he will be devoted to the one and despise the other" (Matthew 6:24). This verse is a statement about one's priorities, and therefore about one's relationship to God. It uses the word *devote* as a synonym for *love*. To be devoted is to cling to, to give oneself to. This statement calls to mind the ancient Hebrew conception of devotion as setting a person or an object aside for the service of God.

The most dramatic statement of the centrality of love in the teaching of Jesus is found in the "twin commandments": "You shall love the Lord your God with all your heart, and with all your soul, and with all your mind. This is the great and first commandment. And a second is like it; You shall love your neighbor as yourself. On these two commandments depend all the Law and the Prophets" (Matthew 22:37–40; cf. Mark 12:28–34, Luke 10:27–37). This was Jesus' answer to the frequently discussed question, Which commandment is the greatest? Many rabbis looked for ways to sum up basic religious obligations in one or two simple, easily remembered statements. Jesus' answer was such a summary.

Jesus' summary was a skillful blending of Leviticus 19:18 and Deuteronomy 6:4. While Jesus was not the first to make this combination, for him it summarizes the essence of religious obligation. In it the insep-arability of love for God and love for neighbor stands out. The question asked for one commandment; the answer cited two, as if they were two sides of the same coin, as if the one does not exist without the other. A right relationship with God entails a right relationship with neighbor. A right relationship with neighbor is based upon a right relationship with God. The significance of this concept cannot be overemphasized. The way one relates to a neighbor is determined not by the worth of the neighbor but by the character of God.

Another word of great importance in this statement is *neighbor*. Acknowledging the obligation to love one's neighbor, one may limit responsibility by restricting the definition of *neighbor*. Jewish people in Jesus' day used the word much as we do: our neighbor is someone who lives near us who is like us—someone of the same race, class, religion, education, and socioeconomic status. In Luke's report of this conversa-tion (10:25ff), Jesus answered the question, "Who is my neighbor?" by telling the parable of the Good Samaritan (vv. 30–37). Although that story offers no definition, it removes all limitations from the obligation to love. With this story, Jesus suggested that love recognizes no distinctions between people.

Another important understanding of the nature of love is brought out in the action of the Samaritan in the parable. One gathers that he did not pause to consider what his duty might be. Rather, he reacted spontaneously and quickly to the need of the victim. The word *compassion* describes his feeling for the victim, and the words that follow describe his efforts to relieve the situation. To love is to do something. In the New Testament the word *love* is almost always a verb, almost never a noun.

The Character of the Disciple. Jesus was not a systematic teacher of theology or of ethics. He did not engage in the kind of discourse that may have characterized the teachers of his day, and that certainly has characterized Christian thinkers since his time. He would not have been at home with Greek philosophers who spent a great deal of time discussing the virtues to be cultivated and the vices to be avoided. Rather he wanted to bring people into a relationship with God that would reshape their character. He assumed that the kind of person one is determines the kind of thing one does. For him, the crucial point is: "Either make the tree good, and its fruit good; or make the tree bad, and its fruit bad; for the tree is known by its fruit" (Matthew 12:33). "For figs are not gathered from thorns," he said, "nor are grapes picked from a bramble bush" (Luke 6:43). "For out of the abundance of the heart the mouth speaks" (Matthew 12:24). While he did not assume that a good person automatically does good things, he did assume that character determines conduct.

The character formation on which Jesus focused was not simply an individual matter, not one of a person entering into a solo relationship with God. Jesus never seemed to believe that one could know God apart from a community of faith or that one could maintain a relationship with God while isolating oneself from other believers. While he did not discuss that matter, he lived in community with his disciples and invited others into that community. He was not concerned, in other words, merely with the conversion of the individual but with people living and functioning as a part of the family of God. While individuals made their own decisions about their involvement in that community, about their life of faith, they did not make them in an abstract situation but within the context of a fellowship.

The key question for conduct, therefore, is: What kind of person are you? Jesus never described an ideal person. Yet he consistently recommended certain ways of thinking and feeling, ways of acting, ways of relating to other people, ways of regarding oneself, ways of regarding

God. As we read the Sermon on the Mount and the other collected teachings of Jesus, as we read his parables, as we read the reports of his conversations, as we read his scattered comments, we may discover certain themes emerging and may begin to get a feel for the kind of character that can be designated *Christian.*

One quality of character that Jesus stressed was *humility.* This word refers to the way in which people must see themselves before God. It describes their response to the awareness that they live in the presence of God. It recognizes an ideal that is beyond them, that they have not yet attained, that they may never attain. Their recognition of their failure before God leads to a sober assessment of their status in relationship to other people. The person who is humble before God, according to Jesus, cannot be arrogant with other persons. The humble person does not seek preferential treatment, does not impose upon other people, does not presume an unwarranted status. The humble person does not make claims about personal achievement or about personal abilities. When Jesus' disciples asked about greatness in the Kingdom, he replied that "Whoever humbles himself like this child" is the greatest in the Kingdom of heaven (Matthew 18:1–3).

A second quality of character which Jesus praised was *sincerity.* Although he did not use the word *sincere,* so far as the record goes, he often spoke of a life that can stand up under the closest scrutiny. Frequently he condemned hypocrisy, deliberate deception, the pretense that you are something when you know you are something else. He spoke in harsh terms of certain scribes "who devour widows' houses and for a pretense make long prayers" (Mark 12:40). He talked about people who honestly thought that they were correct when they were self-deluded. He warned his disciples, "If then the light in you is darkness, how great is the darkness!" (Matthew 6:23). He denounced the Pharisees who blindly stressed minor matters and neglected major ones (Matthew 23). By way of contrast, he urged his disciples to be openly and simply honest (Matthew 5:33–37), to be "pure in heart" (Matthew 5:8), to be trusting (Matthew 5:42), to be "as wise as serpents and as harmless as doves" (Matthew 10:16).

A third quality of character which Jesus often praised was *faithfulness.* Many of his parables stressed this quality. Although most of them had to do with an uncertainty about the end of the age, they emphasized the idea that in light of that event his disciples should be diligent in their service. He insisted that people are stewards of possessions entrusted to them by God and that they owe unlimited service to God. He said that "he who is faithful in a very little is faithful also in much; and he who is dishonest in a very little is dishonest also in much" (Luke 16:10). Faithfulness was for Jesus a quality of character that reflected one's basic loyalty to God.

The Example of Jesus

The ideal of *the imitation of Christ* has loomed large in the minds of the disciples of Jesus throughout the history of the church. In spite of the fact that a discovery of the historic Jesus is extremely difficult, if indeed it is possible at all, most Christians accept as their model the portrayal of Jesus which they find in the Gospels. As R. E. O. White says, "the imitation of Christ is, in truth, the nearest principle in Christianity to a moral absolute." He continues:

> The law of love may be held a second Christian absolute: but without the example of Jesus, the law remains an abstract form rather than a concrete ideal, while without devotion to the person of Christ the law lacks incentive and enabling moral energy. When all allowance is made for varying interpretation, the imitation of Christ remains the heart of the Christian ethic. (*Biblical Ethics*, p. 109)

What we learn from the example of Christ reinforces what we learn from his teachings. There is no inconsistency, no failure on his part to be true to the insight that he has voiced. He announced the coming of the Kingdom of God and he lived as one joyfully acknowledging the sovereignty of God. Proclaiming love as the fulfillment of the Law and the Prophets, he expressed that love in his way of life. He extolled certain qualities of character and without being self-consciously good he exemplified those qualities in his own life.

Jesus' example conveys one idea that is more implicit than explicit in his teachings: Every individual is of infinite worth and is to be treated with respect. The reports of his work show that he made no distinction between people: men and women, Jews and Gentiles, righteous people and sinners were all respected as individuals, as people with whom God was concerned. He did not deal with all people in the same way; what he did was conditioned by circumstances and by the responses of individuals. But never did he act as if anyone were worthless or beyond the pale of God's concern. He treated the rich young ruler and the blind beggar with equal respect. He dealt graciously with a Pharisee who invited him to his home for a meal and with the woman of the city who entered that same house and anointed his feet. He was concerned about people who fell through the cracks of society: widows, little children, lepers, and demoniacs. Although he did not idealize them, neither did he turn aside from them. He looked upon them all as children of God.

For Jesus, life in response to God was a life of active effort to meet the needs of people. The word *compassion* is often used to describe his emotional reaction to seeing people in distress, and he always made some effort to relieve the distress. If there was a keynote for his ministry, it was

Isaiah 61:1–2, which he read and discussed in a service in the synagogue in Capernaum early in his ministry:

> The Spirit of the Lord is upon me,
> because he has anointed me to preach good news to the poor.
> He has sent me to proclaim release to the captives
> and recovering of sight to the blind,
> to set at liberty those who are oppressed,
> to proclaim the acceptable year of the Lord. (Luke 4:18–19)

The story of Jesus' career is the story of an active ministry to the kind of people described in this passage.

THE ETHICAL TEACHINGS OF PAUL

Paul identified himself completely by his relationship to Jesus Christ. He did not see himself as the creator of a new system of theology or of ethics but as a proclaimer of the Gospel of Jesus Christ. Rather than reporting the facts of Jesus' ministry, however, he discussed the implications of the Gospel for disciples of Jesus. As he faced problems and dealt with issues, he tried to make the kind of judgment that he thought Jesus would make. Whether he was in fact consistent with the spirit of Christ can be debated. Whether he added to the teachings which he believed came from Jesus is likewise an open question. There can be no doubt, however, that he believed that in all that he taught he was true to the Gospel. For his moral judgments Paul probably was more indebted to his Jewish background than he realized. He had, after all, received rabbinical training with Gamaliel, one of the most important teachers of his day. He thought of Jesus as the Messiah, though his understanding of Messiahship was quite nontraditional. He talked about Christians as the New Israel and he used the Jewish Scriptures freely to bear witness to Jesus as the Christ. Even so, however, in his moral teachings it was Jesus and not the Law that was fundamental.

Theology and Ethics

For Paul, as for Jesus, the starting point in thinking about human life was the idea of the sovereignty of God. This fundamental Hebrew conviction was the basis for all his thinking about the place of human beings in the world and about human responsibility. God is the creator, the sustainer, and the judge. God is the one who makes demands of people, who gives people the power to meet those demands, and who stands in judgment over them for their failures. This concept of the sovereignty of God gave a tone to all of Paul's statements about moral obligation. Although he gave full play to human responsibility for decision making, Paul never left the impression that he thought that human decision determines the good or the right. Good and right are rooted in the sovereign will of God.

Paul believed in the universality of sin. His statement that "all have sinned and fall short of the glory of God" (Romans 3:23) affirms his deep-seated conviction that no one has escaped the corruption of evil. He thought of sin as a basic alienation from God, a failure to be true to the insight that one has into God's purposes and demands. That alienation results in a wide variety of actions that demonstrate the self-love of people, their determination to do what they wish rather than to obey the will of God. It is of such nature and is so deep-seated that no individual can overcome it. According to Paul, therefore, human beings are victimized by their own sinful nature. Although he talked about powerful spiritual forces of evil at work in the world and in the lives of persons, he did not think of them as responsible for sin. It is persons themselves who are responsible. But so profound is the problem that people are incapable of overcoming it.

For Paul, Christ was the solution to this human predicament. In Christ God acted to redeem people. In Christ God took the initiative to make people true sons and daughters of God. For Paul, the incarnation, the life of Christ, the death on the cross, and the resurrection constitute one redemptive act. In all that he was and did, Christ was the revelation of God's love, the work of God in redeeming people. Paul summed it up in the affirmation, "God was in Christ reconciling the world to himself" (2 Corinthians 5:19).

This new life becomes a reality in the person who responds in faith. Paul insisted that one is saved "by grace through faith." Jews who had the Law and Gentiles who did not have the Law, he thought, were equally helpless. Because they were on equal footing, they were both reconciled to God in the same way: by accepting God's love offered in the person of Christ. They could do nothing to effect their salvation; salvation came to them as the gift of God's grace. The appropriate human response to God's initiative is to acknowledge one's sinfulness and helplessness and to throw oneself upon the mercy of God. One who does that is assured of God's forgiveness and enters into a new life.

This new relationship to God, according to Paul, entails a new way of living. Believers are not merely forgiven for their sins; they are also given power to overcome sin. Paul constantly urged his readers toward Christian conduct, saying to them, in effect, "You *are* Christian; now *act* like it." He urged them to resist evil and to do good, to work out their own salvation. Sometimes he was quite specific in his judgment about what they should or should not do and at other times he spoke in more general terms. Always he conveyed a sense of moral urgency, however, as if one constantly has to make decisions. His understanding of this new life in Christ is the framework for his ethical teachings.

An Ethic of Responsible Freedom

This new way of living into which the Christian enters requires the responsible use of freedom. Paul's phrase, "You are not under law but under grace" (Romans 6:14), sums up his understanding of how one is saved and has significant implications for the moral life. If we are not under law in receiving God's gift of salvation, are we then under law in moral obligation? Once we have been saved without obedience to the Law, does the Law dictate how we are to act?

For Paul, the moral standards expected of the disciple of Christ were higher than those expressed in the Law. Even as he insisted that the believer is free from the Law, so also he insisted that freedom should not be used as "an opportunity for the flesh" (Galatians 5:13). He talked about "the works of the flesh" as "fornication, impurity, licentiousness, idolatry, sorcery, enmity, strife, jealousy, anger, selfishness, dissension, party spirit, envy, drunkenness, carousing, and the like." By way of contrast, "the fruit of the Spirit is love, joy, peace, patience, kindness, goodness, faithfulness, gentleness, self-control" (Galatians 5:19–23). Paul rejected the idea that Hebrew rituals were obligatory for Christians, but he did not actually discuss the relationship of the Christian to the Old Testament moral laws. Had he been asked to do so he probably would have remained consistent and argued that they were not obligatory either. Yet he was convinced that certain ways of acting were inconsistent with the new life of the believer and that other ways of acting were a natural consequence of one's relationship to Christ (cf. Ephesians 4:22–5:14; Colossians 3:1–17). He was not hesitant to specify which was which.

In most of his letters Paul spoke on moral issues, some personal and some social. He said more about such matters in his letters to the Corinthians than in any others, perhaps because of the special problems faced by the Christians in that large city notorious for its immorality. On the basis of what he said, we may state several considerations which guide the Christian in responsible decision making.

Respect for the Church. Paul had a profound respect for the church, as indicated by figures of speech which he used to refer to it: the body of Christ, the temple of God, the household of faith, the household of God. He stressed the dependence of the members of the church on each other and the importance of the contribution of each person. In a passage dealing with divisiveness within the church in Corinth, he appealed to the Christians there to overcome their differences. He asked, "Do you not know that you are God's temple and that God's Spirit dwells in you?" (1 Corinthians 3:16). Although he did not say, "Surrender your own judgment to the church," he did say, "Remember that what you do affects the temple of God."

Respect for Your Self. When one makes decisions on the basis of a legal system, the question is, Is there a law against it? If there is no law, then presumably the conduct in question is legitimate. Because Paul insisted that "we are not under law but under grace," some people concluded that moral considerations were irrelevant and that any conduct was permissible. Their view is summed up in the phrase, "All things are lawful for me." Paul suggested, however, that another affirmation should guide one in making decisions on moral issues: "Not all things are helpful" (1 Corinthians 6:12). Thus in pondering a moral issue we might ask, What good results are to be expected from this way of acting? If results are considered good because they move us toward a desired goal, what is the goal of the Christian life? While the goal can be described in various ways, our answer must deal in some way with our relationship to God in Christ, to one's commitment to the will of God as that will is known in Christ.

To this suggestion about making moral decisions Paul added another affirmation: "I will not be enslaved by anything" (1 Corinthians 6:12). In pondering a moral issue one might therefore ask: "Does it tend to get control of me, to dominate my actions?" If so, it endangers the very freedom which is so important to me.

Following up on their line of reasoning that "all things are lawful," some people had apparently concluded that any "natural" conduct was legitimate (1 Corinthians 6:13ff). They had specific reference to sexual activities. Paul rebutted that idea by affirming that for the new life of the Christian, "immorality" was neither natural nor normal. While he had other comments about extramarital sex activity, his basic argument was that it was not appropriate to the new life in Christ. His concluding statement was, "You are not your own; you were bought with a price. So glorify God in your body" (1 Corinthians 6:19–20).

Respect for Your Brother. Paul's understanding of the church as the body of Christ and as a fellowship of believers involved a sense of concern for and respect for the members of that fellowship. While he did not think of Christians as responsible only for fellow Christians, he believed that such a special relationship entailed a special responsibility. Much of what he said had to do with the way Christians deal with one another. In 1 Corinthians 8 he concluded a discussion of a divisive issue in the church, the question of whether a Christian could eat meat that had been offered to an idol, by saying, "If food is a cause of my brother's falling, I will never eat meat, lest I cause my brother to fall" (8:13). He did not intend to surrender his conscience to anyone else, as he made clear in the next chapter. He was unwilling to make rules for anyone else and he was unwilling for anyone else to make rules for him. But his sense of responsibility for his brother was a principle by which he made decisions about what he would do. The church at Rome had a similar question: How do you deal with the fact that members of the church reach differing conclusions about what is appropriate personal conduct? Insisting that people ought not to pass judgment on one another, Paul said, "It is right not to eat meat or drink wine or do anything that makes your brother stumble" (Romans 14:21). This is not the place to discuss "eating meat or drinking wine." It is important, however, to stress the concern for what happens to a brother.

The same consideration is found in Paul's urging that Christians should "love one another" and "care for one another." The "strong ought to bear with the failings of the weak" (Romans 15:1). Christians are to "bear one another's burdens" (Galatians 6:2). They are to pray for one another, to share with one another, to exhort one another, to "rejoice with those who rejoice and weep with those who weep." They are even to suffer wrongs from a brother rather than to seek justice in the courts (1 Corinthians 6:7–8). They are to submit themselves to one another out of reverence for Christ. Their actions, therefore, are to be determined in part at least by how those actions affect fellow Christians.

Respect for Outsiders. Paul's basic objective for people who were not Christian was their conversion to Christian faith. A Christian's chief responsibility for other people was the presentation of the Gospel. Apart from that emphasis, Paul referred to non-Christians mainly by stating how Christians should deal with their enemies and how they should react to expressions of hostility. The principle of nonretaliation dominates those statements. He urged the Roman Christians, for example, to "bless those who persecute you," to "repay no one evil for evil," to "live peaceably with all," to forego vengeance, and even to give food and drink to the enemy who needs them (Romans 12:14–21).

An Ethic of Love

Paul was faithful to the teaching of Jesus in making love the central imperative. He said to the Romans, "Owe no one anything, except to love one another; for he who loves his neighbor has fulfilled the law" (13:8). He stated the same idea in his letter to the Galatians, "For the whole law is fulfilled in one word, you shall love your neighbor as yourself" (5:14). These exhortations echo Jesus' statement that all the Law and the Prophets depend upon the requirement of love for God and love for neighbor (Matthew 22:37–40).

In several significant passages Paul probed the deeper meaning of love which, in his judgment, was at the heart of the life of the Christian. The best known such passage is 1 Corinthians 13. This magnificent poem, unlike most of Paul's writings, is a polished, literary product. The first three verses speak of the value of love, verses 4–7 speak of the characteristics of love, and verses 8–13 speak of the permanence of love. The second section, therefore, verses 4–7, most fully tells what love is like. An examination of the things that Paul says love does, and of the things that he says love does not do, brings out the fact that love creates and maintains a unity between people. The works of love draw people together; the things that love avoids separate people.

Another important chapter in which love is characterized is Romans 12. This passage begins a section in which Paul gives practical advice on a number of matters of conduct. Not until he gets to the middle of the chapter does he use the word *love*, but its use there makes it clear that this is the concept he is discussing in the entire passage. In this chapter he talks about the importance of humility, of a concern for the unity of the fellowship, of diligent service to one another, of sharing, and of nonretaliation. Within that broad and unorganized collection of exhortations Paul says, "Let love be genuine; hate what is evil, hold fast to what is good; love one another with brotherly affection; outdo one another in showing honor" (12:9–10).

Most of what Paul said about love refers to the relationship of Christians to one another. For him it seemed self-evident that Christians belong to one another and have a responsibility for one another. If love of the brethren did not actually characterize the churches, it certainly should do so. Sometimes, therefore, Paul praised churches because they evidenced this quality (cf. 1 Thessalonians 4:9). At other times he rebuked them for not acting on the basis of love (cf. 1 Corinthians 1–3). At all times he spoke as if those who acted in love for fellow believers were acting in the spirit of Christ. So significant was the church for him that he thought that one of the worst things a Christian could do was to act with disrespect for it. In rebuking the Corinthians for the way they were celebrating the Lord's Supper he exclaimed, "Do you despise the church of God and humiliate those who have nothing?" (1 Corinthians 11:22).

An Ethic of a New Life

For Paul the essence of ethical behavior was the new life in Christ. He was convinced that in Christ people enter into a new relationship with God, that they become new persons as a result of that relationship, and that as new persons their lives are different. As we have seen, he cited certain actions as "works of the flesh" and others as "fruit of the Spirit" (Galatians 5:22). By using these terms he implied that people are fully responsible for the evil that they do, but that they deserve no credit for doing good things. The new way of life of the Christian is the result of faith. As God's work in the person, it is the natural, expected expression of Christian character.

At the same time, however, as Paul wrote to churches he constantly dealt with moral issues and urged believers to act in a Christian way. The members of the Church at Corinth, for example, were at odds with each other over their allegiance to different leaders. They were going to court to settle issues between each other. They were indifferent to a case of sexual immorality within their fellowship. Paul felt compelled to instruct them in the right way of dealing with those matters and to urge them to act properly. Again, the fact that he warned the Galatians about the sins of the flesh suggests that they were having difficulty at that point. His words to the Ephesians about "fornication and all impurity or covetousness," about "filthiness, nor silly talk, nor levity" (5:3–4) suggests that their lives were not entirely above reproach. His plea to the Colossians to "put on" certain characteristics and to "let the peace of Christ rule in your hearts" (3:12–17) suggests that they needed prodding. Paul recognized that a new way of living was not an automatic consequence of a person becoming a Christian.

For Paul, therefore, a moral life is a consequence of Christian faith and is possible only within the context of the Christian community. He sees Christians as constantly struggling with the forces of evil, and therefore with pressures toward immoral conduct. He sees them as trying to be faithful and as constantly vulnerable. He sees them as having no degree of success in that struggle apart from the grace of God. Realistic enough to recognize failure, he talks about the continuing need for forgiveness. Recognizing the possibility of success by the grace of God, he continually urges people to rely upon the Spirit of God. He knows that the struggle will go on as long as time lasts and he anticipates the final victory of good over evil only at the end of time. The anticipation of that final victory, however, is not an escape into otherworldliness but a reason for faithfulness in the present struggle. For him, therefore, the moral struggle is an essential ingredient of faith.

Far from having to do only with a world to come, salvation is for Paul essentially a moral concept. Although it is a gift of God's grace, and in no sense earned, it is quite directly related to conduct. Paul considers it sheer nonsense to think that what one does is unimportant. One who is justified (i.e., a Christian) is expected to maintain a rigorous self-discipline, to live a life far more exemplary than that which is spelled out in the Law. Justification is not a substitute for righteousness but a precondition for it. Although Paul does not expect the Christian to live by the Law he expects of the Christian a righteousness that exceeds the Law. For him, the Lordship of Christ means following the example of Christ and obeying his word. Redemption means moral transformation, so that the Christian is a new person in Christ Jesus. The sharp break with the past is not simply a matter of belief and of worship. It is a new way of acting which results from a new character and which draws on newly discovered resources. For Paul, life *in Christ* is life *like Christ*. His crowning statement is, "For to me to live is Christ" (Philippians 1:21).

SIX
FAITH WORKING THROUGH LOVE

In the discussion thus far, a general approach to the making of ethical decisions has begun to emerge. Chapter one outlined the field of ethics, Chapters two and three described some alternative approaches, and chapters four and five presented some theological and biblical concepts. We can now draw these concepts together and propose a system for making decisions on ethical issues. The framework for this approach is provided by Paul's statement, "For in Christ Jesus neither circumcision nor uncircumcision is of any avail, but faith working through love" (Galatians 5:6).

FAITH

At the heart of one's religious life is a faith relationship to God. Faith is not something which one possesses as one owns a book or a piece of wearing apparel. Neither is it something that one does, as one utters a word, writes a check, or strikes someone. Rather it is an attitude or a disposition, like love, fear, admiration, or resentment. Its nearest synonyms are trust and confidence. In this sense, faith is a condition, a way of life.

Paul often spoke of faith as if it had a starting point. He looked back on the time, vivid in his memory, when he first believed in Christ. For him, however, that initial act was the beginning of a relationship, not an action complete in and of itself. Furthermore, he did not make his own experience standard for everyone, insisting that his way was the only valid one. He recognized that people enter the relationship in many different ways; for him, it was the relationship and not the manner of entry that was significant.

Faith and Salvation

The idea that faith is the way of salvation presupposes two important ideas about human nature: all human beings are made in the image of God, and all human beings are sinful. These contrasting ideas explain the tension which we feel between good and evil. Because the image of God is in all of us, both the desire and the potential for good is in all of us. Because we are sinful, we are attracted to evil, are indeed capable of massive evil, and find that even our best efforts are tarnished by our sinful nature. An awareness of this dual character of human nature should prevent us from being judgmental in our attitudes toward other people and from being smug and self-righteous about our own actions.

The solution to this human dilemma is the grace of God. *Grace* is a word for God's loving, kind, merciful outreach to human beings. In classical Greek the word means whatever affords joy, pleasure, or delight. In the New Testament the word is used for the one thing that affords human beings the greatest possible good: God's action on our behalf. This action is completely unearned, totally undeserved, and is therefore an unconditional gift. It is God's acceptance of us in spite of our sinfulness and with our having done nothing to persuade God to look upon us with favor. Although God reaches out to us in many ways, the supreme manifestation of God's grace is the coming of Jesus Christ to redeem us. The essence of the Gospel, therefore, is found in the declaration that "in Christ God was reconciling the world to himself" (2 Corinthians 5:19).

The result of Christ's work in us is a transformation of character. Our nature, which has been marred by self-love, is transformed into a new Christian nature. The sense of oneness with God, made possible by our being created in the divine image, but broken by our sinfulness, has been renewed. In Christ God has done for us what we could not do for ourselves. Faith is our response to that grace. Prompted by what God has done and is doing, it is our constant "Yes" to God.

Salvation entails a new way of life. We are saved, says Paul, "for good works" (Ephesians 2:8–10). One consequence of our new relationship with God is a new character, and therefore a new pattern of acting that expresses both a concern for personal purity and a concern for the well-being of other people. For Paul, at least, the difference made by salvation was sharp and clear. "Once you were darkness, but now you are light in the Lord," he said to the Ephesians (5:8). You once walked in an earthly way, he said to the Colossians: fornication, impurity, passion, evil desire, covetousness, anger, wrath, malice, slander, foul talk. But now you have "put on the new nature" which involves compassion, kindness, lowliness, meekness, patience, forgiveness, love (Colossians 3:5–17). A new moral nature, therefore, is an essential ingredient of salvation. One who comes under the Lordship of Christ becomes a new self. New motives compel one to new decisions, and new resources make it possible for one to implement those new decisions. A new goal integrates one's life and gives a new direction for moral development.

Life in the Christian Community

By virtue of being Christian, one has a special relationship with other believers. The church is the community of people who believe in Jesus Christ. As the central figure, Christ makes the distinction between the church and all other communities of faith. Long before it was organized, the church existed as a community. It came into being when people began to associate themselves with Christ and it grew as other people became his disciples. People were a part of the church not because they joined something but because they acknowledged Christ as Lord. That kind of relationship continues to the present, transcending time and place, ignoring cultural and ethnic differences, paying no attention to theological niceties, and disregarding organizational considerations.

Within the context of the Christian community, the goal of life is what Paul called *mature manhood* (Ephesians 4:13). The idea that the believer may mature within the church reflects the possibility of people falling short of the ideal. It was Christian people whom Paul urged to give careful attention to basic moral ideals, whom he urged to grow in their love for one another. Only occasionally does the New Testament hint that one who falls short of certain standards should be excluded from the fellowship. Far more often it speaks of helping one another, of striving for goals not yet attained, of seeking forgiveness for failure and asking for strength to resist temptation. The Christian life is a pilgrimage toward a goal that has not yet been achieved. The significance for Christian ethics of this life within the community of faith cannot be overemphasized. The church is the context for our living, the environment in which we develop toward mature manhood. For the Christian, all questions about behavior are to be asked and answered within the context of the community of faith, both with regard to the judgment of that community and with regard to the impact of a decision upon that community.

How does the community of faith affect us? First, we become believers through the community. That community is the group through whom the faith has been perpetuated. Extending back to the time of Jesus, it provides the basic information about the person and work of Christ. More than that, in it Christ is now present in the world and through it speaks to the world. That speaking is done in worship, in religious instruction, and in an outreach into the world.

Second, we understand the Scripture through the church. The Scripture is uniquely the possession of the church. The community of faith makes it available to the world and is concerned that it be understood as a vehicle for the Living Word. While we may study the Bible in the same way that we study other literature, that is not quite enough. We can understand the Scripture best by reading it as a part of the community of faith. As Elton Trueblood observed, we can see a stained glass window best from the inside.

All of this means, third, that we learn from the community of faith. We do not surrender judgment to the church. The church does not have all the answers. Like all other institutions it changes, and its judgments change. It must acknowledge its fallibility. It must be open both to the critic on the outside and to the prophet within. Yet it *is* the community of faith, it *is* devoted to the truth, and it *does* acknowledge the leadership of the Holy Spirit. As conscientious believers seeking to make moral judgments, we will do well to consider carefully what the church teaches.

Fourth, as believers in Christ we share in the life of the church. Because there is a corporate identity, we who constitute the fellowship are involved in corporate actions. We are a part of the brokenness of the church, its racial segregation, its discrimination against women, its investments in South Africa. We are also a part of its ministry to the poor, its championing of oppressed minorities, and its efforts to bring peace to the nations. The silence of the church is our silence, and so are its moral judgments. At times we would like to dissociate ourselves from something that the church does; at times we wish to speak when it is silent. But we are always a part of that community to which we speak and to which we listen.

Finally, as a part of the church we are responsible for its well-being. Its spiritual and moral health is our concern. If we are aware of an insensitivity on its part, ours must be the word that irritates. If we are aware of inappropriate action, ours must be the word of alarm. If we are aware of division, ours must be the healing word. Always we must speak the truth in love.

Using the Scripture

Although *the sole authority of the Scripture* is a basic Protestant principle, Protestants are far from united on the meaning of the phrase. Beliefs range from the idea of infallibility through "where the Bible speaks, we speak; where the Bible is silent, we are silent," to "we take the Bible as our starting point." In spite of these differences, however, we all take the Bible seriously and think that in some way it has a bearing upon our life in the world.

A proper use of Scripture in making moral decisions must take into account the nature of the Bible. In simple terms, it is the written record of God's self-revelation. Basic to an understanding of that record is a knowledge of the circumstances under which it was written, the literary forms in which it was written, and the situation of the people for whom it was written. The writers encountered God in the historical process and reported that encounter in their own way. Who they were affected what they said and how they said it. A vital part of who they were was their encounter with God both in day-by-day living and in unusual circumstances. The truth of the Bible is therefore not to be found in its specific statements about what God said or did but in the response of those ancient persons to God—and in the response to God that is evoked in the modern reader.

The Bible, then, is a vehicle of God's self-revelation. Regardless of the experience of the writers, if for us there is no encounter with God in the reading of the Bible, then *revelation* has no meaning for us and the teachings of the Bible are irrelevant. If, on the other hand, the Living Word comes through the written word, then for us the Bible is authoritative.

But authoritative in what sense? If the words of the Bible are not directives, not specifications about what must be done and what must not be done, then is it authoritative at all? If it is not intended to secure compliance, then why bother with what it teaches? The encounter with God which the authors reported was real. It was not merely an emotional experience, an amorphous feeling of being in the presence of God. It was a sense of divine judgment and of divine compulsion. In ethical terms, it was an understanding of a way of life that pleases God as contrasted with a way of life that displeases God. The details of how one is to act in specific circumstances vary because the conditions of life vary, but the perspective is constant. That perspective was stated in a dramatic way by Micah: "What does the Lord require of you but to do justice, and to love kindness, and to walk humbly with your God?" (6:8). It was summed up by Jesus: "You shall love the Lord your God...You shall love your neighbor as yourself" (Mark 12:30–31). It was summarized by Paul: "He who loves his neighbor has fulfilled the law" (Romans 13:8). It was reiterated by James, who said that pure and undefiled religion is "to visit orphans and widows in their affliction, and to keep oneself unstained from the world" (1:27).

If the requirements of true religion can be summed up in such a simple manner, why bother with anything else? Is any other teaching necessary or helpful? This stated norm needs to be understood by seeing its application in a variety of circumstances. Insight into the implications comes through the explanation and the application. Many of our problems, though not all of them, have parallels in the Bible. The ways in which people of faith responded to their encounter with God in those crises provide a pattern for our response in similar circumstances.

Worship and Morality

A major function of the church—and of the individuals who make up the church—is worship. To worship is to acknowledge God's supreme worth, to present ourselves before God in praise and adoration, to acknowledge our dependence and to express our devotion. We can do these things both in the company of fellow believers within the context of a planned service of worship and in solitary and intensely private experiences. Worship does not depend upon a mood, although a spirit of expectancy is conducive to it. It does not require presence in any particular place or the use of any particular symbols, although accustomed places and symbols may facilitate it. It does not require a given pattern, although familiar procedures may be the means by which we turn attention to God. Places, symbols, and patterns are valuable to the extent that they enable us to offer ourselves to God.

Isaiah's description of his vision of God in the temple (Isaiah 6:1–8) brings out the elements that are common to most worship experiences. First was an awareness of God's presence: "I saw the Lord sitting upon a throne, high and lifted up." An awareness of God's presence is awesome, for God is the transcendent, sovereign Creator and Sustainer of the world and all that is in it, while we are dependent creatures. The second element was an acknowledgement of sinfulness: "Woe is me! For I am lost; for I am a man of unclean lips, and I dwell in the midst of a people of unclean lips." The awareness of God, in all of God's purity, makes one aware of one's own sinfulness and leads to a confession of sin and a petition for forgiveness. The third element was an experience of renewal. Because Isaiah's mission was to be one of the spoken word, his confession of sin focused on his "unclean lips," and his experience of forgiveness involved a sense of his lips having been cleansed and purified. When the burning coal touched his lips he was told, "Your guilt is taken away, and your sin forgiven." The final element was a willingness to do the will of God. Only after being cleansed could Isaiah make that kind of commitment. As his initial reaction to his vision was an awareness of his own unworthiness, his final reaction was an offering of himself.

Worship, then, involves us in a reciprocal relationship with God. God reaches out to us, and we respond by offering ourselves. This offering is the connection between our praise of God and our work in the world. Worship is not a preparation for work, nor is work a substitute for worship. The two are so inseparably united that together they constitute the life of faith.

We are affected by worship in three basic ways. First, worship incorporates us in the Christian community. In worship, both corporate and private, we function as a part of the body of Christ. We are united in prayer and service with all other people who share in the community. Even private, individual experiences of worship do that because we enter those experiences as a part of a broader fellowship. We come to private worship from involvement with other Christians and we return to such involvement. Even in our solitude, therefore, we continue to worship with them. Corporate worship experiences, however, unite us in a unique way. When we worship together, the shared experiences of praise, confession, renewal, and commitment strengthen the bond between us.

Second, worship gives us insight into the meaning of faith. Whether private or corporate, it almost always involves the use of Scripture, the basic document of our faith. It involves meditation, in which we try to make some sense—rational and/or emotional—of life. It involves prayer, in which we place ourselves before God and open ourselves to God's leading. The essential function of the Holy Spirit is to teach. That does not mean the imparting of facts but the giving of insight, the prompting to move in a given direction, the urging to act in a given way. A person torn by emotion and unable to decide on a purely rational basis what to do may learn through worship what is the best course of action.

Third, worship renews the individual. We do not worship for the purpose of gaining strength but for the purpose of praising God. One consequence of the experience, however, is a sense of personal renewal of commitment and of the ability to fulfill that commitment. Because God is the source, we draw from God through worship. Worship is therefore a sacrament—a means by which God's grace reaches us.

The word *liturgy* comes from the Greek *leiturgia*, which is sometimes translated "worship" and sometimes "service." Indeed, when Paul wrote to the Roman Christians about their *leiturgia* he referred to what they did when they gathered in worship, to their personal relationships with one another, and to their responsibilities in the community at large (Romans 12). The fact that one word can be used to cover all three activities indicates that the three are not so different from one another as we imagine, that they are in fact a part of the whole. From a Christian perspective, then, morality cannot be considered in isolation from worship.

LOVE

If a relationship to God is at the heart of our religious life, so is a relationship to other people. So intimately connected are the two, in fact, that they cannot be separated. When Jesus was asked, "What is the greatest commandment?" he replied; "The first is, 'Hear, O Israel: The Lord our God, the Lord is one; and you shall love the Lord your God with all your heart, and with all your soul, and with all your mind, and with all your strength.' The second is this, 'You shall love your neighbor as yourself.' There is no other commandment greater than these" (Mark 12:29–30). Asked about one commandment, he gave the two as if they were one. Love for God is incomplete without love for neighbor; love for neighbor is not a free-standing relationship but depends on love for God. For Jesus, one side of the coin is faith, the other side is love.

The Nature of Love

In the command to love God, the word *love* implies the concept of *faith*. That meaning, however, is not all that the term implies. It involves also a grateful obedience to God's will. "This is the love of God, that we keep his commandments," said John (1 John 5:3). When we love God we are in a relationship in which what we want most is to do God's will.

God wills that we love our neighbor. Here the word *love* means an unselfish concern for the welfare of another person. It is not primarily an emotion which, like all other emotions, changes in response to external factors. It is a rational, deliberate acceptance of responsibility for another person. Neither is it a response to certain desirable qualities in another person. The reason for it is not to be found in the object of love. Jesus said nothing about people deserving our love but a great deal about our responsibility to love. Christian love does not therefore depend upon reciprocation from the other person. We must love regardless of how the other person acts. Although love may turn an enemy into a friend, it does not always happen that way. When it does not happen, we are still under obligation to love.

To love someone is to seek that person's good. This does not necessarily mean doing what that person wants, because what one wants may not necessarily be what is best. We are not required to surrender our judgment. Acting in the interest of another, we may even alienate that person. Yet we cannot refrain from seeking the best for that individual.

Love is a personal relationship. It is not regard for people in general but for persons in particular. There is no such thing as "the poor" or "the sick" or "the criminal." There are individuals who are poor, sick, or criminal. To love is to deal with these persons. We find the perfect illustration of such love in the ministry of Jesus.

Love is universal in its range. When Jesus said, "You therefore, must be perfect, as your heavenly Father is perfect" (Matthew 5:48), he was concluding a statement about God's love for everyone. The Old Testament command, "You shall love your neighbor as yourself," was well known to the Jews of Jesus' day. But in practice they limited their obligation by restricting the meaning of "neighbor" to other Jews. In the parable of the Good Samaritan, Jesus removed the possibility of that restriction. The Christian obligation to love extends to all people.

Love creates a community between persons. All of the actions of love which Paul cites in 1 Corinthians 13 bind people together; all of those things which he says love avoids divide people. Thus love ignores all such artificial barriers between people as race, wealth, class, and nation.

The Demands of Love

The specific demands of love are endless, varying with the circumstances in which we live. On the basis of the New Testament teachings, however, we can generalize. The first requirement is an attitude of concern and respect for other people. Jesus' interpretation of the Law of Moses consistently focused on attitudes rather than on actions. While he did not suggest that what we do is not important, he insisted that what we think and feel are primary. Even a "good" action based upon a wrong motive is unchristian. Conversely, a right attitude, although it is no guarantee that our judgments are wise, means that we are trying to act in the best interest of the other person.

A second requirement is that love must be expressed. We cannot love and leave alone. To ignore someone is to act as if that individual were not really a person. When Jesus talked about the responsibility to love he always spoke of doing things. When, for example, he said, "Love your enemies," he added "and do good, and lend, expecting nothing in return" (Luke 6:35).

Love requires forgiveness and the pursuit of reconciliation. The only phrase in the Lord's Prayer which Jesus interpreted was the petition, "Forgive us our debts, as we also have forgiven our debtors" (Matthew 6:12). Jesus commented, "For if you forgive men their trespasses, your heavenly Father also will forgive you; but if you do not forgive their trespasses, neither will your Father forgive your trespasses" (vv. 14–15). He even said that unreconciled differences with a brother prevent one from truly worshipping God (Matthew 5:23–36). When Peter asked how often he should forgive an offending brother, Jesus replied that there should be no limit to forgiveness (Matthew 18:21–22). This principle for dealing with an enemy is not merely nonretaliation. It is active, generous treatment of wrongdoers in a positive effort to establish a good relationship with them.

Jesus had a special concern for the unfortunate. He saw his mission as a ministry to the poor and neglected (cf. Luke 4:18–19). Often he used service to such people as an illustration of the true character of neighborly love. Obviously he saw deeper needs, needs of the spirit, and these he did not neglect. But an indifference to the physical and emotional needs of the unfortunate is utterly foreign to his religion and therefore to the religion of his disciples.

Jesus' demand for love involves the demand for justice. In this emphasis he was the heir of the great prophetic tradition. Although he did not often use the terms *just* and *justice*, the concept was fundamental to his thought. When, for example, he said, "You shall love your neighbor as yourself," he implied a standard by which we might measure our obligations to our neighbor. When he discussed either the value of the individual or the will of God he was talking about a standard of right conduct to which his disciples owe their allegiance. In Christian thought, therefore, justice is not merely giving all persons their due. Rather, it is acting toward them as God acts.

The Source of Love

These demands of love are impossibly difficult. The person who takes faith most seriously is the one who is most aware of failure. Talking in the abstract about what love demands is easy, but dealing with unlovely people is an entirely different matter. A legalistic morality is relatively simple because we can measure our achievements by the code and catch ourselves up at the points where we fall short. But the radically unselfish concern and the constant self-giving demanded by love are entirely beyond our grasp. We cannot act with utter and complete disregard for ourselves.

In this radical sense, therefore, love is a quality which only God possesses. It is God's way of dealing with people, a way in which we are utterly incapable of acting. But if this is so, then what becomes of our duty to love? Why did Jesus say, "You shall love your neighbor as yourself"? Although love cannot originate with us, it does come from God through us to our neighbor. The First Epistle of John elaborates this idea which is summarized in the simple and direct statement:

> Beloved, let us love one another; for love is of God, and he who loves is born of God and knows God. He who does not love does not know God; for God is love. In this the love of God was made manifest among us, that God sent his only Son into the world, so that we might live through him. In this is love, not that we loved God but that he loved us and sent his Son to be the expiation for our sins. Beloved, if God so loved us, we also ought to love one another. No man has ever seen God; if we love one another, God abides in us and his love is perfected in us. (1 John 4:7–12)

Although love cannot originate with us, then, it comes from God through us to our neighbor. We can act in love even though we cannot originate love. While we cannot by our own will begin to love our neighbor, we can respond to God's call. We can be instruments of God's love at work in the world. Whether God's love reaches our neighbor depends in a sense upon our willingness to permit the divine love to flow through us into the world.

The essence of the covenant which God has made with us is summed up in the Old Testament phrase, "I shall be your God and you shall be my people." It is caught up in Jesus' statement about the wine at the Last Supper, "This is my blood of the covenant." As people of the covenant, we participate in God's work in the world. We learn what reason alone cannot tell us, we are motivated by the love of God, and we are enabled by the spirit of Christ embodied in the community of faith.

Love and Justice

When we think of Christian responsibility we tend to think in individual terms. We think of our relationships with other people and of what we should or should not do as we deal with them. We are concerned about such matters as whether to give money to a poor person who asks for help, or whether to retaliate when someone does something to offend us, or whether to take advantage of the ignorance of a person with whom we are doing business. We concentrate on personal matters like keeping our temper, or speaking the truth, or whether to use drugs. We deal with such intimate questions as whether to have an abortion, or to run the risk of becoming involved with someone married to another person, or to withdraw life-support systems from a member of our family who is critically ill. We see Christian responsibility, in other words, as having to do with individual conduct.

There is, of course, some justification for this way of thinking. Jesus' teachings were directed to individuals and they dealt with personal responses to all kinds of circumstances. Whether those teachings are valid or whether they are applicable to present-day living can be debated. Whether they can be interpreted as having a bearing upon social policy can be debated. But that they are intensely personal is clear. Jesus talked about a person loving his enemy, about returning good for evil, and about going the second mile. But can a nation love? Can a race of people deal with another race? People do not function as "a nation" or "a race" or even as "a family." They function as individual citizens of a nation, as persons of a given racial group, as members of a family. It was to such individual functioning that Jesus spoke.

Is there, then, a Christian responsibility for the social order? Can we deal *as Christians* with social issues? Can we deal with racial discrimination in any way other than trying as individuals to be fair and honest and accepting of all people? Can we deal with the problem of war other than by praying that it will never break out again? Can we deal with the disintegration of the family other than by trying to maintain the stability of our own family life? Can we deal with the second-class status of women other than by ignoring the stereotype that specifies what is and what is not appropriate for women?

Most Christians believe that they do in fact have some responsibility for the social order. There is no general agreement, however, on what that responsibility is. Many Christians, perhaps most, believe that the way to build a better world is to work through individuals. At the simplest level this is interpreted to mean the effort to make Christians of everyone. Many people assume that one who becomes a Christian undergoes a change in character and begins to act morally. The more Christian people there are the better society will become. At a deeper level this individualistic approach assumes that the more one is imbued with the spirit of Christ the more one is likely to act in a Christian way. Experiences of worship, the teachings of the church, and association with like-minded Christians will coalesce to bring the individual into deeper insight into the character of the Christian life and a more compelling motivation to follow the example of Jesus. At both levels this individualistic approach assumes that because better individuals make for a better world, the Christian solution to social problems is simply to help individuals to become Christian and to help Christian individuals become more Christ-like.

This individualistic approach fails to come to terms with serious social problems. It ignores the fact that people do not fall into the neat categories of good and bad. The continuing problem of Christians is that they are always torn between good and evil, that they are constantly having to struggle with choices, and that they do not always follow the way that they believe to be right. Furthermore, an honest Christian acknowledges that people who do not have Christian, or even religious, convictions share the same concerns, and that often the course of action which they take is good and just. The fact that one is a Christian, in other words, is no guarantee that one's decisions are correct or that one's actions are moral. Nor does the fact that one is not a Christian mean that one's decisions are wrong or that one's actions are immoral.

In addition, this individualistic approach fails to get at the root of many problems. We are what we are in social context: we have a biological and a cultural heritage; we are members of families; we are influenced by our peers; we are subject to the laws of the state; we are affected by what we see and hear. Acceptance of the Christian faith does not automatically result in a correction of our attitudes on social problems. The values and ideals of a white, Protestant Christian are not always the same as those of Christians who are not white and Protestant. The values and ideals of a Boston Catholic Christian are different from those of one who is not a Catholic from Boston. The attitude implicit in the phrase "the way we have always done things" affects our judgment on educational, economic, political, religious, and moral issues. Our decisions are not made on the basis of our faith alone but are powerfully conditioned by our other loyalties as well.

The individualistic approach fails to recognize the character of social institutions. The functions of the state are not individual but corporate. The state, for example, builds roads, maintains a postal system, and goes to war. The state deals with criminals, takes care of the poor, and sends people into outer space. Individuals may approve or disapprove of state actions, they may express their opinions, and they may try to alter the course that the state is taking. But however responsive or unresponsive the state is to individual opinion, the state acts. In varying ways the same situation exists with the economic system, with religion, with education, and with social custom. It even exists with the specific company for which a person works, the local school which a person attends, or the congregation to which a person belongs. Individuals act within the social context; but the social context also acts upon the individual.

This last fact points toward a conclusion about Christian responsibility in dealing with social issues. If we are concerned about feeding hungry people, we must work through the structures of society—the economic order and the government—to deal with the causes of poverty. If we are concerned about peace between peoples, we must work through the political structure of which we are a part. If we are concerned about the mistreatment of any group in our society, we must work through the agencies which perpetuate that mistreatment. This approach in no way minimizes personal relationships. It recognizes, however, that individual problems are often symptoms of a much broader social situation and that the structure must be corrected if the situation is to be improved.

When the practices of racial segregation in public facilities were being challenged in the 1950s and 1960s the cry was often heard, "You cannot legislate morals." The people making that protest were ignoring the fact that the laws requiring segregation, enacted in the post-Reconstruction era, had in fact done that very thing. Experience since those laws were struck down, furthermore, has proven that legislation can in fact do a great deal in changing not merely practices but attitudes as well. In the 1970s and 1980s the status of women in society and the attitudes of people toward the rights of women have been altered in the same way. This is not to suggest that all problems can be dealt with through legislation. It certainly is not to suggest that Christians should try to impose their moral standards upon others by having them enacted into law. It is to suggest, however, that many of the moral issues which we face are social in nature and that the appropriate and effective way to deal with them is to work through the structures of power.

Here the relationship between love and justice becomes crucial. We have said that in the Old Testament there is frequent expression of concern for justice. We have observed also that Jesus focused on the concept of love, even to the extent of saying that all the requirements of the Law and the Prophets were summed up in the commandments to love God supremely and to love one's neighbor as oneself. Since he said little about justice, are we to conclude that it is not a Christian concern? If a Christian ethic entails a concern for both love and justice, how are the two related to each other?

Joseph Fletcher (*Situation Ethics*, 87–102) insists that "love and justice are the same, for justice is love distributed, nothing else" (p. 86). He speaks of justice as "Christian love using its head, calculating its duties, obligations, opportunities, resources." For him, *love* and *justice* are simply synonymous terms, so that neither is superior to the other, neither is derived from the other, neither is in conflict with the other, neither uses the other. The two words should create the same image in one's mind and we could drop either term from our vocabulary without losing any substance at all.

Interestingly enough, Fletcher agrees with Paul Ramsey at this point. Ramsey says that "obedient love" is the central category in Christian ethics. He defines justice as God's way of dealing with people, as God's "righteousness" which he says is neither "corrective" nor "distributive" but "redemptive" (*Basic Christian Ethics*, p. 14). The standards of human justice, he says, are drawn from the righteousness of God and are therefore redemptive. Taking Paul as his model, he avoids giving a simple definition of love. He says that 1 Corinthians 13 "defines by *indication*, pointing not to anything generally experienced by all men everywhere, like blueness or fatherhood, but, as we shall see, to Jesus Christ" (p. xvi). He describes love as neighbor-centered, nonpreferential, nonresistant, obedient, and universal. He correctly observes, therefore, that the concept of obedient love focuses on the ideas of covenant and the reign of God, concluding that the two are the same thing, that to obey the covenant is to do justice (p. 388).

DECISION

To make good decisions on specific issues, one needs a pattern for determining what love requires. One cannot make sound decisions without guidelines, without a basis for evaluation, without some criteria by which to say, "I ought to do this" or "I ought not to do that." As a matter of fact, most people do have certain rules of conduct, whether those rules are explicitly stated or not. One who has a set of deliberately chosen and rationally stated principles by which to operate is in a position to make good decisions.

Accepting love as the essence of Christian moral obligation, then, one needs to ask, "What does love lead me to do?" Here we offer certain general principles as guidelines for answering that question:

1. The human race is one. The "differences" that exist between people (race, class, culture, education, and so on) are of only secondary importance.
2. Every individual is of infinite worth. Everyone, therefore, is to be dealt with not as a tool or a thing, but as a person, as an end and not as a means.
3. Material values are secondary to personal values.
4. Every person has certain basic human rights which must be respected at all times. At the least, these rights include life, physical well-being, reputation, and property.
5. Each person has a responsibility to seek the good of other people.
6. Often one value or duty must be sacrificed to another.
7. Because the universe is orderly, it is often (though not always) possible to anticipate the consequences of a given course of action.

These principles are not rules of conduct. They say nothing directly about cheating on tests, about premarital or extramarital sexual intercourse, about working for an institution with whose policies one disagrees. They say nothing directly about care for aging parents, about cleaning up the slums of the city, about eliminating discrimination against minorities, about dealing with corruption in government, about the situations in the Near East and in South Africa. They say nothing about national defense or nuclear energy or protection of the environment. Can we come any closer to making decisions about these kinds of situations? Certainly we can predict with some degree of accuracy the results of contemplated actions. We can be sure that good is more likely to be attained by one course of action than by another. While each situation is unique, there is a regularity or similarity in the patterns of human relationships. On the basis of that regularity or similarity, we can become more specific about what we should or should not do. We can establish certain patterns of conduct.

Are these patterns of conduct "rules"? We might draw a parallel with the concept of the laws of nature. A law of nature is simply a prediction based upon an observed regularity. It says, "This is the way things operate." On the basis of this regularity we can say, "If we want to get this result, then that is the way we should act." A pattern of conduct or "rule" in the realm of morality is the same sort of thing. It is a generalization or a prediction based upon observation. It does not control; it is not arbitrary; it is not without reason. It is the observation that a given way of acting brings certain results. Knowing that, we can say, "If we want this result, then that is the way we should act." Such formulations are tentative, always subject to correction by additional information. But they are useful ways to make day-by-day decisions.

Our social order presupposes such moral generalizations, and we can best seek the good of others by giving critical allegiance to them. As a case in point, consider the academic community. It is the responsibility of an instructor to share information with students as completely, honestly, and objectively as possible; to stimulate their thinking, to test them fairly, and to evaluate their work carefully. It is the responsibility of the students to do their own work as effectively as they can. The instructor cannot seek the good of the students, as love requires, by neglecting the basic responsibilities of the position. The student cannot seek the good of the instructor and the good of fellow students, as love requires, and cheat on tests. While this academic system may not be the best of all possible systems, it is the one within which we live and work, and within it we implement our love by following certain rules. Circumstances may sometimes arise which will call for a suspension of a rule; but in the long run the normal procedures provide the framework for serving the best interests of all concerned.

In addition to such general rules covering social relationships, there are also rules of personal conduct which we choose on an individual basis. While we cannot generalize those personal rules and try to enforce them on everyone else, we can respond to the leading of God by choosing for ourselves a particular pattern of acting. Using Lehmann's terms, "as a believer in Jesus Christ and as a member of his church," we might choose to act in this way or not to act in that way. The establishment of such personal rules is not only permissible but inevitable. Either deliberately or by default, we do in fact establish for ourselves a pattern of conduct. Sound decisions are best made by careful and deliberate choice.

These rules or patterns of conduct have to do with action rather than with motive. They are guidelines for the expression of those principles which we have just discussed, and which are in turn elaborations of the concept of love. They are thus instruments of love. They serve as norms or standards by which day by day we can make loving decisions and choices. They are not directives or preset solutions. Rather they are guides for acting in normal situations and patterns for helping make decisions in abnormal ones. They provide a standard by which we can measure the new, the different, the novel, and the challenging, in terms of what is familiar. They are not absolutes which permit no variation; we can readily make exceptions when they are warranted. Indeed, only because we have rules for the usual situation can we know when extraordinary measures are called for.

This approach can be illustrated with examples from the ministry of Jesus. In his day the written law prohibited work on the Sabbath. By traditional interpretation, or the oral law, a large number of activities that were unlawful on the Sabbath were identified. In addition, custom decreed attendance at synagogue services on the Sabbath. Even the most casual reader of the Gospels will observe that Jesus did indeed respect the Sabbath and the purposes for which it was intended. He frequented the synagogues; he rested; he acknowledged that the Sabbath was created for the benefit of humankind (Mark 2:27). When the occasion called for it, however, he worked on the Sabbath (cf. Mark 3:1–5). Apparently he saw no contradiction between observing the Sabbath on the one hand and making exceptions in order to meet human need on the other.

Furthermore, since rules are always closely related to life in a given context, the rules must change as the context changes. This too can be illustrated from the teachings of Jesus. Once he was asked about the Old Testament law which permitted a man to divorce his wife if "she finds no favor in his eyes because he has found some indecency in her" (Mark 20:2–23; cf. Deuteronomy 24:1). Whatever the reason for the law in its original form, in Jesus' day it worked to the disadvantage of women. In the first century A.D. women were almost totally dependent upon men. A divorced woman, therefore, may very well have had no one to care for her and no means of caring for herself. Jesus' alteration of the Old Testament law, whether it was unique to him or not, represents his awareness of the necessity of changing rules that prove to be damaging rather than helpful to women.

Thus far, although the concept of living by rules has been discussed, nothing has been said about *whose* rules. It has been implied, however, that moral rules are not imposed upon us by an external authority. Rules are valid for us when we deliberately give our allegiance to them. That rule is valid for me, as a mature Christian person, whose guidance I choose to accept.

That is not to say that we start from nothing and arbitrarily create a set of rules by which to govern ourselves. We could not do it that way, even if that were best, because of all the influences from the past that have made us what we are now. Each of us has learned a great deal from our family, from our peers, from the church, from educational institutions, from all of the experiences which we have had. Those teachings have become a part of us. As adults, we have both the freedom and the responsibility to examine critically what we have received from the past. Our examination of any rule should take into account the reason for its creation, its adequacy for dealing with the issue, and the relationship between the present situation and the past. The rules of conduct which we have received from the past may indeed represent the wisdom of experience. If they do, we will do well to preserve them in some fashion. If they do not, we will do well to abandon them. The fact that a rule is old does not make it either true or false. The fact that it has survived, however, does suggest that it merits examination.

One fact that makes the creation of rules of some sort both possible and necessary is the universality and the permanence of certain qualities of human nature. Certain desires, needs, and drives characterize all people, regardless of time and place. Those universal characteristics give rise to a variety of patterns of personal and social relationships. Moral rules have come into being in various societies as embodiments of human experience. Of course, individual differences must be taken into account in all human relationships. It is the similarities, however, which make it possible for us to approach each new experience with some degree of confidence based upon the experience of others.

In Christian thought, the rules by which we operate are cast within the framework of our relationship to God. Christians talk a great deal about *the will of God*. The starting point for their understanding of the will of God is the Bible. Now, quite obviously, Christians vary widely in their view of how the Bible was written, how it is to be understood and interpreted, and consequently how its authority is to be accepted. All Christian thinkers, however, take it seriously as a record of God's self-disclosure. For this reason Christian ethicists of all schools of thought try to show that their approach to ethical issues is essentially in keeping with the spirit of the Scripture.

It is furthermore generally assumed that God is reliable and orderly, not whimsical or capricious. We can talk about love, justice, and righteousness, about honesty, fidelity, and integrity, because of the unchanging nature of the One upon whom the whole structure of the universe rests. Those rules which we make for ourselves are properly the ones we find to be the logical conclusion of this understanding of the way God deals with the world.

Another element in consideration of the idea of the will of God is the concept of the discipline of the Holy Spirit. Whatever else we mean by the leadership of the Spirit, we mean that God is at work in the world and in our lives. This is not to suggest that in all circumstances, or even in any circumstance, we might get a clear vision of the will of God—a vision that will lead us in an entirely new direction. But it is to suggest that as we use the best that is available by way of the teaching of the Scripture, the wisdom that has come from the past, and a knowledge of present circumstances, we may be further enlightened by the presence of the Spirit. In this way we can establish helpful patterns of acting. Rules of conduct established in this way are not matters of whim or of prejudice, but of personal decision, commitment, and acceptance.

Rules, then, can serve well as guides for day-by-day conduct. That is to say, we do not need to try to make every decision in life as if we have never before encountered a similar situation. Once we have decided that we are going to be honest, for example, and once we have decided that honesty prohibits us from using someone else's work as our own, then for us the matter is settled. We do not have to approach every book with a mental debate as to whether we shall or shall not use the author's material as if it were ours. We do not have to debate before each test as to whether we will or will not copy answers from the person beside us. One decision can settle the issue.

Rules are also helpful in preventing us from making decisions on the basis of self-interest rather than of love. If we are threatened in any way, our first thought usually is to save our own skins. Most of us are willing to do that even at the expense of someone else. A student who for any reason has delayed to the last minute the preparation of a paper, for example, is at that point hardly able to debate the morality of plagiarism or of turning in a paper acquired from someone else. All that the student can think about is the urgency of turning in a paper. The last minute is not the time to debate issues of personal integrity; it is the time to act on decisions made in more deliberate circumstances.

Rules help us avoid the undue influence of emotions. Our emotions are an integral part of our total makeup and therefore are an important element in the decision-making process. They often lead us to take actions that are quite unwise, however. Some of the stronger emotions, not merely the negative ones such as fear and anger, but also the positive ones such as compassion and desire, tend to disrupt the reasoning process. Since love is concerned with what happens to people, this "ecstatic impulse of self-giving" needs the direction of careful thought and decision. Rules arrived at in a careful manner are more reliable than impulsive reaction.

In addition, rules help us preserve the wisdom of experience. They help us incorporate in future actions what we have learned from our own mistakes and successes. Indeed, because many of the rules by which we operate are those taught us by our parents, by educational experiences, by the church, by wise men and women of history, we are the beneficiaries of a sort of collective wisdom. Certainly the content of that collective wisdom varies, and obviously not everything that has been passed on is properly called wisdom. Furthermore, even if something were valid for the past, it may have no relevance to the present. The process of determining our own pattern of action, however, makes it quite possible for us to examine what we have received and to appropriate the good and the relevant to our own day-by-day living.

Such rules protect the rights of other people. If it is a fact that each individual has inherent rights which we must not violate, they help us to identify those rights. They give some clue as to what we need to do to help secure those rights and what we should avoid doing so as not to interfere with other people's pursuit of those things that are properly theirs.

Some regularity in our day-by-day conduct, then, some pattern of behavior, some norm by which we can regularly operate and from which we can vary when love so dictates, is essential. Rules carefully arrived at by deliberate consideration, made our own by personal acceptance and/or commitment, and used conscientiously under the discipline of the Spirit of God can be indicators of the way love leads us to act.

SEVEN

HUMAN SEXUALITY AND THE MARRIAGE RELATIONSHIP

William is twenty-two years of age and Mary is twenty-one. They knew each other in high school but did not date. They lived in the same neighborhood and their families were acquainted with each other. They attended the same church and for a time were involved in some of the youth activities. In late high school years, however, both of them gradually became less involved in the church. After he was graduated from high school, William continued to live at home and attended the local university. Mary attended a business college and after graduation found employment in a neighboring community. For a time she shared an apartment with a longtime friend. William and Mary started dating when he was a junior at the university. After his graduation he accepted employment in a city in another state. Mary soon gave up her job, found work in the city where William was living, and moved into the apartment with him. Neither set of parents knew initially about the living arrangement, but gradually sensed what it was. They were distressed when they realized the truth and did not understand why William and Mary did not marry. Mary wanted to marry but William was unwilling to make the kind of commitment which he considered necessary to marriage. The two fell into a pattern for sharing apartment expenses but made no well-thought-out arrangement for joint ownership of property. They entered the relationship without any planning; they simply began living together.

This narration is not a true story about a specific couple but a composite constructed from details of a number of couples. Such living-together arrangements, increasingly common, raise a number of questions that are important from a Christian perspective. What is the nature of human sexuality? What is the place of sex in the man-woman relationship? What is the nature of marriage? What are the appropriate constraints under which Christians live?

THE CURRENT SCENE

The family of the past is usually sentimentalized and idealized: the man is portrayed as the breadwinner and the woman as the homemaker. They married because they were in love and they entered marriage knowing what would be expected of them and what they could expect from their mates. As mates they were loving and faithful, as parents they were wise and kind. Their children were dutiful, they accepted the values which their parents passed on to them, and they had a bright future.

That portrait, of course, is a caricature. Never has one family pattern been characteristic of even a majority of the people. There have been differences between black families and white ones, between working-class families and upper-class ones, between southerners and midwesterners, between Christians and Jews, and peoples of other religions and peoples of no religion. There have been male-dominated and female-dominated families. There have been childless couples, single-parent families, and extended families living in the same household. There have been happy families and unhappy ones. But never has there been a "typical" one.

Yet sociologists have been able to generalize about the age at which most people marry, the percentage of marriages that fail, the percentage of women who work outside the home, the average size of family, and so on. They have described patterns of behavior, discussed factors that contribute to success or failure in marriage, and predicted consequences of certain ways of acting. Such generalizations are now more difficult. The most significant single element in the present situation is the fact of rapid change. The way men and women relate to each other, the way they make their decision about marriage, what they expect in marriage, how they adjust to one another, how their marriage affects the other aspects of their lives, what they do if they find their marriage to be unsatisfactory—all of this is so varied and is changing so rapidly that no pattern is discernible.

With change the order of the day, there seems no place for absolutes. Until the 1960s most people assumed that "right" and "wrong" were defined by generally accepted standards of conduct. That is not to suggest that everyone lived by the standards; obviously many people violated them. Yet they were acknowledged by most people. At present, however, the standards themselves are challenged. Although people have to make choices about their own conduct, and although they choose what seems to them to be right, most are unwilling to say that other people should make similar decisions. As in the period of the

Judges in the Old Testament, "every person does that which is right in his own eyes."

Nowhere is change more evident than in the area of man-woman relationships. The movement of women into employment outside the home has given them far more freedom than they have ever had before. An increasing number find great satisfaction in their careers. Many delay marriage, and many others choose not to marry at all. In marriage, the income of women is becoming more and more important. Furthermore, an increasing number of married women are deciding not to remain in marriages which they find to be unsatisfactory. No longer, therefore, do women identify themselves exclusively, or even primarily, in terms of their families.

This change in the status of women involves important role changes for both women and men. Those changes are reflected most obviously in the more casual and equalitarian relationships between unmarried people. As yet, however, they have not materially altered the pattern of relationships within marriage. In few marriages is the woman's career given equal consideration with the man's. In few do men share fully in household responsibilities, and in few do men assume responsibility for child care equal to that of women. The slow pace of change within the family is not due simply to the unwillingness of men to change; it is due also to the unwillingness of women to relinquish their traditional functions. But changes outside the home inevitably will result in changes within the home.

Another factor which affects the pattern of man-woman relationships is the development of safe and effective methods of contraception. In an earlier day the possibility of an unwanted pregnancy was a significant deterrent to sex activity both before marriage and in marriage. With the development of the oral contraceptive in the 1960s, however, the danger of an unwanted pregnancy has been greatly reduced. Furthermore, the availability of simpler and safer methods of abortion has created the possibility of terminating unwanted pregnancies at little cost, with little loss of time, and without the fact of the pregnancy being known by other people. The possibility of sex without fear of an unwanted pregnancy has made a profound impact upon the man-woman relationship. It should be noted that the possibility of contracting AIDS has reintroduced the element of fear.

In this new setting people live and function as sexual beings, and many do so without any sense of certainty about their sexual nature. They are subject to the pressures of the sex drive, to the influence of their peers, to the concepts presented by the communications media, to the teachings of their family, and to the ideals enunciated by the church. Since we are not accustomed to thinking philosophically, most of us never arrive at a rational and morally defensible position. The establishment of such a position, however, is an integral element in the formation of a Christian ethic.

Our understanding of our sexuality must be developed within the context in which we live. Sexuality is not isolated from the other aspects of life; rather it is involved in all of our relationships with other people, and thus in our political, business, educational, religious, and recreational activities. While it is not the determining factor in all that we do, we do not cease being sexual beings when we do business, play, pray, engage in political activity, or do anything else.

One aspect of our sexuality is the biological factor. Indeed, one can think of sex as a biological function only. In that sense the sex drive, like hunger or thirst, is a physically based need. It is oriented immediately toward pleasure and the release of tensions, and ultimately toward procreation. For its satisfaction sex partners can be interchangeable. In this sense sex functions among human beings exactly as it does among the lower animals. While an adequate understanding of sex cannot stop with this biological aspect, no discussion of human sexuality can ignore it.

A second factor, one which is of major significance in our society, is the fact that many people—perhaps most—treat the man-woman relationships as a game. Two people are attracted to each other, they flirt with one another, they tease one another. At the outset they have no serious interest in one another, though that may develop. For the moment they simply enjoy playing the game. The game does not necessarily culminate in sexual intercourse, although it may. If it does, the intercourse does not necessarily involve any commitment beyond the present moment. Indeed, for many people a part of the game is to avoid commitment.

A third element of sexuality important in our culture is romantic love. In our marriage mythology we assume that this is the only sound reason for a couple getting married, that this is all that they need to create a sound marriage, that if they are in love they should marry, and that if they are not in love they should not marry. This kind of love idealizes the other person. It has been defined as "a gross exaggeration of the difference between one person and everyone else in the world." It is a response to all of those attractive features which one finds in the other, and it is a desire to possess that person for one's own. The highly romantic and unrealistic situations depicted in the afternoon soap operas and the R-rated motion pictures tend to confuse both the married and the unmarried about personal relationships in and out of marriage.

Against this background the traditional Christian understanding of sexuality and marriage represents a difficult ideal. Stated in simple terms, that ideal calls for chastity before marriage and for fidelity within marriage. It considers marriage to be a permanent relationship and divorce for any reason to be a failure. Because of the power of the sex drive, one must be extremely careful about personal relationships. Because the games that men and women play are so highly sexual, a married person must not indulge in them. Even if romance and excitement disappear from a marriage, a couple must remain true to the vows which they have made.

The period of courtship is the time for fun and games; the period of marriage is the time for more serious matters.

All of this is not to suggest that the traditional concept of marriage is totally negative. On the contrary, in this view romance matures into a deeper and more meaningful love. Sex has a more profound meaning than the satisfaction of a biological urge. The security of marriage is more satisfying than the uncertainties of romance. Marriage, indeed, is seen not as restricting but as liberating. Even those people who fail to achieve that kind of marriage think of their failure as a personal matter, not an inadequacy of the system.

A CHRISTIAN INTERPRETATION OF SEXUALITY

A Theological Perspective

It is ironic that Christianity, which professes to help people relate to God and to the world, has actually given little help in dealing with a reality so basic to human nature that some people consider it the source of all human activity. In the late fourth century the great theologian Augustine expressed a negative attitude toward sexuality. Because of his own personal spiritual struggle he came to believe that the sex drive was in itself evil. Although sexual relations were permissible to married people who wished to have children, he thought, celibacy is the holiest way of life. His view came to dominate the thinking of the early church and his influence is still felt. Until quite recently this negativism expressed itself in our country in a puritanism which drew a curtain around sexuality. Sex was a taboo subject, not to be discussed in polite society, and certainly not in mixed company. "Dirty" jokes were jokes about sex. Children were taught nothing about sex, neither at home nor at school, and certainly not at church. Although some Christian theologians tried to discuss sexuality in a relevant way, they could not alter the thinking of the church as a whole. When the sexual revolution struck full force in the 1960s, therefore, the church was ill prepared to give guidance.

In sharp contrast, the Bible is quite open in its treatment of sex. Without deifying it, as did some ancient religions (and, in a sense, as does our modern overemphasis), the Scripture recognizes sex as a normal and important part of human life. Without titillating, it reports many facets of the sex life of the people of the Bible. Without any hint of "naughtiness" it reports their failures.

On the basis of biblical teachings we may make several affirmations about human sexuality. First, sex is a part of our God-given nature. In biblical terms, all creation is the work of God and God has made us the way we are. In the older creation account God's creation of humankind was not complete until woman was created as a complement to man (Genesis 2:7, 18–22), and the climax of the story comes in the statement of the unity of the couple (Genesis 2:24). In the later creation account humankind was made "male and female" (1:27) and was commanded, as were the other creatures, to "be fruitful and multiply." Sexuality, therefore, is characteristic of all human beings. The power of the sex drive is unrelated to how attractive or unattractive one is. A physical or a mental handicap does not make one immune to the sex drive. Older people do not cease to be sexual beings, and neither do people who take religious vows. The strength of the sex drive is unrelated to the marital status of a person. We are all sexual beings whose drive is affected by circumstances but not destroyed by them.

Second, our sexuality is good, not evil. God made us the way we are and all of God's work is good. Like everything else that God made, we can abuse and corrupt it. We can even use it to destroy ourselves. But that possibility is the possibility to do something evil with what God has created as good. The importance of this affirmation lies partly in the fact that it is in sharp contrast with the view long held by the church. It lies also in the fact that although this present generation is quite open and free in its enjoyment of sex, the sad consequences of the abuses of our sexual nature are all too common. The goodness of sexuality is affirmed in spite of the guilt that many people feel about even normal and legitimate sex feelings and activities. The damage is done by the use of sex in the power struggle between men and women, the violation of human beings by other human beings, and the jealousies, frustrations, and insecurities that disrupt personal relationships. The goodness of this aspect of our nature needs to be understood by a generation that in its frantic search for pleasure finds little joy in self-expression.

Third, sexual intercourse is best understood as a relationship rather than as something that two people do. The vulgarisms often used to refer to coition speak of one person doing something to another. The biblical term for the legitimate sex relationship, *to know*, conveys a very different attitude. Knowledge does not simply mean an awareness of facts, an intellectual acknowledgement that something is true; it is an experience of reality. To know someone is to be involved with that person at the deepest possible level. For a man and a woman to know each other sexually is to enter into a communion that is far more than physical. Andrew Lester says:

> We "know" what we lack, as either a male or a female, by experiencing it in intimate, revealing relationships with one of the opposite sex. This intimate "knowing" reaches its most profound level in intercourse. A human being, whether male or female, knows himself and his own potential through experiencing the powerful fulfilment of intercourse. This person also comes

to know his partner in a way that cannot be achieved through any other avenue of experience. (*Sex is More than a Word*, 22–23)

From a Christian perspective, the mutuality of this relationship is of major significance. This concept is implicit in the older creation narrative which focused on the man's need of companionship (Genesis 2:18–25). It is more directly affirmed in the later creation account which speaks of humankind being created as male and female, as the two essential parts of the one entity (Genesis 1:26–28). No biblical writer, however, has stated this idea more forcefully than the apostle Paul. He said to the Corinthians:

> Each man should have his own wife and each woman her own husband. The husband should give to his wife her conjugal rights, and likewise the wife to her husband. For the wife does not rule over her own body, but the husband does; likewise the husband does not rule over his own body, but the wife does. (1 Corinthians 7:2–4)

In a later statement about the total man-woman relationship, he said, "Be subject to one another out of reverence for Christ" (Ephesians 5:21). While his discussion of mutual submission was not limited to the sex relationship, it includes it.

Fourth, the sex relationship has two basic functions. The first is reproduction. This function, affirmed in the command to "be fruitful and multiply," is assumed throughout the Scripture. The second is the establishment and the maintenance of the unity of a man and a woman. While other factors are involved, unity is incomplete without coition. This is the implication of the words of Scripture, "so that they are no more two but one flesh." Once a man and a woman have come together in coition, their relationship can never again be as though it had not happened. For this reason Paul warned, "Do you not know that he who joins himself to a prostitute becomes one body with her?" (1 Corinthians 6:16). Undoubtedly he overstated his case. There is nothing magical about coition, and two people who have no intention of a relationship beyond a temporary physical union are not necessarily changed by that act. Yet coition does create a kind of identity between two people who come together to express their love and their acceptance of one another. In addition, it continues to express that unity. When a man and a woman who love each other come together sexually they do not merely satisfy sexual desire. They come together because they are one and coition is the most meaningful expression of that oneness.

Fifth, the sex drive needs to be regulated. Just as there are good and legitimate means for satisfying the yearning for food, so are there good and legitimate means for satisfying the sex drive. As hunger can be satisfied in ways that harm a person, so can the sex drive be satisfied in ways that are damaging. The fact that sex is a natural, God-given function does not imply that no limits are to be set upon its expression. While sex repression is demonstrably dangerous, sexual license is no less so. The voluntary establishment of limits and the exercise of restraint is a sound way of dealing with the sex drive.

This does not mean that one must turn to an external authority which has prescribed what may and what may not be done. It means rather that the Christian needs to make decisions about how to channel the sex drive so as to make it a positive, constructive, and creative force in life. We have already observed that in the making of decisions the Christian uses a number of resources, one of which is the Scripture. Three general principles permeate the biblical teachings about sex. First, casual and promiscuous sexual encounters are prohibited. Second, so central is the sex relationship in marriage that to have intercourse with a person is to enter into a union with that person that amounts to marriage. Third, any kind of forced relationship is a violation of a person and thus a violation of the will of God.

A final theological affirmation is the fact that personal integrity is not a matter of action so much as it is one of motive and attitude. Jesus employed this principle in interpreting the commandments having to do with murder, adultery, divorce, honesty, and justice (Matthew 5:21–48). Thus it is persons rather than actions that are moral or immoral. That is not to say that actions do not matter; they matter a great deal, as Jesus affirmed when he said that "you will know them by their fruits" (Matthew 7:20). But whether one is loving or unloving determines how one acts, and there are many ways of expressing both kinds of attitudes. Sexual purity, therefore, has to do not merely with what one does but with one's attitude toward other people.

Questions about the Relationship

Sex and Freedom. One of the most important forces for social change in the twentieth century has been the development of safe and reliable methods of contraception. Before this development the possibility of an unplanned pregnancy was a basic factor in the maintenance of standards of conduct between men and women, in marriage and family relationships, and in the presence of women in the labor force. But "the pill" has changed all of that. After telling her friends that she could count more than seventy men with whom she had had sex, a college student added, "It's no big deal because I am on the pill."

The freedom afforded by contraceptives, however, is not quite as full as the student assumed. There remain some unresolved problems associated with the pill, as well as with other contraceptive devices. In addition, AIDS, at first thought to be a problem for homosexual persons only, is now known to be spreading among heterosexuals as well. In time those problems may be resolved, however, and the safety which the young woman incorrectly assumes is already here soon may become a reality.

The question, therefore, is important. Is sex really a "big deal"? The answer is yes. Sex is a part of who we are; it is basic to our being human, to our being persons. Sex activity is not merely gratification; it is expression. Our objective, therefore, is not "to have fun," but to enrich our lives through our sexuality. While that cannot be achieved by imposing rigid taboos, neither can it be achieved by stripping it of its significance. To every activity in which we engage we bring our total personality: our appearance, our mental ability, our interests, our sense of humor, our accomplishments, and our ambitions. We cannot separate these elements from one another or from our sexuality. To realize that our personality has many facets which cannot be separated from one another is to realize that we never act as a mind only or as an emotional being only or as a sexual being only, but that everything we do involves our total personality. Our sexuality, therefore, is only one part of a cluster of human qualities. If sexuality crowds out all of the other aspects of a personal relationship, then that relationship is seriously impoverished.

Sex and Love.   We have said that coition is the most intimate possible way for a couple to express their love for one another. Does that mean that the sex relationship should always be that? In our modern mythology of romance we have tied love and sex together by assuming that love makes coition right. By that mythology the only criticism of the young woman who has gone to bed with more than seventy men is that she could not possibly have loved all of them!

Does the fact that a couple are in love justify the sex relationship whether they are married or not? Circumstances may prohibit a couple from marrying: they may still be in school, or they may not be able financially to establish their own home, or their parents may object. One or the other of them may be married to someone else. One or the other of them may have financial, emotional, or legal obligations to someone else which at the moment makes marriage impossible. Should they express their love in the sex relationship?

This question is not easily answered. In arriving at an answer, however, several factors should be considered. For one thing, love is not easily identified. That is to say, the distinction between being in love and not being in love is not a clear one. People do not really "fall" in love—or at least most people do not. They are often suddenly attracted to other people. Sometimes people to whom they are attracted respond to them and sometimes not. Sometimes they are quickly excited by a new relationship or by the possibility of one. Such attraction may result in a deep attachment or it may not. But love is not created instantaneously; it is developed over a period of time.

Another consideration is the fact that love does not always lead to marriage. Most people are in love with several different persons before they marry. More than half the engagements entered into in this country are broken because people who had believed that they were in love decided that they were not, or that in spite of their love their planned marriage could not succeed, or that they were not ready to marry at that particular time, or that other circumstances made marriage impossible. Being in love, therefore, is a tenuous basis on which to decide something as important as whether to engage in the sex relationship.

A third consideration is the context in which these two persons are in love. That is to say, they do not exist in isolation from other people and their relationship is therefore not exclusively their own. They are son and daughter, they are brother or sister, they are students or workers, they have friends, they are a part of a community of faith, they are children of God, and they are disciples of Christ. They have a past from which they have benefited, as well as from which they bear scars. They have a present in which they function with varying degrees of success and satisfaction. They have a future whose foundation is now being laid. While each person decides in the situation what to do, the situation is not simply the fact that two people are in love. It is the fact that each of those persons comes from a background, exists within a broad community, and has a future. This consideration is not the simplistic question, "What would other people think?" It is the recognition that their lives and the lives of other people are profoundly affected by what they decide.

Sex and Marriage. In traditional Christian thought, sexual intercourse is to be reserved for marriage. That ideal is usually stated in terms of "chastity before marriage and fidelity in marriage." Christians generally have affirmed it even when they have not adhered to it. They have affirmed it in the face of clear evidence of increasing premarital and extramarital sex activity in American society. They have affirmed it in the face of challenges mounted by sociological and psychological studies which question the belief that family life is threatened and personal happiness is endangered by such activity.

The traditional Christian view draws strong support from both the Old Testament and the New. Without concentrating on specific regulations, we can generalize. The Old Testament law speaks of intercourse as appropriate only within the context of marriage. Prostitution was prohibited for Hebrew women, and the men were warned against patronizing prostitutes. A man who had intercourse with an unmarried woman was required to marry her, and one who had intercourse with a married woman was to be executed.

Jesus did not say a great deal about the sex relationship, perhaps because the people among whom he lived had such high standards. The Gospel according to John (7:53–8:11) reports one instance in which he spoke forgivingly to a woman taken in adultery rather than agreeing to the punitive requirement of the law. In his interpretation of the law against adultery he focused on the essential inwardness of morality by speaking of lust rather than of the overt act (Matthew 5:27–28). He did not reject the ideal to which he was an heir, but reinterpreted it and focused on redemption rather than punishment.

Writing to churches located in the Gentile world, where the moral standards were quite different, Paul was much more articulate and specific in his affirmation of what was moral and what was not. Although he insisted that one is saved by grace and not by obedience to the Law, he regarded the Law as a sound guide to moral conduct. He understood the Law to prohibit all sex relationships outside marriage, which he labeled "immorality" (*porneia*). To the Corinthians he said, "Do not be deceived; neither the immoral, nor idolaters, nor homosexuals, nor thieves, nor the greedy, nor drunkards, nor revilers, nor robbers will inherit the Kingdom of God" (1 Corinthians 6:9–10). He said the same thing, in other words, to the Galatians (5:19–21), to the Ephesians (5:3), and to the Colossians (3:5–6). While he recognized the legitimacy of the sex relationship within marriage, he considered immorality a sexual aberration. "The body is not meant for immorality," he said, "but for the Lord, and the Lord for the body" (1 Corinthians 6:13). He considered sex outside marriage so serious a matter that he affirmed that "no immoral or impure man...has any inheritance in the kingdom of Christ and of God" (Ephesians 5:5).

Does this traditional and biblical stand remain valid today? A large body of research reveals that an increasingly large percentage of our population, including many Christians, no longer subscribe to that ideal. Furthermore, researchers have discovered no evidence of a relationship between premarital sex activity and success or failure in marriage. Most contemporary Christian ethicists, however, while avoiding a legalism which prohibits all premarital sex activity, nevertheless recommend the traditional position as the best way. One such person is Richard Hettlinger, who says:

> I would ask whether the act of intercourse, with all its unique quality and intimacy, can be rightly or meaningfully experienced apart from the permanent commitment of marriage. Does not love, in any profound sense, remain unfulfilled until the couple are actually responsible for each other? And if so, can the act which expresses and seals the unity of love be justified in advance of that moment? (*Living with Sex*, p. 137)

He seems to leave the door open, however, by saying:

> If intercourse is accepted mutually after full and free discussion by a couple planning to be married, if there is a clear acceptance of the possibility of

pregnancy and a readiness for the sacrifices it will involve, and if they are mature and established in their respect and love for each other, it is quite possible that the act will be little different in its significance for them if it precedes marriage. (p. 139)

But how do these conditions differ from the status of marriage? All that is lacking is the legalizing and the formalizing of the relationship by a ceremony approved by church or state or both.

What is the place of the sex relationship within marriage? Is it at the heart of a marriage or is it secondary to other matters? Does a satisfactory sex relationship signal a successful marriage and an unsatisfactory sex relationship an unsuccessful one? As traditional Christianity has considered abstinence from premarital intercourse to be the moral course to follow, so has it considered fidelity in marriage to be the right way. Today few Christians challenge that concept, though some have been persuaded to adopt the "open marriage" stance advocated by the O'Neills in the 1970s (Nena and George O'Neill, *Open Marriage*). Infidelity, however, whether approved by one's mate or not, seriously upsets the stability of a marriage. The sex relationship is best reserved for the most intimate communion between husband and wife. To engage in it with someone other than one's mate is to deny the essential oneness of which the Scripture speaks. Fidelity, on the other hand, is the natural result of that oneness. The love between a man and a woman is actually an exclusive relationship in which there is no room for competition.

Sex expression is intended for the mutual benefit of husband and wife. With surprising insight and clarity, Paul stated that fact in 1 Corinthians 7:3–5:

> The husband should give to his wife her conjugal rights, and likewise the wife to her husband. For the wife does not rule over her own body, but the husband does; likewise the husband does not rule over his own body, but the wife does. Do not refuse one another except perhaps by agreement for a season that you may devote yourselves to prayer; but then come together again, lest Satan tempt you through lack of self-control.

Not always has this insight into the mutuality of the relationship been understood. Many women have regarded sex as a burdensome responsibility of marriage. If they enjoyed sex they were ashamed to admit it. It is both possible and desirable, however, that the wife as well as the husband find meaning in sex. For that reason the word *gratification* is not the best term to use in reference to sex, because it implies an act of self-seeking. *Expression* is better because in the sex relationship, properly understood, each partner expresses love and commitment to the other and seeks to please the other. Because it is the most intimate of all human experiences, it is the most complete expression of love and the most profound way of knowing another person.

A CHRISTIAN INTERPRETATION OF MARRIAGE

In modern American mythology, love, sex, and marriage constitute an inseparable trilogy. In fact, of course, the three are easily separated. Love does not always express itself in coition, and it does not always lead to marriage. Sex, in the form of coition at least, is entirely possible apart from love and apart from marriage. Marriages that are both loveless and sexless do in fact exist. Like all other myths, however, this one expresses a reality. There is a connection between love, sex, and marriage because all three are concerned with the basic human yearning for intimacy and for acceptance. For that reason, it is appropriate to consider a Christian interpretation of marriage in connection with a Christian interpretation of sex.

Most Christian marriage ceremonies include phrases similar to the one in *The Book of Common Prayer* which says that marriage "is an honorable estate, instituted by God." That affirmation is usually reinforced by reading the passage in which Jesus quoted the Old Testament statement that God instituted marriage: "Have you not read that he who made them from the beginning made them male and female, and said, 'For this reason a man shall leave his father and mother and be joined to his wife, and the two shall become one flesh' " (Matthew 19:4–5; cf. Genesis 2:24).

Human beings were created in such a way, therefore, that the coming together of a man and a woman, not merely sexually but in a personal bonding, is a normal experience. To ask, "What is the purpose of marriage?" is no more logical than to ask, "What is the purpose of sleep?" A more appropriate question is, "What are the functions of marriage?" Stated in ideal terms, marriage functions in two basic ways. First, it provides a supportive structure for the birth and nurturing of children. Obviously some children are born and reared outside such a relationship, and obviously not all married couples have children. Yet marriage is the socially and religiously approved setting for such activity. Second, marriage provides the setting for the fullest possible personal development of each partner in self-giving and affords the deepest sense of security and acceptance possible in human society. While not all marriages function effectively in this way, no other relationship holds out the possibility in the way that marriage does.

Three words traditionally used to describe the Christian concept of marriage are *monogamy, unity,* and *indissolubility.* In our society monogamy is firmly established in law, and few people seriously challenge it. The high rate of divorce and remarriage, however, has altered the pattern so that monogamy is not taken to imply a permanent marriage relationship. It should be noted that the growing emphasis on the equality of women is thoroughly consistent with the concept of monogamy. Taken seriously, the ideal of monogamy leaves no room for the subordination of one person to another, no room for the well-being of the one to be completely controlled by the other, and no room for the future of one to be at the mercy of the other. If monogamy is understood in any sense other than a legal one, it means an exclusive and mutual commitment of two persons to each other.

The concept of unity is currently challenged on two fronts. First, there is question as to whether it is possible. Can two persons, with different backgrounds, different personalities, different attitudes and tastes, and different temperaments, come together and form a unit? However much they love each other, do they not always retain their own identity? Do they not always remain distinct individuals? And second, is it desirable? Does anyone really want to give up individual interests, ambitions, aspirations, and possibilities? Should we not be more concerned with the development of individual potential rather than with its elimination?

If unity means the loss of individual identity, then it is neither possible nor desirable. Marriage should nurture each partner so that the personality of each can be developed to the fullest. Personality never develops in isolation, however, but through interaction with other persons. Neither does it act in isolation, but in relationship with others. Furthermore, our lives are never static nor stationary. They never cease growing and developing. The concept of unity in marriage means that a husband and a wife contribute to the development of each other in such a way that their lives grow together. They depend upon one another and they support one another. They are always in tension between *I* and *we*, and in their efforts to resolve that tension they try to see the one in light of the other.

When is such unity achieved? Most marriage ceremonies include the quotation, "What therefore God hath joined together, let not man put asunder," and the person officiating pronounces the couple "husband and wife." Obviously that pronouncement does not impose a unity in any sense other than a legal one. Many who go through the ceremony are never really united. Any unity that is achieved by a couple begins when they single each other out from all the other potential marriage partners. Everything that they do together is a part of the unifying process, both before the ceremony and after it. The unity cannot be said to have been established at any specific point. Rather, so long as character and personality develop and grow, just so long are a couple in the process of becoming one.

Yet the significance of the marriage ceremony should not be minimized. What the sociologists call "the rites of passage" are important not only in signaling a change in status but also in establishing that new status. That is why we need ceremonies associated with birth and death, with attaining maturity, with religious affiliation and status, and with marriage. It is not only in the eyes of the world that a marriage ceremony establishes a union between a man and a woman; it is also in our own eyes that our status is changed and that we become husband and wife. A religious ceremony acknowledges the conviction that the union is, in a sense, an act of God. In Christian terms the ceremony is at the least an acknowledgement that one's status is changed in the eyes of God, and at the most an acknowledgement that the creation of the union is the work of God.

Neither should the consummation of a marriage by the act of sexual intercourse be minimized in the creation of the unity. Since that act gathers up and expresses the total personality, there is something profound and irrevocable about the commitment made in it. It is the consummation of love and self-giving. Beyond it there is nothing which can effect that union more perfectly nor express it more adequately.

The concept of indissolubility is closely related to that of unity. Most Christians, while acknowledging that some developments do in fact destroy a marriage, nevertheless insist that the ideal calls for a permanent union. Following the reports of Jesus' teachings on divorce in Mark (10:11–12) and Luke (16:18) rather than the ones in Matthew (5:311–32 and 19:3–9), the Roman Catholic Church teaches that no marriage which was valid and consummated can ever be dissolved. (That church does sometimes *annul* marriages which were contracted in violation of certain regulations.) At one time Protestant churches generally followed Matthew's account and accepted the possibility of divorce on the ground of unfaithfulness. At present, most Protestant churches, while they uphold the ideal of permanence, nevertheless recognize a variety of causes for failure and permit the remarriage of divorced persons.

Are the Protestant churches ignoring the teachings of Jesus when they acknowledge the possibility of the termination of a marriage? To answer this question we need to consider why Jesus taught what he did and try to determine whether he would say the same thing today. While we cannot answer those questions certainly and completely, we do know that women of his day needed the protection which his position represented. The only Old Testament law on the subject permitted a man to divorce his wife if he found "some indecency in her" (Deuteronomy 24:1). The intent of the word *indecency* was debated in Jesus' day. It was generally given a quite liberal interpretation, and divorce, though impossible for a woman, was quite easy for a man. A single woman, however, was in an untenable position in that society. A woman depended upon her father until she was married, and then upon her husband. Because there were no careers open to women by which they could earn their own living, they had to have some man to care for them. To divorce a woman, therefore, was to deprive her of all security. Today most women are quite capable of fending for themselves and indeed an increasing number are quite pleased to do so. Because they do not have to have husbands, they are not victimized by divorce in the same way that they were in Jesus' day. While the ideal of a permanent union remains, and while the satisfactions of such a union remain important, the economic consequences of failure are not nearly so damaging to women.

Permanence is probably a better word than *indissolubility* to describe the ideal. *Indissolubility* has an extremely legalistic connotation, implying that there is no way out of a marriage no matter how bad things may get. *Permanence*, however, implies an ideal that is closely related to *unity*. It suggests that the unity of a couple is not something that they are locked into but that it is something that they work to achieve and to maintain.

HOMOSEXUALITY AND CHRISTIAN FAITH

What has been said thus far has been said about heterosexual relationships. It is becoming increasingly apparent, however, that many people are homosexual. Just how large that number is cannot be determined, but estimates range between 5 and 10 percent of the population (Margot Joan Fromer, *Ethical Issues in Sexuality and Reproduction*, p. 81).

The definition of *homosexual* is by no means as precise as most people assume. Alan Bell declares that

> the homosexual experience is so diverse, the variety of psychological and social and sexual correlates so enormous, that the word 'homosexuality,' used as a kind of umbrella term, is both meaningless and misleading. ("Homosexuality, an Overview," in Harold L. Twiss, editor, *Homosexuality and the Christian Faith*, p. 9)

Recognizing the difficulty of drawing a sharp line, however, it is helpful to make a distinction between those who are essentially homosexual and those who are not. Fromer defines a homosexual as "a person who feels a strong erotic attraction to persons of the same sex, who has the ability to be sexually aroused by members of the same sex, and who prefers to engage in sexual activity with members of the same sex" (p. 79). Homosexuals fit no stereotype and are found in every racial, cultural, religious, and socio-economic group. They work in every trade, business, and profession. Like heterosexuals, they frequent social places and activities where they may meet each other, they are attracted to each other or they dislike each other, they enter into casual relationships, they form partnerships that last only for a time, and they form enduring relationships.

How do we explain the fact that a significant number of people feel "a strong erotic attraction to persons of the same sex"? The general public tends to think that individuals deliberately choose the homosexual way of life. If that were the case, then clearly they could choose not to be homosexual if they wished to do so. No serious student, however, views the situation that way. In the past homosexuals have been subject to such hostility and even abuse that no rational person would deliberately make that choice.

One approach to an understanding of homosexuality is to think of it as a completely natural phenomenon. In this view, some people are born homosexual. Although the psychological factor is clearly involved in the development of their sexual disposition, their genes have set the pattern and defined the limits. Any effort to deny or to alter this fact is doomed to failure because it is an effort to act contrary to the dictates of nature. Although a number of studies have been conducted to discover whether this is the case, the findings have not been entirely consistent. There is enough evidence, however, to indicate that this possibility needs further exploration.

A second possibility is the idea that the homosexual disposition is psychologically caused. Most students who take this approach consider it an arrested or a distorted psychosexual development which is the result of an abnormal relationship with one or both parents. Some regard it as a mental illness, and indeed for many years the American Psychological Association classified it as such. In 1973 that association removed it from the list of mental illnesses, but some psychologists still consider it as such. If it is an illness, it is subject to treatment and perhaps to being cured.

A third approach is to stress social and cultural conditioning. According to this view, the "accident" which leads an individual into his first homosexual experience, the conditioning effects of that experience, and the impact of the social attitudes and codes about such sexual contact are important to future behavior. One homosexual contact does not necessarily lead a person into homosexuality, as a large percentage of the people in our society know. Yet many students believe that in some instances that first experience plays a significant role in influencing the development of a pattern of homosexuality. Especially vulnerable, they think, are children of parents whose attitudes and discipline lead them to inhibit normal sexual behavior. One who has been reared with the attitude that normal sexual relationships are dirty may develop an aversion to heterosexual relationships and thus lay the foundation for deviation from the usual pattern.

There is probably no one explanation of the fact that a given percentage of human beings are homosexual. Rather the explanation is multidimensional. Some people find themselves in this status for one reason, some for another, and some for more than one reason. Biological, psychological, and sociological factors combine with individual experience to bring about this result. This confusion makes more difficult our effort to look at the situation from a Christian perspective.

The legal status of homosexuality is currently changing. Most people now believe that what consenting adults do in private should not be subject to legal regulation, and approximately a third of the states have exempted consensual homosexual activity from legal regulation. Yet laws concerning homosexual activity remain on the books in many states and the penalty for conviction of a "crime against nature" is imprisonment varying from ten years to life. During the 1970s several court cases challenged these laws as vague and unclear, but the Supreme Court upheld them (Meredith Gould, "Statutory Oppression: An Overview of Legalized Homophobia," in Levine, *Gay Men*, p. 55). Although those laws are now rarely enforced, they remain on the books because they reflect the attitude of the majority of people.

Court decisions have often upheld the right of both private agencies and government to refuse to deal with homosexuals. No federal or state legislation prohibits private employers from refusing to hire homosexuals, although some local governments have adopted regulations against the practice. In most states there are no laws which prohibit a landlord from refusing to rent to a prospective tenant whom he knows or believes to be a homosexual. In the past, homosexuals have not been allowed to enlist in the armed forces of the United States and people have been discharged when the fact of their homosexuality has been disclosed. While recent court action has upheld the right of homosexuals to remain in the service, the regulation still states that "homosexuality is incompatible with military service" and that the presence of a homosexual person "seriously impairs the accomplishment of the military mission" (Fromer, pp. 98–101).

Homosexuals are often denied the courtesy and respect which other people take for granted. They are treated in ways "ranging from half-hidden scorn to open hatred," says Morton Hunt. "People avoid them, exclude them, whisper or joke about them, stare at them with open hostility" (*Gay*, pp. 59–60). Some family members refuse to have anything to do with them and others pretend not to know about the homosexuality. According to one survey, most Americans consider homosexuality morally wrong and most think that homosexuals should not be allowed to serve as judges, school teachers, or ministers. Many would deny them the privilege of being doctors or governmental officials; most think that homosexuals try to become sexually involved with children; and most say that they try to avoid associating with homosexuals (Levitt and Klassen, "Public Attitudes toward Homosexuality," reprinted in Levine, *Gay Men*, pp. 20–35).

This public sentiment parallels the attitude of the churches. Until about 1970, according to Seward Hiltner, most churches and most theologians said little about homosexuality ("Homosexuality and the Churches," in Marmor, *Homosexual Behavior*, p. 219). When they did speak they either condemned it as a sin or expressed a concern for it as an illness. In recent years, however, the place of homosexuals in the church has been seriously debated. The hierarchy of the Roman Catholic church continues its vigorous condemnation while many priests and lay people challenge the church ruling. Most Protestant churches are moving cautiously toward some support of the civil rights of homosexuals and toward some acceptance of homosexuals within the church. Meanwhile, finding themselves unwelcome and uncomfortable in the mainline Protestant churches, many homosexual Christians have identified themselves with the Metropolitan Community Church.

In our attempt to consider homosexuality from a Christian perspective we must look at the biblical teachings. Although the Bible does not often speak to this subject, in every instance in which it refers to homosexual practices it condemns them. In the Old Testament there are three pertinent passages:

1. Genesis 19:1–11: The city of Sodom, doomed to destruction because of its sinfulness, lost its opportunity for reprieve when the men of the city attempted the homosexual rape of God's emissaries who were visiting Lot.
2. Judges 19:22–30: In a situation similar to the Sodom event, certain men of the tribe of Benjamin attempted the rape of a visiting Levite.
3. Leviticus 18:22 and 20:13: A part of the Holiness Code, these regulations include homosexuality in a catalogue of a variety of sexual offenses for which severe punishment is spelled out.

In the New Testament the only passage in which homosexuality is discussed at length is Romans 1:16–32. This passage is a part of Paul's discussion of the world's need for Christ. Paul says that both Jews and Gentiles are sinful and that both are saved in the same way: by grace through faith. In that discussion he portrays homosexuality not as sin but as God's punishment on the Gentiles for their sin of idolatry. Other New Testament references to homosexuality are found in lists of sinful practices: 1 Corinthians 6:9–10, Jude 7, 2 Peter 2:6–10, 1 Timothy 1:8–11.

Both the Old Testament and the New, then, treat homosexuality as a sin. How applicable is this view to our present situation? Christian ethicists are divided in their judgment. Some unequivocally call homosexuality sinful. Edward Malloy, for example, after an examination of a wide variety of literature on the subject, and after consideration of the psychological and sociological theories, concludes: "I am convinced that the homosexual way of life, as evolved in the social structures and practices of the homosexual sub-culture, is irreconcilable with the Christian way of life" (*Homosexuality and the Christian Way of Life*, p. 328). Lynn R. Buzzard says, "Both the specific injunctions of Scripture, the general teaching of the Scripture and our general understanding of the nature of men and women makes homosexuality *ab*normal, *un*natural." He says both that the attitude of God toward the homosexual is that "God really cares about him and loves him" and that "the attitude of God toward the homosexual is that he/she ought to repent" ("How Gray is Gay?" in Twiss, *Homosexuality and the Christian Faith*, pp. 51, 53). This understanding, it should be noted, assumes, as Buzzard does, that even if homosexuality is not a deliberately chosen way, it can be deliberately rejected. "There is increasing evidence," says Buzzard, "that some, if not all, homosexuals can change if they really want to" (p. 53).

Others regard homosexuality as a tragic fact of life that must be accepted. This is the stance of H. Kimball Jones, for example (*Toward a Christian Understanding of the Homosexual*). Homosexual relations, he says, can never have the same potential for human fulfillment that heterosexual relationships do, but they are the only possibility for such fulfillment that some persons have. The validity of "mature homosexual relationships" must be recognized for individuals for whom "there is really no other practicable answer" (p. 108). While homosexuals should be encouraged to "maintain a fidelity to one partner when his only other choice would be to lead a promiscuous life filled with guilt and fear," there can be no such thing as a valid marriage between homosexuals because at best the relationship remains "an unnatural expression of human sexuality" (pp. 108, 109). He concludes that while homosexuality can be "a relatively creative and fulfilling way of life for the responsible homosexual," a homosexual relationship is doomed, by its very nature, never to pass beyond a certain point. "Two homosexuals," he says, "can never complement one another in the same sense that male and female can" (pp. 109–110).

Still other Christian ethicists think of homosexuality as a fact of life within which some persons can function as Christians in the same sense that heterosexuality is a fact of life within which other people can function as Christians. They do not regard one's sexual orientation, in other words, to be a determining factor in one's relationship to God. In discussing Paul's statement about homosexuality (Romans 1:16–32), for example, David Bartlett points out that Paul's major point is that no one is justified by his own goodness but by grace through faith. This passage is not about homosexuality but about the need of all people for salvation. "The discussion of a variety of sins, including idolatry and self-righteousness," Bartlett says, "is used to point toward *everyone's* need for God's gracious and redemptive mercy in Christ" ("A Biblical Perspective on Homosexuality," in Twiss, *Homosexuality and the Christian Faith*, p. 31). Bartlett uses the same method in discussing Paul's statement to the Galatians, "For in Christ Jesus neither circumcision nor uncircumcision is of any avail, but faith working through love" (Galatians 5:6). He says that for the words "neither circumcision nor uncircumcision" we could substitute "neither heterosexuality nor homosexuality" (Twiss, p. 39). He believes that the recognition of homosexuality as an "unchangeable affectional preference" requires us to reject an ethic "which insists that homosexuals should either try to engage, unhappily, in heterosexual relationships, or remain celibate" (Twiss, pp. 34–35). The gifts of God's Spirit, he says, are "equally available to heterosexual people and to homosexual people" (p. 38).

What, then, can we assume about homosexuality and the Christian way of life? Two observations can be made. First, since the best evidence suggests that people do not choose to be either heterosexual or homosexual, but either are born with a given sexual orientation or are molded by psychological or sociological conditioning, there can be no credit or blame for either heterosexuality or homosexuality. One's sexual preference is a matter entirely beyond one's control in just the same sense that the color of one's eyes is beyond one's control. It is simply a fact of life which one accepts.

Second, the Christian homosexual has the same obligation to deal responsibly with his/her sexuality that the Christian heterosexual does. Here we must be a bit more tentative because the Scripture does not deal with homosexuality as a viable option. We may assume, however, that except for the matter of procreation, sex functions in the same way for the homosexual that it does for the heterosexual. If that be true, could we assume that homosexuals may commit themselves to one another in loving and caring relationships? That the ideal for such relationships is monogamy, fidelity, and indissolubility? That their union be one in which there is mutuality of responsibility and privilege? One which will help each partner to develop as a whole person? That sex is only one part of a total personal relationship?

"Homosexual acts between persons who intend a genuine union in love are not sinful nor should the church consider them as such," says Norman Pittenger ("The Morality of Homosexual Acts," in Batchelor, *Homosexuality and Ethics* p. 139). He outlines the conditions under which such relationships are genuinely moral by saying that the two persons must be committed to each other rather than using each other, that there must be no element of coercion, that the two must intend some loyalty to each other, that each must welcome and appreciate the personality of the other, and that the relationship must involve a union of lives in which the identity and the freedom of each is preserved (p. 140). This outline is in fact a description of an ideal marital relationship. We have no problem in assuming that, while the ideal described in this statement is difficult for a man and a woman to achieve, it is possible for them to do so by the grace of God. Can we also assume that, by the grace of God, two people of the same sex can achieve it?

LIVING-TOGETHER ARRANGEMENTS

One campus minister observed that every couple for whom he had performed a marriage ceremony during the past five years was already living together at the time of their marriage. Another campus minister challenged the obvious conclusion by saying that only a few couples for whom he had performed ceremonies were already living together. Who can say which minister was dealing with the more typical group? No one knows how many unmarried couples are living together in this country. The U.S. Census Bureau tries to count them and lists approximately 1.5 million "households which contain two unrelated adults of opposite sexes." Those figures are probably unrealistically low.

Why do unmarried people take up residence together? Obviously sex has a great deal to do with it, but it cannot be the full explanation. After all, sexual activity is not restricted to people who are living together. Marvin Mitchelson says, "In my opinion, this modern phenomenon is caused by a quest for personal freedom without wanting to flee from the pleasures of having a mate" (*Living Together*, p. 17). Judi Loesch shows more insight when she comments;

> Young people don't want to stay with their parents. They're not ready for marriage—not yet—because they don't really know themselves, and they've got a lot more changing to do. And they're lonely. Very lonely." ("Unmarried Couples Shouldn't Live Together," *U. S. Catholic*, July, 1985, p. 16)

A common, if not universal, human characteristic is a yearning for intimacy, for a sense of belonging to someone else, for a sense of security in an exclusive personal relationship. Many people who, for a variety of reasons, are not willing to make the commitment required of marriage nevertheless enter into this kind of relationship seeking such sharing.

What happens to these relationships? After a time—the average lifetime of a living together arrangement is approximately three years—a couple is likely either to separate or to formalize their relationship in marriage. That is not to suggest that the arrangement is intended to be a trial marriage. Most couples entering into such arrangements do not look beyond the arrangement itself. They do not expect it to be permanent—indeed, if they did they probably would marry at the outset. They realize that marriage may follow, but they also realize that it may not. No statistics are available to indicate what is the most frequent development.

Living-together arrangements may be described as quasi marriages. They are like marriage in that there is a pattern of sex relationship that involves more than the physical act itself. This relationship has meaning for both partners, though not necessarily the same meaning. It is a way of communicating, though what is communicated is not always understood and if understood is not always appreciated. It is intermingled with the total personal involvement, being affected by everything else in the relationship and affecting everything else.

Like marriages, living-together arrangements involve an agreement on certain economic considerations. Clearly there has to be some agreement on the financial obligations of each partner. Beyond that, there are the routine affairs of housekeeping. What about preparing meals and washing dishes? What about housecleaning? What about the care of clothes? What about care when one is ill? What about the acquisition of common property? Even more subtle are relationships. What adjustments must be made about the time each owes the other? What consideration is due when the regular schedule is upset? What is done about differing opinions as to what is important? What of different preferences about food or TV programs? What about the timing of certain activities? The list goes on infinitely. Two people who begin living together must make a big adjustment, whether they are married or not.

Like marriage, a living-together arrangement entails a growing emotional involvement on the part of a couple. That involvement is affected both by happy experiences and by unhappy ones, by conflict and by making up, by shared activities and by communication about those activities which are not shared. It is profoundly affected by the routines that develop, and it is affected by the upsetting of those routines. For good or for ill, two people who live together, whether married or not, become a part of each other.

But these arrangements are only quasi marriages. They have no legal status. While marriage is defined by law, and to a certain extent is regulated by law, a living-together arrangement is not. That fact becomes important in a consideration of the rights of both parties both while the relationship lasts and when it is terminated. It is sometimes a problem when one is looking for work and more often when the couple decide to acquire property. That consideration is so important that Mitchelson recommends written agreements which protect individual rights, with a particular focus on property (*Living Together*). These agreements, he believes, are legally enforceable. Paul Ashley agrees, but issues a strong warning: in some states intercourse between unmarried people is illegal and is subject to prosecution. In most places there are strong mores disapproving of unmarried people living together. He writes that "couples who choose to flaunt the law or even the mores of the community in which they dwell should not enter into any written contracts which are predicated on their personal relationship" (*Oh Promise Me But Put It in Writing*, p. 64).

Neither do these arrangements have religious sanction. To many people that consideration may seem unimportant. It is interesting, however, that while only two-thirds of the people in this country have a formal relationship with a religious group, more than 90 percent of the people who marry look for a minister, priest, or rabbi to conduct the ceremony. And they usually want a religious ceremony—with vows, prayers, and Scripture—the whole works! This is not to suggest that people become religious at the time of their marriage. It is to recognize the importance which most people seem to attach to religious sanctions for their marriage. And that is something that is missing from living-together arrangements.

Even more significant a difference is the lack of commitment that characterizes living-together arrangements. By definition they are not expected to be permanent. The usual marriage ceremony contains the phrase, "till death us do part." People who make that vow intend it at the time. While a high percentage of marriages do not turn out to be permanent, they are begun with the expectation that they will be so. The couple promise themselves, the world at large, and even God, that they will make it so. That commitment, realistic or not, but clearly a part of marriage, is missing from a living-together arrangement. Living-together arrangements are by definition tentative.

Presumably Christian young people contemplating entering a living-together arrangement have already made their decision about the matter of the sex relationship outside marriage. If that decision was made without giving careful thought to the religious and ethical issues, they would do well to think about them before they take up residence together. If they have given attention to them, however, and have decided that their faith does not require them to refrain from sexual intercourse before marriage, then there remain several other questions about other aspects of living together to which they need to give attention.

First, what emotional resources do they have that will sustain the relationship under the inevitable pressures of living together? The simple fact of being together so much of the time places a strain upon a relationship. The disruption of an accustomed way of life, the differences of personal habits, the eccentricities of each individual, the difficulty of having time for oneself, the impossibility of each meeting all the expectations of the other—all of these and many more are tension-creating factors. That romantic involvement which we label *love*—and which is chiefly a physical attraction—is not adequate to deal with them. Obviously a couple can learn to handle the strain of a relationship if they choose to do so. But the question is, what will make them want to do so? In other words, what takes the place of the commitment which provides the framework within which a married couple deals with these matters?

Second, does it matter what other people think? Put another way, can a couple make their own decisions without regard to what other people think? One of the presuppositions which underlies ethics is just this point. Each individual does indeed have both the right and the responsibility of decision making. For Christians, decisions are made within the context of the Christian community. One source of guidance is the tradition of that community. Christians, therefore, should quite properly consider those "other people." How are our parents affected by what we do? How is our relationship with our parents affected by our decision? How do we relate to the church? How do we relate as individuals and as a couple to the broader community? To raise these questions is not to predetermine the answer; it is to say that Christians need to take into consideration the fact that those "other people" are persons to whom they relate, and that those relationships will be affected by the decision.

Third, and closely related to the second, is the question of the importance of "a piece of paper." If a couple love each other do they need a piece of paper to make them remain together? If they do not love each other, why should they remain together? The legal importance of the piece of paper has already been discussed, and its religious significance has at least been hinted at. But what of its emotional importance to the couple? Apart from such mundane matters as respectability and property rights, does the piece of paper make any difference in their relationship? The piece of paper might be compared to a sacrament. A sacrament is "an outward sign of an inward grace." Is it a necessary sign? Does the grace exist without the sign? Do we need the sign to confirm in our lives the experience of grace? These questions about sacrament are applicable to the piece of paper. Is there something within us which wants (if it does not require) that confirmation? Does the paper provide an emotional sense of security? Does it offer a challenge? Does it make the relationship more stable and more meaningful than it could otherwise be?

A final question that needs consideration is, how will the relationship be terminated? This question is important because, as we have indicated, nearly all couples either marry or terminate the relationship after about three years together. Before entering a relationship, therefore, one needs to contemplate the end. Although no one knows what percentage of such arrangements lead to marriage, one should not assume that those marriages which take place all turn out to be stable and happy ones. Mitchelson says that "many people will tell you that getting married ruined a perfectly good relationship" (p. 137). Those people are wrong, of course, for the premarital relationship clearly had reached the point where a change of some sort was going to take place. Some couples, though we have no way of knowing how many, form good marriages. Apparently those persons believed that their relationship would be better if they were married, and their belief proved to be correct. Others, however, contract marriages that soon end in divorce. The failure of those marriages cannot be due to their changing a relationship that was good and happy, because had the relationship been ideal the couple would not have felt any need to change it. Apparently they married in an effort to prevent a breakup of the relationship, but they failed in their purpose.

The other way a relationship is terminated is by separation. It is generally assumed that such a separation is easier than divorce because there are fewer legal entanglements and only the couple are involved. That may be true of short-lived relationships, but the longer the couple live together the more complicated it becomes. One reason for this fact is that a couple invariably begin to acquire joint property, and the more they have the more difficult becomes an equitable distribution of that property when they separate. In addition, while it is assumed that each person would take out of the arrangement those items which that person brought into it, there are often conflicts as to who owned what. Another, more serious reason, however, is the emotional difficulty of separation. What ties a married couple together is not so much the law as it is emotional involvement: shared experiences, shared concerns, shared conflicts. They have been related to each other in a highly complex way, and when that relationship is terminated, by divorce, separation, or death, there is a profound sense of loss. The same thing is true of the involvement of a couple who live together without marriage; the longer they remain together the more their lives become intertwined. When they separate, even if the separation is mutually desired, there is a sense of loss that is exactly the same as in the case of divorce. And the problem is complicated by the absence of any kind of structure within which to deal with it.

EIGHT

LIFE AND DEATH: ISSUES IN BIOMEDICAL ETHICS

New methods of research and new technologies have resulted in dramatic developments in health care during the past fifty years. One consequence of these dramatic developments has been the shifting of the responsibility for decision making from the physician to the patient. We like to be able to say to the physician, "You're the doctor. Do what you think best. I just want to get well." But increasingly, patients are faced with questions, not just of getting well, but of choosing between two undesirable courses of action, or of choosing between two good alternatives, or of deciding whether some of the things that *can* be done *should* be done. Should a pregnant woman who does not want to give birth to a child have her pregnancy terminated? Should a couple who want a child but cannot have one without following some extraordinary procedures resort to such measures? Should a person risk an organ transplant which offers hope of prolonging life for only two or three years? What steps should be taken to prolong the life of a family member who is dying? Should we ask a physician to follow procedures that ease the pain but shorten the life of that person? Scientific and medical research have opened up a wide variety of possibilities. Any one of us may be compelled to make agonizing decisions about what will be done when we are the patients, or when members of our family are the patients. In this chapter we shall consider five basic issues in biomedical ethics: abortion, biomedical parenting, responsible parenthood, organ transplants, and euthanasia.

ABORTION

On January 22, 1973, the Supreme Court of the United States handed down a decision in the case of *Roe* v. *Wade* which significantly altered the legality of abortion in the United States. For nearly a decade there had been signs that the change was coming. Through the mid-1960s the laws of every state had severely limited the right of a woman to have an abortion, most states permitting the procedure only when the life of the woman was threatened by the pregnancy. In 1967, however, legislation which was significantly more lenient, but which still maintained certain restrictions, was adopted in Colorado, California, and North Carolina. In 1969 the legislature of the state of New York removed all restrictions in that state, effectively making abortion legal for any woman who elected to have one. No change had been made in Texas, however, when in 1972 a single, pregnant woman challenged that state's law which prohibited abortion except in cases where the life of the woman was in danger. The district court ruled in her favor, the decision was appealed, and in 1973 the Supreme Court upheld the district court decision, declaring that a decision about abortion should be made by the pregnant woman herself, not by some other agency.

Basing their decision on the Ninth and Fourteenth Amendments, the court applied the right of privacy to a woman's decision as to whether to have a child. The court said that a woman's right to an abortion is limited by the state's appropriate interest in safeguarding the health of the woman, in maintaining proper medical standards, and in protecting human life. The last of those interests of the state is of particular significance. The ruling affirms that a fetus is not a person in the sense in which the Fourteenth Amendment uses the term. Yet the potential and the development of the fetus is recognized by the varying regulations according to the trimesters of pregnancy. A state cannot prohibit abortion during the first trimester. In the interest of protecting the health of the woman, a state may insist that during the second trimester abortions be performed only by qualified medical personnel in proper facilities. During the last trimester, when the fetus is considered viable, the state may prohibit all abortions except those that are essential to protect the life and/or health of the mother.

That 1973 decision, however, did not permanently resolve the legal status of abortion in the United States. On July 3, 1989, in a five-to-four decision, the Supreme Court moved toward a reversal of the *Roe* v. *Wade* decision by upholding the constitutionality of a Missouri law which restricts the right to abortion. This *Webster* v. *Reproductive Health Services* decision leaves the door open to test cases which might result in the overturning of *Roe* v. *Wade*. Furthermore, the nation remains divided as to whether abortion is morally right. A number of antiabortion organizations are quite active. Many of them are working to bring about changes in the legal situation. All of them hope to affect public opinion and private judgment. Other groups are equally active in defending the right of women to make a free choice.

Whatever the legal status, the question of having an abortion is a major moral issue for persons who confront it. The fact that its legality is now affirmed, and the fact that relatively safe and simple methods have been devised, make it both possible and necessary to consider the moral implications. Before these developments it was possible to avoid the moral issue by simply citing the facts that it was illegal and that it was unsafe. Though the moral implications are quite thorny, however, from a Christian perspective they are the more important ones. In considering moral implications, it is helpful to review the attitudes current in American society.

First, many people believe that abortion is morally wrong and that it should never be performed under any circumstances. This is the viewpoint of the Right-to-Life movement. The Roman Catholic church has historically taken this stand and has taken the lead in the movement. That movement, however, is not exclusively a Catholic one; many Protestants are a part of it. The people who hold to this view think of the conceptus as having the life of a human being. So far as personhood is concerned, they make no distinction based on the stage of development of the fetus. From the moment of conception, the fetus is treated as having the same right to life as any other human being. They consider the deliberate destruction of a human fetus to be murder. People who hold this view recognize that in some instances a choice must be made between the life of the unborn child and the life of the mother, that there is a life-for-life situation in which the one must be sacrificed to the other. In those circumstances some people concede that the right decision may be to sacrifice the unborn child to save the life of the mother.

Second, some people argue that abortion is wrong except under a limited number of quite specific conditions. It can be justified, they say, only if (1) it is necessary to preserve the physical or mental health of the mother; (2) there is clear evidence that the child would be born with severe physical or mental handicaps; or (3) the pregnancy was the result of rape or incest. This approach implies that while abortion is sometimes the lesser of two evils, it is nevertheless evil. It can be justified only by demonstrating that a higher good is served by an abortion, that greater evil would result from not having the abortion than from having one. It should be observed that while this approach requires some decision making, it is not the woman who makes the decision. The decision that an abortion is indicated is made by the physician.

Third, many people believe that the decision concerning an abortion should be made by the woman alone. They believe that the Supreme Court's decision in 1973 was right not only because it was a correct interpretation of the Constitutional amendments, but also because it is consistent with the dignity and the responsibility of the individual. They believe that a woman has an inherent right to choose to terminate a pregnancy when, for whatever reason, she judges it best for her to do so. They argue that a fetus is not in fact a human being, but only potentially so, and that the rights of a fetus should not be allowed to override the rights of a person. Only when the fetus has become viable, that is, when it is able to live outside the womb, a condition that emerges some time between the twenty-fourth and the twenty-eighth week of pregnancy, may its rights be equated with those of a human being. Before that time a woman has the moral right to terminate a pregnancy.

If the first view is correct, there is no moral issue to be decided. The distinction between right and wrong is clear, and the only problem for the Christian is to take the difficult path of doing the right thing. If the second view is correct, the freedom and the responsibility of the pregnant woman are quite limited. It is the physician who must decide whether any of the conditions has been met. Only after the physician has determined that there is adequate cause does the woman have the option of choosing to terminate a pregnancy. If the third view is correct, then the woman has the full responsibility, at least until the fetus is viable, of deciding whether to terminate her pregnancy.

From a moral perspective, the most important issue to be resolved is that of when personhood appears. The official view of the Roman Catholic church is that it begins from the moment of conception. In a pastoral declaration, Pope Pius XII said, "Innocent human life, in whatever condition it is found, is withdrawn, from the very first moment of its existence, from any direct deliberate attack." He calls this right of freedom "from any direct deliberate attack" a "fundamental right of the human person" which is "as valid for the life still hidden within the womb of the mother as for the life already born and developing outside of her." Thus he makes no moral distinction between killing a child before birth and killing one after birth. (Quoted in Richard A. McCormick, "Abortion," *America*, June 19, 1965, p. 898.)

Many Protestants agree with this view. The line of reasoning about abortion runs: (1) Human beings do not have the right to take the lives of other human beings because all life is the gift of God. (2) Human life begins at the moment of conception. (3) Abortion at any stage in the development of the conceptus is the termination of human life and therefore is always wrong. Some people, not quite willing to assume that personhood appears from the moment of conception, say that since we cannot be sure when it happens, in order to avoid terminating the life of a human being we must act as if it did begin with conception. The end result, therefore, is the same: abortion is always wrong.

This line of reasoning focuses on the assumption that the fetus is a person. Is that in fact the case? Life clearly does not originate at the moment of conception, because both the sperm and the egg are alive before they meet. Individuality, however, is established genetically at the moment of conception. From the time of conception through birth through maturing to death that individuality develops as the potential is actualized. But that individuality is not the same in the various stages of development, and the fertilized egg is quite different from the newborn child. The Bible insists on the value of persons. Indeed, most of its moral teachings focus on safeguarding human rights, and among those rights the right to life is basic. Those biblical teachings, however, speak of persons dealing with other persons who are functioning with an independence which unborn children do not have. Of course a fetus is alive: it moves, it shows sensitivity to pain, and early in its development it has a heartbeat and brain waves. Does that make the fetus a person? The lower animals also move, are sensitive to pain, have brain waves, and in addition are independent entities, but they are not persons. The potential of the fetus makes it different from anything else alive, but does that difference make it a person?

Unfortunately, the Bible gives little help in answering this question. Indeed, only one Old Testament regulation has to do with unborn children. Exodus 21:22–25 prescribes a fine for a man who accidentally causes a woman to have a miscarriage. That law, however, reflects the importance of children to the Hebrews rather than the sanctity of the life of the unborn child. Furthermore, it deals with a miscarriage which is the result of violence directed toward a third party, not toward the woman or toward the fetus, and therefore with an accident rather than with deliberate termination of a pregnancy. It requires a rather vivid imagination to extend the Bible's stress on the worth of individuals and the value of human life to include a fetus at any stage of development.

That is not to suggest that the fetus is insignificant. The fetus is not simply another part of the woman's body, as dispensable as the tonsils or a fingernail. The fetus has a potential which no other part of the body has: if nature is allowed to take its course, and the fetus is allowed to develop normally, it will become a person. It must be respected for what it can become. Its right to life is not that of a fully developed human being, but its significance lies in its potential of becoming a person.

A second consideration is that of the clash of values. This problem can be as thorny an issue as the question of when the fetus becomes a person. A woman who is pregnant but wishes not to be does not have a choice between good and bad; she must choose one value to be sacrificed to another. On the one hand is the value of the fetus which has the potential of becoming a person. On the other is the specific circumstance which makes her pregnancy undesirable. That circumstance may be the embarrassment of an unmarried pregnant woman, financial problems, disrupted career plans, difficult marital relationships, unsettled family circumstances, health problems for her or for the unborn child, or even a threat to her life. What is to be sacrificed to what? Does the unborn child have absolute priority? How important is the health of that unborn child? Does the physical or mental health of the woman have absolute priority? How important are her career ambitions? How important are the personal relationships within her family? How important is her family's ability to take care of children? Whose best interests will be served, and whose damaged, by her decision?

A woman making a decision, therefore, is not choosing between having an abortion on the one hand and maintaining traditional family values on the other. Most people value the family quite highly. Most—though by no means all—expect parenthood to be a part of their lives. A woman does not necessarily reject motherhood for all time when she rejects motherhood at a particular time. Neither does she reject motherhood when she decides that one child—or two or three or any other number—is enough. She may indeed be acting in the interest of her family by choosing to have an abortion. Traditional family values have to do not with the number of children but with the quality of life provided for all members of the family—mother, father, children, and perhaps members of the extended family.

These considerations lead to another important question. Who should be involved in the decision-making process? For obvious reasons the woman ultimately makes the choice. While many pressures may be brought to bear upon her, in the last analysis she determines what course to follow. In making her decision, should she be guided by the judgments of anyone else? One other person who should be involved in the decision-making process, if possible, is the father of the child. This is obviously true if a woman is married. After all, the child was conceived within the context of that marital relationship. Not only does the husband have rights and responsibilities in regard to what is done, but also the relationship between husband and wife is seriously affected by the decision. Beyond that, the mutuality which has been described as the ideal of the husband-wife relationship would preclude a unilateral decision on such an important matter.

If, however, the woman is not married, the involvement of the father of the child is more difficult, if not impossible. An unwed father may be unwilling to have any part of the decision and even try to avoid his responsibilities. Many unmarried couples break up when the woman becomes pregnant, sometimes at the initiative of the woman but more often at the initiative of the man. The woman is then left with the full responsibility of deciding what to do and of implementing that decision. Even if the relationship between the man and the woman was a casual one, however, the man has both legal and moral rights and responsibilities.

A young, unmarried woman would do well to involve her parents in her decision. Most young women are reluctant to discuss this problem with their parents. Some fear the anticipated reaction of their parents and some do not want to hurt them. Certainly it would be unrealistic to expect parents to be happy about the situation. Most parents probably would be both angry and hurt. But most parents would also be deeply concerned and would attempt to help their daughter not only to decide what to do but also to follow through on her chosen course of action. A young unmarried woman ought not to be alone in making and carrying out a decision either to have an abortion or to carry the child to birth.

In making her decision, a young woman would be well advised to consider all the alternatives open to her. Besides abortion, there are several viable ones. The first is marriage. Before the liberalizing of the law on abortion, and before the medical developments which made abortions fairly simple and safe, this was a frequently chosen option. It was often said of a couple that "They had to get married." They did not have to marry, of course, but that seemed the best option open at the time. Clearly a couple should not marry simply because the young woman is pregnant. If the couple were anticipating marriage, however, and were waiting because of educational status or economic circumstances or some other reason, it might be well to alter their plans and marry earlier than they had planned. A second option is for the woman to carry the child to full term and rear the child as a single parent. That has been done with happy consequences by a number of women, and in increasing numbers women are choosing this option. A third possibility is to give birth to the child and give it up for adoption. While it is usually difficult for a mother to give up her newborn child, this has proved to be a good decision for large numbers of people. (See Ruth A. Pierce's *Single and Pregnant* for a discussion of these options.)

It should never be assumed that abortion is an easy solution to a problem pregnancy. While it may be the best alternative, it does not resolve all problems. Rachel Smith, who says of herself that she is both antiabortion and prochoice, observes:

> Why can't we see abortion for the human tragedy it is? No woman plans for her life to turn out that way. Even the most effective contraceptives are no guarantee against pregnancy. Loneliness, ignorance, immaturity can lead to decisions (or lack of decisions) that may result in untimely pregnancy. People make mistakes.
>
> What many people seem to misunderstand is that no woman wants to have an abortion. Circumstances demand it; women do it. No woman reacts to abortion with joy. Relief, yes. But also ambivalence, grief, despair, guilt. (Rachel Richardson Smith, "Abortion, Right and Wrong," *Newsweek*, March 25, 1985)

BIOMEDICAL PARENTING

While an unwanted pregnancy is a problem for some people, childlessness is a problem for others. Approximately one out of every ten couples in this country is infertile. While in the past some have simply accepted the fact, others have dealt with the problem by adopting children. The widespread use of contraceptive devices and the increasing resort to abortion is now reducing the number of infants available for adoption. The practice of adopting older children and children of different ethnic background, however, is increasing.

Modern medical technology offers another approach to the problem of childlessness. In the nineteenth century there were some experiments with the artificial insemination of human beings, using techniques long employed with great success in the breeding of animals. After World War I the procedure, though uncommon, came to be accepted as valid. It has become quite common since World War II, and it is now estimated that each year more than ten thousand children are conceived in this way in the United States.

The technique itself is fairly simple. By means of instruments a physician introduces semen into the woman's uterus where it may fertilize an awaiting ovum. If the problem of conceiving is a physical malformation on the part of the man, such as a low sperm count or impotence, then semen from the husband may be employed (Artificial Insemination by Husband or AIH). If the husband is sterile or if there are medical or genetic reasons why semen from the husband should not be used, then semen from a donor may be used (Artificial Insemination by Donor or AID). While successful impregnation does not depend upon the source of the semen, there are more moral questions about the use of semen from a donor than about the use of semen from the husband.

A recent (1977–78) development in the techniques of overcoming the problem of childlessness is *in vitro* fertilization. This involves the removal of a ripe ovum or egg from the woman's ovary and placing it in a laboratory dish with sperm from the husband. If, as it is hoped, one of the sperm fertilizes the ovum, the resulting embryo is cultured for a brief time and then returned to the woman's uterus. There the embryo may implant itself and grow and develop as if conception had taken place in the normal way. This technique is not so effective as normal conception, for only about one in ten attempts is successful, whereas 50 percent of all naturally fertilized ova result in recognizable pregnancies. The most common use of *in vitro* fertilization is to overcome the infertility of a woman.

Artificial insemination with semen from a donor has made it possible for a couple to nurture from the time of conception a child who is biologically the child of the woman but not of the man. Surrogate motherhood makes it possible for a couple to rear from birth a child who is the biological child of the husband but not of the wife. As far back as biblical days a childless woman sometimes gave a female servant to her husband so that he could have a child by her. The achievement of this result by artificial insemination, however, is recent. Exactly how long it has been practiced we do not know, but in the early 1980s it was done openly, with some physicians making known their availability to arrange such pregnancies, some attorneys making it known that they would handle legal arrangements, and clients entering into such arrangements knowing at the outset what the cost would be. The legality of contracts with surrogate mothers is still unsettled.

In discussing the morality of these procedures, several theoretical considerations are important. The first is the question of whether the artificial insemination of a woman with semen from a donor is a violation of the husband-wife relationship. This question is equally applicable to the insemination of a surrogate mother. The position of the Roman Catholic church, enunciated by Pope Pius XII in 1949, is that this procedure constitutes adultery because it is a violation of God's plan that husband and wife should have mutual, nontransferable rights to each other. It is an invasion of the wife's reproductive system by someone other than her husband. In fact, according to the Pope, even AIH is wrong because it substitutes another method for "natural sexual intercourse" and is not therefore a personal union of husband and wife.

Protestant theologians who oppose artificial insemination, although not speaking in such absolutist terms, are concerned about what they see to be a separation of procreation from the husband-wife relationship. Thus they even see a problem with artificial insemination using semen from the husband. They consider procreation in this way to be a matter of medical technology rather than one of a loving relationship between husband and wife. Paul Ramsey, for example, speaks of these techniques as irreversibly removing "a basic form of humanity: the basis in our creation for the covenant of marriage and parenthood" (*Fabricated Man*, p. 130). He sees a necessary linkage between "the love-making and the life-giving 'dimensions' of this one-flesh unity of ours" (p. 133).

Not all Protestant theologians agree, however. Joseph Fletcher brushes aside any suggestion that artificial insemination is an adulterous act. He believes that to think of it as such is to think of marriage fidelity as merely a legal relationship rather than a personal one (*Morals and Medicine*, p. 121). James Nelson likewise focuses on the intent of the man and the woman who resort to these measures. He says that when there is mutual consent, when it is chosen as an act of love, and when the child so conceived is accepted in the "parenthood covenant" of the husband and wife, then it can hardly be considered adultery (*Human Medicine*, pp. 72–73).

A second consideration, important to many people, is that the semen used in artificial insemination must be secured by masturbation. The traditional teaching of the Roman Catholic church is that masturbation is inherently sinful because it is a sex act separated from that procreative intent which is normative for every sexual act. Protestant ethicists who object to masturbation as sinful do so for other reasons. First, they think that in masturbation sex is separated from a personal relationship and thus is deprived of its fundamental meaning. And second, the sexual fantasy associated with masturbation, not tied in with a real partnership, promiscuously cultivates lust with a disregard for the personhood of other individuals.

It must be admitted that most ethicists do not spend a great deal of time discussing the question of the morality of masturbation. It is probable that the traditional teaching of both the Catholic church and the Protestant churches that masturbation is sinful is rooted in the Old Testament attitude which stressed the importance of procreation so much that it considered it wrong for a man to "spill his seed upon the ground." Discussing the issue of artificial insemination, therefore, most Protestant ethicists see no need to raise any objection at this point. Helmut Thielicke, for example, speaking of AIH, calls masturbation for this purpose "fundamentally and radically different" (*The Ethics of Sex*, p. 256). And speaking of AID, James Nelson, while saying that the donor is "prostituting" his sex functions, insists that unlike ordinary prostitution this act in no way damages anyone's marital union (*Human Medicine* pp. 73–74).

A third consideration, relating to surrogate motherhood, is quite complicated. That has to do with a woman being paid to bear a child for another woman. The issue of the legality of the practice has not yet been fully resolved. Rightly or not, it has been compared with the illegal buying and selling of children who have been either kidnapped or purchased from people desperate for money. Indeed, courts in Kentucky and in Michigan have handed down decisions declaring surrogate motherhood illegal because it is a form of buying and selling babies. While a 1987 court in New Jersey upheld the validity of a surrogate mother contract, the supreme court of that state reversed that decision. At present it appears that courts will not sanction such contracts.

Whether the practice is illegal, however, is not our major concern. What we are concerned about is whether the practice is in fact the buying and selling of children. What actually determines to whom a child so conceived and born belongs? Is it a contract between a childless couple and a woman who needs money? If so, parenthood is a matter of law. Is it a question of whose sperm and egg unite? If so, the child belongs to the man as well as to the surrogate mother and he has all of the rights and responsibilities of fatherhood. If one woman bears a child for another, what difference does it make whether the semen came from the other woman's husband or from some other man, perhaps even the husband of the surrogate mother? What difference does it make whether the fertilization of the egg was in vitro or by AID or by sexual intercourse? Is the problem that of one person handing over a child to another in exchange for money? Does that constitute a treatment of the child as a commodity? Or, on the other hand, are all of these questions unimportant in light of the fact that a childless couple find a way to satisfy their deep desire to have a child of their own?

Because these procedures for overcoming childlessness are relatively new, the implications have not yet been fully explored. There seem to be few moral problems with artificial insemination with semen from the husband; there are more when the semen is provided by a donor; and the problems are even thornier in the case of surrogate motherhood. This is not to suggest that the practices should be avoided because there are problems, but rather that anyone considering them should know the problems and be prepared to deal with them. A number of those issues are:

1. What are the parental rights of the husband whose wife was inseminated with semen from a donor? Of the woman for whom another woman was a surrogate? Of the surrogate mother? Are adoption proceedings necessary?
2. Is it right to pay semen donors?
3. Is it right to pay surrogate mothers?
4. What steps should be taken to insure that the donor or the surrogate mother did not transmit disease or genetic defect?
5. What kinds of records should be kept? Should children who later want to know about their biological parents have access to those records, as do adopted children?

RESPONSIBLE PARENTING

Today most couples who marry plan eventually to have children. They expect to decide when they shall have a child, however, and they expect to determine how many children they shall have. While many factors will enter into their decision, a major one should be their prospect of bringing a normal, healthy child into the world.

The prospect that a child will come into the world normal and healthy is not at all certain. The human race now faces what some people call a genetic crisis. Inherited diseases and handicaps are increasing at an alarming rate, and current medical practice seems unable to do much about the problem. Seven percent of all children born in the United States have birth defects, and over a million persons a year are hospitalized because of such defects. In addition, there is evidence that genetic factors seem to be linked to a wide variety of illnesses.

While we cannot anticipate all potential genetic difficulties, we can identify many couples who are at high risk of producing a child with serious handicaps. Even a healthy person may be a carrier of a disease. Tay-Sachs disease, for example, a disorder that leads to blindness, paralysis, and death, usually before the age of four, is common among Jews of Eastern European origin. Sickle cell anemia, a painful and life-shortening disease, is found chiefly among blacks. Although only a minority of people in these groups are affected, people who are at high risk or who are carriers need to make informed decisions about whether to have children. If a couple learns that any child they bring into the world may be born with handicaps, several alternatives are open to them. First, they can gamble, believing that the odds are in their favor. If the odds are one in four that their child will have sickle cell anemia, for example, then they are three in four that their child will not have that problem. They may even prepare themselves to take care of an afflicted child if that should be necessary. Second, they may decide not to have a child, and to rely upon contraceptives. That decision, of course, is essentially the choice not to have a child *at this time*. It should be noted, however, that contraceptives are not altogether reliable. This decision can be reversed at any time by simply ceasing to use contraceptives. Third, they can decide that one or the other of the partners will be sterilized. That is essentially a permanent choice. While some vasectomies have been reversed, the success rate of that procedure is not high.

By a variety of tests, the most widely employed of which is amniocentesis, it is possible early in a pregnancy to diagnose the health status of a fetus. A couple who are already expecting a child and learn that there are serious problems have two options. First, they may decide upon an abortion. We have already discussed the moral implications of that issue, and it need only be said here that for some people nothing makes abortion right, while for others the fact that the child would come into the world severely handicapped justifies abortion. Second, they may decide to continue the pregnancy. Some prenatal treatment of the fetus is possible in some cases, and we are also learning more about the treatment of some problems in infants. A couple may decide, therefore, to accept the responsibility of providing the best possible treatment both before birth and thereafter.

What has been said has assumed that the decision is to be made by the couple themselves. Society also has a stake in the decision, however. The direct financial costs of caring for handicapped people are sometimes quite great, and because few families can meet all of them, some responsibility falls upon the state and upon private agencies. In addition, the indirect costs for health care, for education, and for continuing support are immeasurable. Some efforts have been made, therefore, to pass legislation limiting or even removing the individual right of decision in certain types of situations. For the most part, those efforts have failed because there is a serious question as to whether they are a violation of individual privacy.

Persons faced with problems such as the ones described here might be guided by three considerations. First, the best decisions require the most complete information possible. The prevention of problems is far better than the treatment of problems. Obviously we cannot know everything about a child who has not even yet been conceived, nor everything about an unborn fetus. We *can* know a great deal, however, and the more we know the better equipped we are to decide how to proceed. One who knows that he or she is in a high risk group, therefore, needs to know as much as possible about himself or herself. One who knows that a fetus may be diseased needs to know as much as possible about the condition and the prognosis for that fetus.

Second, we have a moral obligation to care for the helpless. The couple to whom a handicapped child is born, whether or not they had prenatal information about the handicap, are responsible for doing the best that they can for that child. This basic concept in Christian morality is reinforced by the fact that all human relationships involve responsibilities. This responsibility should not be romanticized. To care for a severely handicapped person costs a great deal in money and in time, and even more in energy and emotion. In some cases the expenditure is required over a long period of time. It is emotionally draining, it is confining, it seriously affects one's lifestyle. None of this detracts from the satisfactions that come from caring for one whom we love and who depends upon us. The mother of one paraplegic child said: "We love her. We are proud of her accomplishments. We would not give her up for anything in the world. But I hope that no one else ever has to go through what she and her father and I have gone through." While that mother and father did not choose that demanding way of life, they chose to do everything they could to meet the needs of their handicapped daughter.

Third, we have a moral obligation to all of the people affected by the birth of a handicapped child. Husband and wife have responsibilities to each other, and their relationship with each other will be affected by the care of a handicapped child. The lives of other children in the family are significantly altered. Each person has involvements and responsibilities outside the family—with work, school, the church, and community life in general. There are therefore broader implications for the investment of money, time, energy, and emotions. The needs of one person, even handicapped, cannot be allowed to destroy all other relationships.

ORGAN TRANSPLANTS

Medical history was made in 1954 when the first successful living donor kidney transplantation took place. Since that time surgical techniques have advanced greatly, significantly facilitated by the development of new medicines to overcome the problem of rejection. Today approximately five thousand kidney transplants are done each year, and the success rate is approximately 90 percent. Many surgeons are well trained for the operation and many hospitals are equipped for it.

This development of kidney transplantation was a part of a longer history of tissue transplantation. The first successful cornea transplant took place in 1905. Skin grafts were first successful in the 1920s. The first liver transplant was performed in 1963, and the first pancreas transplant in 1966. Bone marrow, ovaries, and testicles have been successfully transplanted. The prospects for further developments seem unlimited. Perhaps the operation that has claimed the greatest public attention is heart transplantation, with the first being performed in 1967.

The phenomenal developments in the techniques of organ transplantation should not blind us to the failure rate. Although tremendous strides have taken place in dealing with the problem of rejection, it has not been completely resolved. Furthermore, other physical problems may be complicated by the surgery. All surgery, no matter how simple, involves some danger. While that danger can be minimized, it cannot as yet be eliminated completely. The more complex the surgery, and the more experimental it is, the greater the danger.

The medical profession is quite sensitive to moral and ethical issues associated with organ transplantation. Early in the development of the procedures, Dr. J. R. Elkinton and Dr. Eugene D. Robin suggested some ethical guidelines which are still generally recognized as valid:

1. The physician must be concerned for the patient as a total person.
2. There must be a reasonable prospect for success.
3. Therapy must be the only goal.
4. Risk to the healthy donor of an organ must be kept low.
5. There must be complete honesty with the patient and his family.
6. Each transplantation should be done in a way that will increase scientific knowledge.
7. There must be careful, intensive, and objective evaluation of results.
8. Publicity must be careful, accurate, and conservative (cited in Smith, *Ethics and The New Medicine*, p. 121).

In addition to the issues covered in this code, however, there are other moral concerns. One, which has to do with the use of organs from a cadaver donor, is the question of the determination of death. Under no circumstances is it considered right to remove a vital organ from a person who is not yet dead. Yet organs cannot be used for transplants if they are not removed from the body immediately after death. At one time the line between life and death was sharply drawn. When the heart stopped beating and breathing ceased, the doctor could say the patient was dead. But now breathing and the heartbeat can be restarted, and impaired functions can be assisted by artificial means. *Brain death*, considered by some to be the determining factor, is not an entirely satisfactory indicator because it can occur while other vital functions continue. At present the most widely accepted criteria for the determination of death are those stated in 1981 by the President's Commission for the Study of Ethical Problems in Medicine and Biomedical and Behavioral Research: "An individual who has sustained either (1) irreversible cessation of circulatory or respiratory functions, or (2) irreversible cessation of all functions of the entire brain, including the brain stem, is dead" (*Defining Death*, p. 73).

A second issue is the question of who has the right to decide that the organs of a deceased person may be used for transplants. Some persons use *living wills* to make that decision before their own death. Under what circumstances, however, is it right to remove organs from the body of one who has not made such a will? This question often arises in the case of accident victims. Because many such victims are quite healthy, their organs are ideal candidates for transplantation. At present the next of kin may give permission. Does the body belong to them? Is it right to remove organs from the body of someone who had not given approval? On the other hand, is it right to waste vital organs which could save the life of another person? As long as these questions remain unanswered, it seems appropriate to continue with the assumption that the next of kin may make the decision because they are the ones who have the greatest emotional involvement with the deceased person.

A third issue is the allocation of scarce resources. There are many more people who need transplants than there are organs available. How is it to be decided which needy person is to be the recipient? It is taken for granted that an expressed wish of a donor will be respected. It is also assumed that if the next of kin express a desire, it will be respected. If there is no such expression, selection is generally done by a hospital committee. The usual procedure is to eliminate all candidates for whom the prognosis is not good. Then, from those who are left, the one who was first on the list is chosen. Every effort is made to eliminate such considerations as wealth, moral character, and social significance.

A fourth issue is that of risk to the patient. Medical canons require that physicians always act primarily in the interest of their patients, and only secondarily in the interest of furthering medical knowledge and skills. This means, of course, that in the treatment of a patient a physician will employ methods known to have a high success rate. Only after those methods have failed may a physician properly venture out to less predictable ones. The decision to move in that direction is not exclusively a medical one, and certainly should not be made by a physician alone. The patient too must be involved. Of course no surgery can be performed without the consent of the patient, but physicians can present the alternatives either in a persuasive manner or in an objective manner. The patient must have the option of weighing carefully the pros and cons. The patient must be informed of the odds, of the possible consequences both of having the operation and of not having it. In the last analysis it is the patient who needs to understand the risks because it is the patient who makes the final choice.

A fifth issue is a bit more difficult to delineate, but nevertheless is quite important: how is the *person* affected by the receiving of a body organ? Harmon Smith, who is quite positive about organ transplantation, comments, "In contemplating the personal dimension of organ transplantation, I have sometimes wondered how many organs from other persons could be transplanted into my body (presuming immunologic acceptance of them!) before I would no longer be myself" (*Ethics and The New Medicine*, p. 113). What does giving up an organ, or receiving an organ from someone else, living or dead, do to the self? Clearly it does not make one more or less of a self. Yet, as Smith indicates, if one's personality is altered by the formation of a new friendship or the reading of a book or by living in a different culture, can we expect our personality to remain unaffected by something as serious as this surgery?

Joseph Fletcher, however, equally concerned about human values, writes passionately about "Our Tragic Waste of Human Tissue" (Donald R. Cutler, editor, *Updating Life and Death*, pp. 1–27). Human values are not something mystical, he says, but something very much connected with the body. They involve the health and well-being of living people and the possibilities for helping people who are not healthy. To be moral is "to respond to human need, to answer a call for help in a concrete and particular situation" (p. 12). Paul Ramsey, who rarely agrees with Fletcher, is not far from him on this point. Commenting on an invitation he had received to present a theological definition of "the moment of death," he said that it is a medical matter, not a theological one. The theologian, he said, "can only offer his reflections upon the meaning of respect for life, care of the dying, and some warnings of the moral complexities such as are set down here" (Cutler, p. 52). From a Christian perspective, then, the ultimate issue is not merely the treatment of bodies but a consideration of the quality of human life.

When we talk of a living donor, of course, we are talking of the donation of a *paired* organ. Although there have been successful transplants of testicles and corneas, the most commonly donated organ is the kidney. Whether it is morally permissible for a person to donate a paired organ has been questioned on the ground of its constituting a mutilation of the body. That question is more academic than real, however, for the conclusion almost universally has been that it is not only permissible but commendable for one person to make such a sacrifice for another.

The question is more difficult, however, when we ask whether it is the duty of one person to make that sacrifice for another. Does the general Christian duty to help other human beings extend to such an extraordinary action? Does the fact that we are related to a patient, and that therefore the prospects for a successful transplant are greater, mean that we are obligated to make this sacrifice? Does the existence of a family connection put undue pressure on us to donate an organ? Does the urgency of the need of the other person have any bearing upon our obligation? How can we balance the need of the patient with the needs of other people who depend upon us? Can we ask others to sacrifice security so that we can help a third party? On the other hand, if pressure is put upon us, wittingly or unwittingly, to donate an organ for a relative, how free are we to say no? These questions cannot be answered in terms of a generalized duty. Each prospective donor, in the final analysis, must make an independent and unique decision on the question, "What ought I to do?"

THE CARE OF THE DYING

"Dad, how long does it take a person to die?" a child asked his father after a visit to an elderly friend dying of cancer. Commenting on this problem, Vincent Barry cited what he called "main currents in the experience of the dying: loneliness, fear, bitterness, self-doubt. Feelings of uselessness and desertion. Loss of self-governance, control, and participation. Indignity" (*Moral Aspects of Health Care*, p. 281). While facing death has always been a problem for people, it is intensified in our day by modern medicine's ability to delay death when it can no longer hope to cure or to relieve pain or even to prolong life at a worthwhile level. What do we do about a comatose person for whom there is no possibility of recovery? What do we do for an incurably ill person whose remaining days or months are certain to be increasingly, agonizingly painful? How are we to care for people who are surely dying?

We have already discussed the problem of determining when death occurs. Here we need to remember that in medical terms death is a process which includes clinical death (the cessation of breathing and the heartbeat), brain death, and biological death (the permanent extinction of bodily life following clinical death). While the determination of when death occurs is not always easy, therefore, it is a medical question.

More important from a moral perspective is an understanding of what death is. That understanding must be cast within a framework of an understanding of what life is. That human life is biological no one will argue. There is another side to human life, however, which we call personal: self-consciousness, self-transcendence, the ability to relate. In biblical terms this is "the breath of life"; it is "the image of God." In defining death, therefore, we must distinguish between biological death and the loss of personhood.

Among those things for which, according to the author of the Book of Ecclesiastes, there is an appropriate time, is "a time to die." In an earlier day we accepted that statement at face value. In the light of developments in modern medical science, however, we have begun to reject it. Instead, we take every possible step to avert death, both for ourselves and for those for whom we care. Such efforts have enabled many people to live longer, more comfortably, and more productively. Sometimes, however, those measures seem inappropriate. Sometimes it seems that while they can keep the body alive, they cannot keep "body and soul together." And sometimes it seems that the "soul" (or at least the person) is trying desperately to leave. Historically, the science of medicine has had three objectives: to cure the ill, to preserve life, and to ease pain. Modern medical practice succeeds remarkably well in the effort to heal and in the effort to preserve life. While it also does quite well in the easing of pain, at times it seems to place such a priority on the preserving of life that it becomes a bit heartless. Does there come a point at which extraordinary measures should cease and the patient be allowed to die? If so, how do we know when that moment has arrived?

A seriously ill person surely understands something of the situation, and a dying person often senses the imminence of death. Nothing is more certain than death, and people close to it are best served by an open and honest treatment of the facts. At a time when we are accustomed to talking about the responsibilities of physicians and nurses, and about the love and care of family and friends, we do well to consider the rights of patients. Those rights include, at the least:

> The right to be treated as a living human being.
> The right to participate in decisions concerning care.
> The right to be cared for by caring and knowledgeable people.
> The right to freely express feelings and emotions.
> The right to be kept as free from pain as possible.
> The right to honest answers to questions.
> The right to die in peace and dignity.

From this listing of rights of a dying person there is one notable omission: euthanasia. Does one who is dying have the right to a quicker and easier death? Popularly defined as "mercy killing," euthanasia is far more than that. Literally the word means "good death," and is an ideal especially important at a time when for many people there is no dignity in death, but only pain, loneliness, bitterness, and fear. What are the possibilities of Christian love making death good for persons?

Two facts of modern medicine combine to raise serious moral issues at this point: (1) our ability to keep comatose bodies biologically alive almost indefinitely, and (2) our inability to relieve the suffering of many people who are approaching death. Three problems arise from these facts. The first has to do with the way people die now. Today 80 percent of Americans die in hospitals, as compared with 37 percent only thirty years ago. Many die with machines attached to them, with relatives excluded from their rooms, with information withheld from them, and with no one who can or will talk with them about what is happening. What does Christian love and compassion require in that situation? What does it require of the medical personnel? Of the members of the family?

The second problem is the question of whether one must simply wait for death to come, perhaps after long and intense suffering, or whether one may choose to hasten death. In more blunt terms, this is the question of whether one has the right to suicide. Does a terminally ill person have the right to choose death at a time and in a manner that seems best for that person? Or are such actions immoral because they disregard the sacredness of human life? Are they a usurpation of a right which belongs to God alone?

The third problem is whether someone else, out of compassion for a terminally ill patient, might morally help that patient implement a decision to end his or her own life. Are we obligated by love to resist death to the bitter end, regardless of the cost in suffering by the patient? Or does love permit us—perhaps even require us—to assist the patient to escape from the suffering? Many Christians, observing the intense suffering of someone they loved, have prayed that God would bring an end to it by allowing the person to die. If that patient were to ask for help in dying, would refusing to help be a greater act of love than doing so?

The difficult question is whether elective death is sometimes morally valid or whether it is always wrong. *Elective death* means the choice of the time and the manner of dying. There are two facets of this question. One is whether a patient who is conscious and capable of making decisions has the right to make this one and to implement it, either alone or with assistance from someone else. This may mean a prior agreement that life-support systems will not be employed to keep the body alive when hope of recovery is gone, and that heroic measures will not be undertaken to resuscitate the body when breath and heartbeat have stopped. It may mean more direct steps to terminate life, taken by the patient who is capable of doing so, or administered by someone else for the patient who is unable to do so. The other facet is whether someone caring for a comatose patient has the right—or the obligation—to make such decisions on behalf of that patient and to implement it.

Consider first the question of whether a terminally ill person has the moral right to refuse treatment—in the form of medication or surgery or life-support systems—that promises nothing more than a prolongation of the dying process? Is one obligated to allow everything possible to be done to lengthen life? The right of a person to refuse treatment is generally recognized in the laws of this country. Does one have the moral right to do so? If we accept the concepts of freedom and responsibility, the answer must be yes. Every person has the right to accept the inevitability of death.

The next question is whether someone else has the moral right to decide to withhold medication or to withdraw life-support systems from a terminally ill person. That question is much more complicated. Who could make that decision? The medical personnel? The family? How do we know that the time has come to take this step? Is there really a difference between withholding medication or withdrawing life-support systems, which we expect to result in death, and taking positive steps to terminate the life of a patient? If a patient is in a coma and death in a personal sense has already occurred, if therefore the only life remaining is biological, then the moral problems of withdrawing life-support systems, if not eliminated, are greatly reduced.

If a terminally ill person decides, either because of intense suffering or because of the burden which long-term care imposes upon the family or because of some other factor, that a quick death is to be preferred over a lingering one, is suicide justifiable? If so, and if a patient needs assistance in performing that action, is a family member or a friend or a medical staff person justified in providing that assistance? Does one who is dying, in short, have the moral right to choose the time and manner of death? Does one have the moral right to choose a quick, painless death over a long, agonizing one? If so, does one have the right to help from medical personnel, family, or friends?

Although each of these situations has its own implications, the fundamental issue is the same: Do human beings have the moral obligation to struggle against death by every means possible, both for themselves and for other people, until the inevitable moment arrives? Or do human beings have the moral right to exercise some choice as to the time and manner of death? Some important biblical and theological considerations help us deal with that question.

We begin with a look at biblical teachings on the taking of human life. At the outset we must examine the commandment, "You shall not kill" (Exodus 20:13). All of the commandments of the Decalogue are concerned with the covenant community. This law protects members of that community from the threat of death at the hands of someone else. It is a prohibition of the deliberate slaying of one person by another, and other laws in the Old Testament reinforce that prohibition. In the Old Testament the word for *kill* covers both murder and involuntary manslaughter. The point of the commandment, therefore, is that people have a right to life which must not be violated either deliberately or accidentally. The law, in other words, deals with the right of the individual to live rather than on the attitude of another person.

Jesus' interpretation of this commandment against killing dealt with one's attitude toward other persons. He considered anger against another and contempt for that other to be immoral (Matthew 5:21–22). He internalized morality, making it a matter of motive and attitude rather than act and consequences. That teaching was verified by his own dealing with people who were commonly disregarded as unimportant or resented as sinners. It is true that he sometimes used sharp words in speaking to or about the Pharisees. If those words are interpreted as expressions of anger, then the anger was caused not by offenses against Jesus but against the helpless victims of the system. Even in those words, therefore, Jesus expressed a concern for the life of individuals.

While the sixth commandment prohibited killing, the Hebrew law did not prohibit everything that comes under that term. It authorized capital punishment for a number of offenses. The Code of the Covenant, of which the Decalogue is a part, specified death as the penalty for a man who strikes his father or mother, for kidnapping, for cursing father or mother, for murder, and for having kept an animal known to be vicious when that animal killed a man (Exodus 21:12–19). The Deuteronomic Code even prescribes execution for "a stubborn and rebellious son" (Deuteronomy 21:18–21)! Never was the law considered a prohibition of killing in war, presumably because the law was understood as a protection of the rights of the members of the covenant community. Indeed, the Hebrews are frequently described in the Old Testament as having proceeded, with the blessing of God, to the rather merciless slaughter of their enemies.

In some circumstances, suicide was not considered to be wrong. There is no Old Testament law against it. Without any censure the book of 1 Samuel describes Saul's suicide following his defeat by the Philistines at Mount Gilboa (31:4–6). Presumably that course of action was more honorable than allowing oneself to be captured by the enemy. To allow oneself to be killed in support of a worthy cause was recognized by the Hebrews, as apparently by people in all places and in all times, to be praiseworthy. That was the case with the wars of the Hebrews. It is implicit in Jesus' observation that "greater love has no man than this, that a man lay down his life for his friends" (John 15:13). In light of all these facts, we cannot conclude that the Bible teaches either that under no circumstances is it valid to take the life of another person, or that under all circumstances one's supreme moral obligation is to stay alive. The issue, therefore, is under what circumstances it is right to terminate either one's own life or the life of another person.

A second theological consideration is the Christian and biblical understanding of personhood. Because we have already discussed this theological concept (chapter four), here we need only be reminded of the fundamental ideas. Those ideas are:

1. Persons are creatures made in the image of God.
2. Persons are both body and spirit.
3. Persons are self-conscious.

4. Persons are rational beings.
5. Persons make decisions on moral issues.
6. Persons relate to other persons.

A third consideration is a Christian understanding of the nature of death. Is death always bad? Most people seem to think so. Their desire to avoid it is a combination of an unwillingness to lose present relationships and an uncertainty about what lies beyond death. For people contemplating the death of someone they love, of course, the pain of bereavement is what they feel most. Christians share these concerns with all other people. And like other people, Christians are involved in those death-denying activities that include all our efforts to stave it off to the last moment and our refusal to accept the certainty of its approach. Also like other people, they engage in all those rituals that try to cover up with cosmetics the fact that death has indeed come to someone they love.

The people of biblical days were no less anxious about death than are we. They contemplated human frailty. They prayed for continued life and they mourned death. They were anxious about what they left behind, and they were uncertain about what was beyond the grave. In most of their history reported in the Old Testament there was one significant factor in their understanding of death. Behind all references to death was the understanding that humankind was created by God and continues in the hand of God. Individual existence, however, was understood to cease with death. The dead were simply in Sheol, and any continued existence that people had was in the memory of the survivors who honored them. In the later Old Testament documents, however, there was some speculation about the struggle between good and evil and about punishment and reward after this life. That speculation continued during the intertestamental period so that by the time of Jesus the Pharisees, at least, affirmed the resurrection of the dead, with punishment for the wicked and reward for the righteous.

The New Testament writings consistently reflect the idea that the believer is in the hands of a loving God, both in life and after death. This presupposition of the Christian community, reflecting ideas from the late Old Testament and interbiblical periods, was rooted partly in the teachings of Jesus and partly in the fact of the resurrection. In the synoptic Gospels it is not taught directly but is assumed to be true, and certain implications are brought out. In the Gospel according to John it is talked about much more directly as the gift of "eternal life." In the letters of Paul there are frequent, forthright declarations of the expectation of a continuing personal, spiritual existence in the presence of God. Paul's most extensive discussion of the idea is found in the fifteenth chapter of 1 Corinthians, where he talks both of the resurrection of Christ and of the resurrection of the believer. His most moving affirmation is his insistence in the letter to the Romans that nothing—not even death—can separate one from the love of God (Romans 8:35–39).

Among the several principles which Allen Page formulated on the basis of his study of what the Bible teaches about life after death, the following are relevant to our concern:

1. "Life begins and ends with God."
2. "There is the growing hope in the biblical tradition among the faithful that they will be with God beyond death."
3. "Affirmations of hope for life after death are grounded in faith, in the experience of the individual and of the community of faith."
4. "The focus on continued personal existence is sometimes expressed with individual emphasis, sometimes with corporate emphasis." (*Life After Death: What the Bible Says*, pp. 84–87)

As we consider the question of the morality of elective death in the light of medical facts and of Christian theology, we find ourselves struggling with several questions. First, are we usurping God's authority when we elect death either for ourselves or for someone else? God has final authority over human life. While we have important decisions to make about our life, we do not own it. Do we, then, have the right to terminate it? That is a serious question. The basic human sin has been interpreted in a variety of ways, but one way to express it is the attempt to take the place of God. Yet it must be said that we see no problem in interfering by trying to delay death. We take extraordinary measures to keep a body alive even after it is apparent that death can be delayed for only a short time. Few people raise any question about interfering with human life by execution or by war. Why should it be a more urgent issue when a person is trying to die?

Second, what is the best way to demonstrate a sincere concern for the well-being of a patient? For most ill persons the ideal objective of treatment is recovery. If recovery is not possible, then relief of pain is the next objective. Is the terminally ill person for whom there is no relief from intense suffering and for whom things can only get worse, best served by continued treatment or by euthanasia? What is the most loving thing to do in these circumstances?

Third, what makes us reluctant to administer euthanasia? Is it our concern not to do something wrong? If so, are we concerned for our own personal purity or for the well-being of the person who is in deep distress? Does our sense of guilt compel us to keep the patient alive no matter what the cost? This is not to suggest that a concern for our personal purity is irrelevant. After all, there is a strong biblical tradition that God is the source of right and wrong, and that the moral obligation of the believer is to obey God. The issue, however, is whether the idea of the sanctity of human life requires us to take every measure to preserve that life, or whether it requires us to take the awesome step of ending a person's life to provide escape from suffering.

Fourth, is euthanasia an act of mercy? We consider putting a suffering animal "out of his misery" an act of mercy. Does mercy, then, ever require this last desperate measure to relieve the suffering of a human being? Paul Simmons asks:

> Is it more harm to kill a patient who is (1) dying, (2) has no chance of recovery, (3) is in unrelievable pain, and (4) has requested help in dying, or to force that person to go on suffering, helpless to do anything about, and hopelessly frustrated at having earnest, sincere, and rational requests repeatedly denied? (*Birth and Death: Bioethical Decision-Making*, p. 149)

The moral dilemma is not resolved. Intense suffering brings people to the point of being unable to function as whole human beings. Comatose persons have lost those faculties that distinguish them as human. Yet human beings are "a little lower than God." In that context, what does it mean to care for a dying person? It means to act in such a way as to demonstrate that the person matters. It means being with that person as that person tries to cope with the dying process. It means the sharing of our attitudes about living and dying. It means an honesty which "speaks the truth in love," and bares one's feelings as well. It means a respect for that person as one who thinks and feels, as one who desperately holds on to relationships, as one who fears the unknown on the one hand and longs for escape on the other.

NINE
ETHNIC MINORITIES

Howard Thurman says that "one of the central problems in human relations is applying the ethic of respect for personality in a way that is not governed by special categories" (*The Luminous Darkness*, p. 1). Special categories, however, have always been a part of the American scene. Although the United States was once called a melting pot, a better image might have been a mixing bowl, because so many groups in America remain separate from other groups—distinguishable in terms of beliefs, practices, appearance, and language. In earlier days some people were attracted to the United States by the opportunity which they saw here, some came here to escape bad situations in their native land, and some were brought here against their will—all to join people who were already here. Some people were so completely assimilated that they lost all sense of identity with their past, some failed in their efforts to be accepted into the mainstream, and some tried desperately to maintain or to rediscover their connections with their past. In this chapter we shall explore a Christian approach to the problem of allowing our dealings with persons to be governed by special categories.

IDENTIFYING THE MINORITIES

In any society the majority group shares a common tradition, a common language, and a common value system. It controls the economic and political structure in the society. For the whole of society it determines what is right and good, what are proper procedures, what are the limitations under which various peoples work, and the manner in which people

152

may participate in the process. A minority group, in contrast, is a subordinate segment of society, conscious of themselves as a distinct group without their having chosen to be, and assumed to have certain physical or cultural traits by which they are identified. In the United States blacks, Jews, Native Americans, and a number of national groups have such minority status.

Blacks

More than 28.5 million blacks live in the United States, constituting 12.1 percent of the total population. A little more than half of them live in the southern part of the country, and in most southern states the black population ranges between 20 and 35 percent of the total. At one time, the majority of blacks lived in rural areas, but at present more than 75 percent live in metropolitan areas. Nearly 50 percent of the people of Memphis are black, 55 percent of those in New Orleans and Birmingham, and 66 percent of those in Atlanta. Many cities outside the South have high concentrations of black population: New York, Chicago, Detroit, Washington, and Newark all have black populations of more than 20 percent.

Today's problems of black-white relationships are directly related to the fact that the people who were held in slavery before the Civil War were kept in poverty and ignorance long after that war was over and were systematically and effectively excluded from the political process. In the last decade of the nineteenth century and the first two decades of the twentieth century that exclusion was formalized in the South in a body of *Jim Crow laws* which imposed on the people a rigid segregation, the consequences of which we still suffer.

Although theoretically blacks are a part of the mainstream of American society, they are at best a disadvantaged part of it. In 1980 the median income of black families in the United States was only 58 percent of that of white families. Only 11.7 percent of the nation's population in that year, they constituted 28 percent of the low-income families. Although the wages of black employed women almost equal those of white women, the wages of black men are only 73 percent of those of white men. Traditionally, blacks are employed in lower paying and less prestigious jobs than are whites. This fact is explained partly by the lower educational level of blacks, partly by their virtual exclusion from managerial positions, and partly by the persistence of custom. Forty percent of black young people are unemployed, as compared with 15 percent of white teenagers. Although unemployment rates go down as educational level goes up, the difference between blacks and whites continues. The unemployment rate of black college graduates is higher than that of white high school dropouts.

In spite of the fact that racial discrimination in the selling or renting of property is illegal, tradition maintains the pattern of segregated housing in most places. Seventy-five percent of black families live in metropolitan areas, and over 50 percent of them in inner cities. The majority of those who live in cities live in impoverished areas and the percentage is increasing. While there are no statistics on white and black neighborhoods, most urban people live in areas that can be identified as one or the other. This segregated housing contributes to, although it does not fully explain, the continuation of segregation in other spheres such as education, religion, employment, and politics.

In a ruling handed down in 1954 (*Brown* v. *Board of Education*), the Supreme Court reversed the *Plessy* v. *Ferguson* decision of 1896 and declared the "separate but equal" philosophy unconstitutional. Prior to 1954 the southern states had rigidly segregated their schools and by every objective standard the schools maintained for the black population were grossly inferior to those provided for whites. Because there was strong resistance to the Court's mandate to desegregate the schools, more than ten years passed before any progress was made, and another ten before that progress was significant. At present, however, under pressure from the federal government, racial segregation in the public schools has essentially been eliminated. That result has been achieved by the abandonment of the neighborhood school concept, the use of the quota system in the placement of students and the employment of faculty and staff, and the busing of students. In some places one consequence has been the abandonment of the public schools by a significant number of white parents in favor of private education for their children.

The desegregating of higher education was begun immediately after World War II, and at present nearly all colleges, both public and private, are in theory open to applicants without regard to race. Some institutions have made significant efforts to achieve real desegregation in student bodies, in faculties, and in curriculum. The continuing process has resulted in the strengthening of some institutions and the weakening of others. At times it has brought about radical changes in campus life. It has brought a new factor into the competition between colleges and universities in the recruitment of students and faculty. For a time, it brought increasing numbers of black students into higher education, with black enrollment more than doubling in the 1970s and early 1980s. Unfortunately, however, that enrollment trend was reversed in the mid 1980s.

Although as yet they have nothing like a proportionate amount of political power in this nation, blacks are becoming increasingly involved in the political process. Between the end of the Reconstruction era and 1965 blacks were effectively disfranchised. The Voting Rights Act of 1965, however, made illegal all of the laws by which they had been prevented from voting and in addition provided for federal supervision of elections. After a period of a steady increase in registration and voting, they now vote at about the same rate as whites. A small number have been elected to public office, some have been placed in appointive positions, and some have been employed in local, state, and federal agencies. They still do not share proportionately in the political process, however. There is only token representation in the federal and state legislatures, in the judicial system, and in the law enforcement agencies—so few, in fact, that it remains relatively easy to count them.

Jews

Jews are not, strictly speaking, an ethnic group because they share no unique culture pattern. They have no ethos that distinguishes them from other Americans. They came to the United States from different countries at different times, all bringing traditions from the places of their origins. The rate at which they were assimilated into American society varied with a number of factors. Their Jewishness was only one factor, and the character of their Jewishness varied from one national group to another. Yet, because that Jewishness is significant, something that they had in common with one another in spite of the different ways in which it was expressed, they constitute a distinct group.

Jewish people themselves do not agree on a definition of the term *Jew*. It is not a racial designation. Race, after all, is not a scientific category but a popular mental construct which tries to identify a group by certain genetic traits which are reinforced by isolation and intermarriage. The Jews were never fully isolated from neighboring groups and in some places there was a good deal of intermixture with other people. Neither is it a religious designation, because many people who identify themselves as Jews follow no religious practices and avow no faith. Perhaps the most that can be said is that Jews are a group identified and influenced by a common history.

Approximately 5.8 million Jews live in the United States, with more than a third of them in the New York City metropolitan area. Religiously they are divided into three groups. The Orthodox, the largest group, keep as closely as possible to the Mosaic Law and to its elaboration in the Talmud. They are characterized, therefore, by a careful observance of the rituals of their faith. The Reform movement, which originated as a response to the European philosophy of Enlightenment, represents the effort to come to grips with a scientific world view. Reform Jews pay little attention to ritualistic matters and concentrate more upon moral responsibility. Conservative Judaism is, in a sense, a middle way between the other two groups.

Although there has been a long history of discrimination against Jews in the United States, the problem is not now so great. As late as the 1950s there were problems of employment, sometimes covert and sometimes openly stated. Restrictive covenants handicapped Jews in renting or buying property. After the Supreme Court ruled in 1948 that such covenants were illegal, "gentlemen's agreements" achieved the same result. Until the mid 1960s many colleges and universities either refused to accept Jewish applicants or maintained a quota system whereby a limited number were accepted. Private clubs and civic organizations often refused to accept Jewish members, and a number still maintain that practice.

Some overtly anti-Semitic groups were active in this country for many years: the Ku Klux Klan, the Populist Party, the Fellowship Forum, the Christian Forum, the Silver Shirts, and others. Since the mid-1960s, however, attitudes seem to have been changing, and popular polls show that most Americans express favorable views toward the Jews. A continuing problem, however, is the acceptance of the traditional stereotype of Jews as pushy, clannish, and unethical. In addition, many people say that they believe that Jews are more loyal to Israel than to the United States. Nevertheless, overt expressions of hostility are essentially a thing of the past and most Jewish people do not feel insecure about their status in the United States.

Native Americans

Nearly 1.5 million Native Americans live in the United States. Although they are found in nearly every state in the Union, 20 percent of them live in Arizona and New Mexico, 10 percent in Oklahoma, and another large group in California. The largest group in the South live in North Carolina, and in the Northeast the largest group is located in upper New York State. A little more than half of the Native Americans live on reservations, and most of the others in urban centers.

The federal government has not maintained a consistent policy in its dealings with Native Americans. In the early nineteenth century it forcibly moved large numbers to reservations in the West, expropriating their land and allowing it to come into the hands of private business. Late in that century it began to break up the reservations in an effort to assimilate the Indians into the mainstream of American life. In 1929 the government reversed its policy and again encouraged life on the reservation with traditional tribal government, an education that fostered traditional culture, and the development of native arts and crafts. In the 1950s and 1960s it tried again to relocate Indians away from reservations. In the 1970s the national policy was changed once more, and Native Americans on reservations were given control over their own affairs. A conflict of interest over land use, mineral rights, and water rights continues to the present.

While Native Americans differ among themselves as to what their final objectives should be, most want to plan for the survival of their culture and of their identity as a people. Their chief problem is poverty, with one-third of the total Native American population living below the poverty line. Most are unemployed, live in substandard housing, and have only a limited education. Plagued by a variety of diseases, chiefly related to problems of sanitation, food, and shelter, their life expectancy is ten years less than that of whites.

National Groups

The traditional melting pot image portrays the United States as a people whose ancestors came from many different lands and were blended into one new people. Since our earliest days, we think, we have welcomed and assimilated people from a wide variety of places and cultures. The last major wave of immigration, however, occurred in the late nineteenth and early twentieth century, bringing people mainly from southern and eastern Europe. Since that time, and especially since World War II, our government has significantly limited immigration.

Some immigrants have been rather easily assimilated into the general population. Others, however, for reasons of language or other cultural factors, have retained a certain group identity and often have experienced significant discrimination. In our country today many people are known to the majority population primarily in terms of their language or their ethnic origin. While we cannot deal with all such minority groups, we can cite some as typifying the experience of many.

Although Puerto Rico became a possession of the United States in 1898, many Americans consider Puerto Ricans to be "foreigners." For four centuries Puerto Rico was a Spanish colony, and its population is a mixture of the descendants of natives, black slaves, and Spanish settlers. The Spanish culture, including the Spanish language, has long dominated the land. Since 1920, large numbers of Puerto Ricans have come to the mainland, and at present approximately 1.25 million people of Puerto Rican origin live here, most of them in New York City. Because their migration to the mainland has been so recent, their values and culture are essentially Puerto Rican. Many continue to speak Spanish rather than learning English. Although many have dark skins, they do not identify themselves as blacks. Whites generally regard them as nonwhite, and blacks often resent their denial of being black.

Most Puerto Ricans are unskilled and their unemployment rate is more than twice as high as the overall New York City unemployment rate. Their language problem presents complications in job-seeking, in education, in the courts, in social services, and in day by day activities. In addition, they face the problem which all other ethnic minorities face— that of maintaining their cultural identity while trying to move into the mainstream where they can enjoy the full benefits of life in this country.

Nearly 10 million Mexican Americans live in Texas, California, Arizona, and Colorado. Many are descendants of people who lived in the territory acquired from Mexico between 1845 and 1854, and an undetermined number entered this country illegally. Contrary to popular opinion, they are not primarily farm workers, for 80 percent live in urban areas and their employment is as varied as any other group within our society. They generally live in segregated areas and patronize segregated social institutions. Although bilingual instruction is offered in some places, their children encounter serious language problems in school.

The general value system of Mexican Americans is associated with the concept of *La Raza*, which means "the race" or "the people." It implies that the people are held together by certain cultural and spiritual bonds, including their language. Their religion is a form of Catholicism that is more home centered than church centered. Their family ideal stresses the supremacy of the male, who is responsible for the honor of the family, and the proper function of the woman as wife and mother. In the preservation of these cultural values, the importance of the language emerges. "The principal language for Mexican Americans, whether first, second, or third generation," say Marden and Meyer, "is some variant of Spanish....Spanish is spoken in the home as long as one identifies with the Mexican American community" (*Minorities in American Society*, p. 245).

Mexican Americans historically have not been fully involved in the political process. As recently as 1980 only about half of them were registered to vote, and a third of those who were registered failed to vote in the general election. Even the 1975 extension of the Voting Rights Act to protect their rights, the provision of bilingual ballots, and other assistance to voters who do not speak English has made little difference. Consequently, few have been elected to public office at any level.

A number of Asian groups are found in this country, each with its own cultural heritage. Between 1849 and 1880 more than one hundred thousand Chinese, nearly all of them men, were brought to California to meet the demand for a supply of cheap labor. When that need proved to be temporary, the Chinese came to be viewed as a threat to the native population. The state legislature of California passed laws limiting immigration, making the Chinese ineligible for citizenship, and excluding their children from public schools. In 1882 the Congress of the United States passed the Exclusion Act, which outlawed any further immigration from China. This law remained in force until 1943.

At present some eight hundred thousand Chinese live in the United States, chiefly in California. They reside mainly in the cities and until recently were concentrated in "Chinatowns" within those cities. This residential segregation was partly a matter of choice because of kinship and clan ties and because of the desire to preserve the Chinese culture. It was also partly a matter of the resentment of whites who wanted to preserve the character of their own neighborhoods. Today, however, Chinese Americans tend not to live in segregated areas but to be dispersed throughout the cities.

In the late 1880s a number of Japanese immigrants came to the port cities of Seattle and San Francisco and settled in the surrounding areas. Like the Chinese, they were met with serious resentment. Congress passed a number of restrictive measures, and in 1924 terminated Japanese immigration completely. This situation was changed only in 1952, when the immigration laws were changed to comply with the Supreme Court ruling that no one could be denied citizenship on the basis of race.

Prior to World War II most Japanese in this country lived in "little Tokyos" for the same reasons that the Chinese lived in Chinatowns. Custom barred them from certain occupations and directed them into others. Thus they worked in lumber mills and fish canneries and on truck farms. They established grocery stores, restaurants, fruit stands, flower shops, nurseries, laundries, and barber shops. In spite of restrictive covenants which limited their right to buy property, many managed to acquire land and to operate their own farms. Yet they were denied access to public facilities and to private recreational institutions; they were frequently denied service in restaurants and hotels; and they could not be sure of courteous treatment in shops and stores.

During World War II people of Japanese origin were widely suspected of being more loyal to Japan than to the United States. Rumors about a "fifth column" which planned sabotage of war industries and military bases were circulated. Consequently, the federal government rounded up all Japanese in the Pacific Coast states and placed them in internment centers, even though two-thirds of them were American citizens. Some one hundred thousand people were forced to dispose of their property quickly, usually at a great loss. When the war was over they were allowed to leave the centers. Having nothing to return to, few went back to the cities from which they had come, although most remained in the western states. They did not settle in Japanese neighborhoods, however, but scattered throughout the cities to which they moved. They are more fully integrated into American social institutions than they had been before the war, therefore, and more than most other minority groups.

Since about 1975 the United States has admitted more than five hundred thousand Southeast Asian refugees from South Vietnam, Cambodia, and Laos. Some were brought here by the American government and some by church groups or private agencies. Receiving stations in Guam and in the Philippines and reception centers in the United States were set up to prepare them for acceptance into American communities. Efforts were made to secure sponsors and to help them find work. As they have become independent, many have regrouped into communities in Los Angeles, San Francisco, New Orleans, and Dallas. They have encountered some hostility, particularly because of their competition for employment.

The resettlement of these people was not accomplished without difficulty. The language problem was great for nearly all of them. At times it proved impossible to keep extended families together, a matter of great concern to them. Although some were well educated, and although many were skilled in certain occupations, they were rarely able to find employment in the kinds of work in which they were competent. Rather they were hired for jobs that required little skill and offered minimum wages.

There are, of course, many other groups: peoples from Cuba, Korea, the Philippines, India, and so on. So long as they remain identifiable groups, characterized by cultural distinctions, and living, either by choice or from necessity, in segregated areas, they face both social and personal problems related to their status in society.

STEREOTYPE, PREJUDICE, AND DISCRIMINATION

The lives of members of minority groups are shaped, in large measure, by their membership in those groups. The chief instruments by which society shapes them are stereotype, prejudice, and discrimination.

A *stereotype* is the attributing of certain characteristics to all members of a particular group of people. All of us tend to create mental images to help us deal with the large numbers of people whom we encounter daily but cannot absorb as individuals into our lives. By these images we decide quickly what claim people have upon us and how we are to relate to them. We learn from our culture certain ascribed characteristics of members of specific groups. Accurate or inaccurate, relevant or irrelevant, good or bad, complimentary or uncomplimentary, these pictures reflect common beliefs and affect interrelationships within society. Stereotypes are invalid in a number of ways:

1. They highly exaggerate the importance of a few characteristics.
2. They fabricate some supposed traits and make them seem reasonable by associating them with other tendencies that may have a kernel of truth.
3. They either omit or insufficiently emphasize favorable personality traits.
4. They fail to show how other people share the same tendencies.
5. They give no attention to the reason for the tendencies of the minority group.
6. They leave little room for change.
7. They leave little room for individual variation within a group. (Cf. Simpson and Yinger, *Racial and Cultural Minorities*, p. 100)

Prejudice is a rigid emotional attitude toward a group of people, a predisposition to respond in a certain way. In most cases this response is negative. It leads us to expect all members of a particular group to think alike and to act alike, to have the same emotional reactions to situations, to have the same personal characteristics and the same values, and even to have the same innate abilities. We tend to think that we know the most important things about a person, therefore, when we know the group to which that person belongs. We see any personal difference which one may have as merely a variation of the same theme. Prejudice therefore makes it quite difficult for us to see members of the group as individuals, with unique traits and characteristics.

Discrimination is the overt expression of prejudice. It draws conclusions and acts, not on the basis of reason, but on the basis of predispositions. Judgments about employment, for example, or about renting or selling property, or about admission to school, or about any number of other activities, are made on the basis of the applicant's membership in a group rather than on the basis of the applicant's qualifications.

Why is this pattern of stereotype, prejudice, and discrimination so widespread and why does it persist? Four explanations are commonly given (cf. McLemore, *Racial and Ethnic Relations in America*, pp. 105–124). (1) It is culturally transmitted, and people learn to be prejudiced as they learn a language or as they learn manners. (2) Some personality types need this attitude to help them cope with their own problems. (3) Majority groups use the pattern to dominate minority groups for their own benefit. (4) People draw their identity from their group membership, and prejudice is a means of one group distinguishing itself from another. Kyle Haselden adds another important idea. In discussing the problem of race relations in the 1960s, he correctly insisted that prejudice cannot be understood without a recognition of the fact of human sin. He said that the central element in prejudice is "the innate, inevitable, yet sinful self-centeredness of the human soul" (p. 76). He sees self-centeredness as "the essence of sin and prejudice as a specific expression of that sin" (Haselden, *The Racial Problem in Christian Perspective*, p. 77). Since sin is a constant condition of humankind, there is little likelihood that prejudice will ever be removed from human society. That does not mean that we must accept it as valid, but rather that we must always deal with it in a constant struggle for justice.

THE CIVIL RIGHTS MOVEMENT

Current issues in minority group relationships cannot be understood without reference to their social and historical context. One of the most important elements in that context is the Civil Rights movement which emerged after World War II and continues to the present.

On May 17, 1954 the Supreme Court of the United States handed down a decision that proved to be a turning point in the struggle for the civil rights not only of blacks but also of all other ethnic minorities. In 1950 the National Association for the Advancement of Colored People (NAACP) had taken into the courts a case, *Brown v. the Board of Education of Topeka*, which challenged the Southern pattern of providing "separate but equal" educational facilities for blacks and whites. When that case reached the Supreme Court in 1954, that Court decided in favor of the plaintiffs. While many years were to pass before any significant change was made, and while a great deal of pressure of many sorts was required to enforce change, it would be difficult to overemphasize the significance of the decision.

Other forces came into play in the 1950s and 1960s which eventually overshadowed the NAACP. One such force was the Southern Christian Leadership Conference (SCLC), led by the Reverend Martin Luther King, Jr., which for a decade was virtually identical with the Civil Rights movement. King's "Letter from Birmingham City Jail," written on April 16, 1963, was his most effective statement of the philosophy of nonviolent resistance. Urging Christians to obey just laws but to disobey unjust ones, he distinguished between the two by saying, "A just law is a man-made code that squares with the moral law or the law of God. An unjust law is a code that is out of harmony with the moral law" (p. 7). With that distinction, he called upon Christians to "disobey segregation ordinances because they are morally wrong." In campaigns of nonviolent resistance, King and his followers challenged segregation in public transportation, in public facilities, in businesses, indeed in the whole fabric of society. There was violence, sometimes on the part of the onlookers and sometimes on the part of the police, but King and his followers refused to retaliate. While for many people nonviolence was merely a strategy, for King it was a way of life. The result of the movement, however, was both the effecting of major changes in the treatment of blacks and the altering of the conscience of America.

During King's lifetime other groups also challenged segregation. Under the leadership of James Farmer, the Congress Of Racial Equality (CORE) picketed segregated institutions and sent interracial groups of *freedom riders* into the South to dramatize the widespread ignoring of federal regulations prohibiting segregated seating in interstate commerce. The Student Nonviolent Coordinating Committee (SNCC), with Stokely Carmichael as the dominating force, was formed in 1961. The Black Muslims, originating in 1930 as an alternative to Christianity, gained a large following in the 1960s because of their antiwhite teachings.

The role of the government was critical. In June, 1941, under pressure from black leaders, President Franklin Roosevelt issued an executive order prohibiting racial discrimination in defense industries and creating a Fair Employment Practices Committee. In 1948 President Harry Truman ordered an end to segregation in the armed forces. After World War II the NAACP went into the courts to force both state universities and the public schools to desegregate. Congress passed a Civil Rights Act in 1957 and strengthened it in 1960. President John F. Kennedy encouraged civil rights legislation, and President Lyndon Johnson's support was crucial in the passing of the Civil Rights Act of 1964 and the Voting Rights Act of 1965.

Although the civil rights legislation of 1964 and 1965 marked the end of legal segregation, the problems persisted: unemployment and poverty; life in the ghetto characterized by poor health and sanitation; fractured families; a high crime rate; no political power; and a pervasive sense of frustration and hopelessness. The Reverend Martin Luther King, Jr., ceased to be recognized as the undisputed leader of the blacks. Riots broke out in cities both in the South and in the North in 1963, and the same thing happened again each summer throughout the 1960s. When King was assassinated in 1968 his dream of a desegregated America seemed more impossible than ever.

In the late 1960s the Civil Rights movement was essentially replaced by the Black Power movement. Made popular by Stokely Carmichael, this phrase inspired fear in the hearts of white Americans because they assumed that it meant violence. Although Carmichael did not reject that possibility, he realized that blacks were outnumbered and that other types of power were therefore more practical. In the 1966 speech in which he used the phrase *Black Power* he urged blacks to organize to gain political and financial power and to make themselves independent of whites.

One result of the Black Power movement was the development of a sense of pride in being black, the assertion of the values of black culture, and the rediscovery of the African heritage of black culture. While there is some dispute as to the extent to which that African heritage is now apparent, it is clear that in America there is indeed a distinct black culture. Consequently, Black Studies programs were instituted in many colleges and universities. The part that blacks have played in American history has been brought to light as never before, and some efforts have been made to ensure that both blacks and whites are made aware of the distinctive contributions of blacks to literature and the arts.

During the 1970s and 1980s the concept of *affirmative action* was used to establish the rights of blacks and of other minorities. The term was first used in the 1964 Civil Rights Act, and in 1965 President Johnson issued an order requiring all contractors who did business with the federal government to "take affirmative action" to ensure that they dealt with employees "without regard to their race, creed, color, or national origin." Since that time the concept has been used in congressional actions, in executive orders, and in court decisions. Such affirmative action has involved dissemination of information among minority groups, the keeping of records to prove that there has been no discrimination in hiring or dismissing employees, the providing of back pay to people who have been victims of discrimination, and training programs for minority groups.

Opponents of affirmative action have called it *reverse discrimination* because preferential treatment was given to members of groups which in the past have been discriminated against. Affirmative action did not require the hiring of unqualified applicants; it did require that in choosing between qualified applicants preference be given to members of minority groups. As this principle was enforced, employers were sometimes required to hire partly on the basis of ratios of minority to majority employees. The purpose was to bring the minority group up to an appropriate level, and the method worked effectively to that end. Many people argued, however, that one consequence was the substitution of discrimination against one group for discrimination against another. Others insisted that employment partially on the basis of race is at least as fair as many other criteria, such as preference for veterans, seniority rights, the union shop, and tenure in educational institutions. And they argued that it was necessary to break the cycle of inferior education, unemployment, and poverty. At best, however, preferential treatment was a temporary measure, a plan not to maintain racial balance but to eliminate the imbalance that existed.

In the early 1980s the federal government reversed many civil rights policies that had been in effect for several years. The Justice Department, the Equal Employment Opportunity Commission, the Office of Federal Contract Compliance, and the Office for Civil Rights in the Department of Education either slowed down or discontinued their enforcement activities. New guidelines which made significant inroads on the concept of affirmative action were issued in August, 1981, by the Office of Federal Contract Compliance. Early in 1982, all civil rights enforcement measures were placed under the jurisdiction of the Justice Department, thereby eliminating the Labor Department's compliance programs and limiting the functions of the Equal Employment Opportunity Commission.

In spite of the progress that has been made since World War II, black Americans are still disadvantaged. The average income of black college graduates who are family heads is approximately $4,000 per year less than that of white college graduates; whites with less than eight years of schooling earn more than black high school graduates; and the unemployment rate of blacks is approximately twice as high as the unemployment rate of whites. A smaller percentage of blacks than whites graduate from high school, a smaller percentage attend college, and a smaller percentage earn degrees. While segregated housing cannot be maintained by law, it is maintained by custom, and in most cities blacks are still concentrated in areas of substandard housing. Middle-class and upper-class blacks who can pay for better housing usually choose to find that housing in black communities. While most churches affirm an openness to people of all ethnic groups, in fact most Christians worship in segregated churches. The changes that have taken place during the past decades have been motivated partly by a desire to assimilate into American culture and partly by a desire to emphasize the distinctively black culture. Both emphases continue and will continue to have an impact on black-white relationships.

A CHRISTIAN APPROACH

As we have seen, the presence of minority groups is a major fact of American society. Historically, some groups have been assimilated while others have persisted as permanent, distinctive segments of the overall structure. So long as there are distinctive groups, Americans will be required to deal with issues of majority-minority relationships. While each group is distinct in terms of its history, its values, and its characteristics, there is a basic Christian approach to dealing with people which is directly relevant to the issues associated with the presence of all minorities.

Biblical Concepts

In chapters six and seven we have already discussed love (*agape*) as the appropriate way for Christians to relate to other people. With this concept in mind, let us now consider the implications of biblical teachings for dealing with minority groups. An honest study of the Old Testament compels us to recognize its ethnocentricity. The very concept of a *chosen people* makes a distinction between an *in group* and an *out group*. If we have a unique relationship with God, then there must be a difference between us and those people who do not have that relationship. If we are God's specially chosen people, then they are not. If we are united by that covenant relationship, then we have obligations toward one another that we do not have toward people outside of the covenant. It is very easy for us to conclude that God loves us more than God loves other people, that we are morally superior to other people, and that our relationship with God justifies our doing what is necessary to sustain our privileged position. That disposition is applicable not only to enemy nations but also to the "outsiders" who live among us. Clearly this way of thinking is a problem.

The Bible says nothing directly about race. A careful study of those Old Testament passages (notably Genesis 4:8–16 and Genesis 9:25–27) which some people interpret as giving sanction to racial segregation and even to discrimination reveals nothing that supports those views. Those passages teach quite different ideas. The concept of race is a construct of the modern mind, an effort to classify the peoples of the world on the basis of certain relatively common inherited physical characteristics.

The Old Testament, however, does recognize the existence of minority groups. Such people lived with the Hebrews throughout their history. Some who could not claim Abraham as their ancestor came with the Hebrews out of bondage in Egypt and into the Promised Land (Exodus 12:38). After they entered Canaan the Hebrews shared that land with many other distinct groups. After they became dominant, remnants of that other population remained. Some captives of war were held as slaves and even some Hebrews were impressed into slavery because of unpaid debts. At no point, however, does the Old Testament justify such minority status for anyone. Rather, recognizing that it exists, it records laws designed to protect the rights of those minority peoples. The laws dealing with slavery, for example, restrict the power of the master and stress the obligation of the master to the slaves.

The theme of God's concern for all people, by way of contrast, is found in many places in the Old Testament. Both Isaiah (2:2–4) and Micah (4:1–4) dreamed of the day when universal peace among the nations would result from the universal worship of God. Deutero-Isaiah (Isaiah 40–55, composed near the end of the Babylonian captivity of the Jews), though focusing on the imminent redemption of Israel from captivity, is permeated with the note of universalism forcefully expressed in the invitation, "Turn to me and be saved, all the ends of the earth" (Isaiah 45:22). The story of Ruth, set within the period of the Judges, protests the narrow nationalism of the Jews in the post-Exilic period (cf. Ruth 4:18–22). And the prophecy of Jonah is a ringing, dramatic affirmation of God's love for a Gentile people.

Several generalizations based on the Old Testament offer guidance for our consideration of minority groups in our society. First, the Old Testament teaches that the human race is one. Both creation accounts (Genesis 2:4b–2:25 and 1:1–4a) talk about the creation of one species of humankind, and other passages in those early chapters of Genesis (4, 11) speak of the divisions as the consequence not of God's will but of human sin. That wisdom is echoed in the prophetic dream of the reversal of the effect of Babel and the uniting of humankind in the worship of God and obedience to the word of God (cf. Micah 4:1–4; Zephaniah 3:9). Living in harmony with God's purposes, therefore, requires the removal of the barriers rather than the maintaining of them. Second, justice requires a commitment to the protection of the rights of all persons, regardless of the groups to which they belong. No one's rights are lessened by accidents of birth, by social status, or even by deliberate sinful choice. The rights of life, property, dignity, respect, and self-determination are unaffected by ethnic group, sexual orientation, social class, or any other ways in which we classify people. And third, because God's love extends to all people, we may not exclude anyone from our concern. This is a particular emphasis of the Prophets (cf. Isaiah 11:6–9, Micah 4:2, Isaiah 45:22, Micah 5:2–9, Zechariah 2:10–11). If the love of God is inclusive, then our practices must also be inclusive.

The New Testament is even more forceful than the Old in its judgment upon group divisiveness. The Jewish people of Jesus' day made distinctions between groups: Jew and Gentile, male and female, religious and irreligious. We have already examined Jesus' teachings on love as the basic moral imperative, stressing the universal character of that love. A number of other statements are quite to the point regarding minorities. With a memorable and provocative story, for example, Jesus answered the question, "And who is my neighbor?" (Luke 10:25–37). In that story of the Good Samaritan he dramatically confronted the sharpest division of his day, making a hero of a member of the hated minority. Again, after he had healed the servant of a Roman centurion he commented on the man's faith, saying that he had not found that kind of faith even in Israel and adding, "Many will come from east and west and sit at table with Abraham, Isaac, and Jacob in the kingdom of heaven" (Matthew 8:5–13). Yet again, in the parable of the great feast (Luke 14:16–24) he taught that people who had been the recipients of divine favor could disqualify themselves by rejecting God's invitation and that others, despised by the "chosen people," would be entertained at the heavenly feast. In quoting from Isaiah as he cleansed the temple he sounded the note of the universal love of God: "Is it not written, 'My house shall be called a house of prayer for all the nations'? But you have made it a den of robbers" (Mark 11:17; cf. Isaiah 56:7). The Gospel according to John reports an intimate conversation with the disciples in which Jesus asserted that barriers between groups of people have no meaning in the Kingdom: "And I have other sheep that are not of this fold," he said; "I must bring them also, and they will heed my voice. So there shall be one flock, one shepherd" (John 10:16).

By his example as well as by his words Jesus demonstrated that discrimination on the basis of ethnic group was foreign to his religion. When he traveled between Galilee and Judea he usually went through Samaria, ignoring the Jewish custom of crossing the Jordan to avoid going through that area. On one such trip he talked at length with a Samaritan woman and consequently elected to spend two days in the nearby village (John 4:1–43). Several times he went into Gentile territory and ministered to people in those regions (Mark 5:1–20, 7:24–30, 8:27–33). In Capernaum he talked freely with a Roman centurion, healed the man's servant, and commended the man's faith (Matthew 8:5–13). One can scarcely read the Gospels intelligently without concluding that Jesus deliberately ignored the ethnic prejudices of his own people.

The Book of Acts makes it clear that the teachings and example of Jesus were taken seriously by the first-century disciples. Two striking passages in that book bear directly upon the subject of discrimination. The first was a dramatic experience in which Peter was led by the Spirit of God to ignore the Jewish restrictions and to go to a Roman centurion in Caesarea (Acts 10). Later, at the Jerusalem conference where Paul's work with the Gentiles was being challenged, Peter vigorously and successfully defended his own innovation which had preceded Paul's action (Acts 15). The second was Paul's speech at the Areopagus in Athens (Acts 17:22–31) in which he declared that God "made from one every nation of men to live on all the face of the earth."

The apostle Paul insisted that the Gospel removes all barriers between people and that all Christians are "one in Christ." That is to say, the fact of our common relationship to Christ overrides all other differences, real or imaginary, between people. Within the Christian fellowship all differences of sex, language, culture, skin pigmentation, and the like fade into insignificance. Thus Paul insisted to the Corinthian that "just as the body is one and has many members, and all the members of the body, though many, are one body, so it is with Christ. For by one Spirit we were all baptized into one body—Jews or Greeks, slaves or free—and all were made to drink of one Spirit" (1 Corinthians 12:12–13). To the Galatians he wrote, "There is neither Jew nor Greek, there is neither slave nor free, there is neither male nor female; for you are all one in Christ Jesus" (Galatians 3:28). In his letter to the Ephesians he dealt with the subject at some length (Ephesians 2:11–22), stating that the terms *circumcision* and *uncircumcision* no longer had any real significance. Jew and Gentile have been made one in Christ, who "has broken down the dividing wall of hostility" (2:14). The decision at the Jerusalem conference (Acts 15) confirmed Paul's judgment and practice.

The Methods of the Civil Rights Movement

While they have had support from some persons outside the groups, the struggle for liberation of minority peoples has been conducted by members of the groups themselves. Believing themselves to have been held in subjection by the dominant groups of society, they have taken steps to break those bonds. The fact that they have had to struggle alone is a judgment on the dominant majority. One could wish that the majority were sensitive to injustice, that they were concerned for the rights of the minorities, and that they would take the initiative to correct the abuses of power within the system. That, however, has not been the case. Furthermore, the solidarity of the minority groups has been such that they have been unwilling for members of the majority group to take leadership roles in the struggle. Because the majority has often been viewed as "the enemy," one who comes from that group can hardly gain unquestioned acceptance by the minority.

The movements have been well organized group efforts. While individuals have made unique contributions, the group has provided the setting within which individuals have worked. Rosa Park's unwillingness to move to the back of a bus, for example, mushroomed into a mass protest and under the leadership of the Reverend Martin Luther King, Jr., developed into the Southern Christian Leadership Conference (SCLC). The decision of some black students at North Carolina Agricultural and Technical College to try to eat at the lunch counter in a store in Greensboro developed into the Student Nonviolent Coordinating Committee. Many Christians, viewing morality as a personal matter and considering it their duty as individuals to struggle for justice, have been suspicious of organized group pressure. One of the contributions of the Social Gospel movement, however, was the recognition that many problems of our day cannot be dealt with on an individual and personal basis, but rather must be confronted by society as a whole. It is entirely legitimate for Christians to involve themselves in group efforts to bring about a more just social order.

The most dramatic and effective instrument of the black Civil Rights movement was nonviolent resistance to policies which were considered wrong and oppressive. The Reverend Martin Luther King, Jr., a Baptist minister who was profoundly impressed with the work of Ghandi in India, made this method central in his work. He took quite literally the words of Jesus, "Do not resist one who is evil. But if any one strikes you on the right cheek, turn to him the other also" (Matthew 5:39). He led his followers in defying the laws which sanctioned segregation, he led them in protest marches, and he led them in rallies. His followers were accused of creating trouble because their nonviolent activities often were met with violence. King believed that no changes would take place unless something was done to force the dominant group to improve the situation. He acknowledged that one of his objectives was the creation of tension to compel action. Blacks could not work through the structures of power because they had no place in those structures. On religious grounds King was unwilling to resort to violence. And on the same grounds he was convinced that nonviolent resistance was morally right. Motivated by his Christian convictions, he operated in a manner which he considered consistent with the teachings of the Scripture.

Would it be moral for a group to resort to violence in the effort to secure their rights? The riots in the "long hot summers" of the 1960s are a case in point. They grew out of the frustrations of people who lived in poverty in the ghettos of big cities. They resulted in a few deaths, a considerable number of bodily injuries, and property damage in the millions. They did not improve the situation of the blacks or better relationships in any way. Had they achieved either of those results, however, would they have been justified? Looking back on the situation, most whites now praise nonviolence and condemn violence. Do they, however, have the same problem with violence in the service of other causes? If it is wrong in the struggle of a minority group against a dominant group in one country, is it also wrong in the struggle of a nation to establish its independence? Is it wrong in the struggle of one nation against aggression by another? Or is violence sometimes a proper tool in the struggle for the right? If so, how do we know when the appropriate time for violence has come? Is it wrong to use violence in dealing with crime and criminals? Is violence always wrong, in other words, or is it sometimes right and sometimes wrong? Is it wrong for everyone, or is it wrong for some but right for others?

Violence, of course, is not the only form of power which members of a minority can use. As we have seen, the concept of Black Power referred not to armed violence but to educational, political, and economic power. Is it proper for a small group, acting as a bloc and in the interest of a single cause, to be the deciding factor in the election of public officials? Is it proper for blacks, for example, to determine their support of a candidate for mayor or for governor, posts in which the official makes decisions that affect the entire population, on the basis of the candidate's attitude toward blacks? In all fairness, we will have to admit that in our political system this is the way decisions are usually made. Persons are elected to public office who gain support for their stands on a variety of issues. One person supports a candidate for one reason, and another person supports that same candidate for another reason. Many groups use the power of the ballot to gain their objectives.

The same kinds of questions can be asked about the use of other forms of power. Is it appropriate for minority groups to boycott institutions or products? Is it appropriate for minority groups to picket business establishments? Is it appropriate to hold mass rallies? Is it appropriate deliberately to flout traditional customs and practices? Is it appropriate deliberately to offend? Does the achievement of an objective justify the use of methods which otherwise one would not employ? Is a cause, in other words, more important than social custom and convenience?

One of the debated methods that has been used, not by the minority groups themselves, but by the government in dealing with discrimination against minorities, has been affirmative action or reverse discrimination. That method, enforced for a time by the Equal Employment Opportunities Commission, came under fire in the mid 1980s. Is it a morally right method? In an objective sense, if it is wrong to discriminate against blacks it is also wrong to discriminate against whites. Is a white victim of discrimination any less a victim than a black one? If we look at situations case by case, the answer would have to be that discrimination is wrong in any case. If, however, we look at the overall pattern the answer may be different. The long history of discrimination has created a situation in which injustice to minority groups will persist until some step is taken which will correct the imbalance. Minority peoples will continue to live in poverty until something is done to improve the economic, educational, and political structure.

A Strategy for Christian Involvement

Questions of morality are always personal in the sense that they require personal decision and action. How can Christians bring their religious faith and their moral insight to bear upon the problems of division within society? Several suggestions about personal involvement are offered here. First, we need to avoid the assumption that one is good or bad in terms of the group to which one belongs. Truth is rarely on one side alone. We must maintain an objectivity which enables us to evaluate specific objectives, methods, and achievements. Further, we need to learn to respect people with whom we differ. If we cannot do this, we perpetuate the divisions rather than heal them.

Second, we need to inform ourselves as fully as possible about history and about the current situation. People in the majority group need both to know what the facts are and to understand the feelings of members of minority groups. Minority group people need to know the same about the majority. We all need to know what is happening—and what is not happening. Without such knowledge and insight we are likely to accept the status quo and to assume that everyone else is satisfied with it. By doing so we will contribute to the perpetuation of a system in which injustice is done to large numbers of people. Without knowing it, we may contribute to the problems by subscribing to beliefs and ideas which are incorrect and practices that are unjust.

Third, we need to be meticulously careful about our language. Insidious stereotypes are perpetuated by terms used in ordinary conversation, by jokes, and by attitudes and manners. A name, for example, is identified with a person; that is the significance of the commandment, "You shall not take the name of the Lord your God in vain." God's name is sacred because God is holy. By the same token, the terms by which we refer to groups of people are important; terms which the groups prefer should be used, and terms of contempt should never be used.

Fourth, we need to raise questions about the present situation. Most of us tend to face an issue only when a crisis forces it upon us. If no trouble appears on the surface, then we assume that everything is all right. The system may be unfair without either the majority or the minority being aware of the unfairness. The basic question is not whether people are satisfied, or even happy, with less than their full rights; it is whether justice is being done. To answer that question one must look at matters which other people are not looking at and raise questions which other people do not want raised. Christians in the majority group, in other words, should not wait for minority people to cry out for help; they should look for the hidden problems and try to resolve them.

Fifth, this means that Christians should serve as a conscience to society at large. They need to challenge assumptions, to criticize abuses, and to publicize facts. They need to correct mistaken ideas, to protest injustice in business practices or in the courts, to support public information programs, and to resist the exploitation of persons in employment.

These personal, individual activities, however, are the beginning of moral responsibility in these matters, not the end. The problems which we face are not merely personal ones; they are problems with the social structure. It is true, for example, as has often been pointed out, that in an earlier day in the South there were warm, personal relationships between many blacks and whites, that often there was genuine affection between a black person and a white person. Those celebrated relationships, however, were not relationships between equals. Both parties knew that there were limits beyond which they could not go even if they chose to do so. Both were governed by the superior-inferior mentality. And even so, that kind of relationship was the exception rather than the rule. The social structure isolated blacks from whites and kept blacks in an inferior position, and no amount of good will on the part of individuals, black or white, could alter that situation. Only an alteration of the structure could effect improvement.

That being the case, in dealing with the problems of any minority group Christians must deal with the structures of society. Individual friendship and individual morality, as important as they are, are not enough. If better education is needed, the procedures of the institutions which provide that education must be altered—the curriculum, the textbooks, the teachers, the social structures in the school, and the relationships of the school with the community will all be involved. If the law places a group at a disadvantage that law can be changed only by working through the normal political process. If there is discrimination in an industry it will not be corrected by individual protest; the pressure of the larger society will have to bring it about. The Christian who is concerned with observed injustices, therefore, will best work for improvement by working in cooperation with other concerned persons to alter the formal structures of society.

Fundamentally, Christian responsibility in this area is that of exercising influence. Again, we are accustomed to thinking of influence as a personal, one-to-one matter, something that is most effective when it is done unobtrusively. It is that, but only in part. There are vast areas of our life that are not intimate and personal but social, and it is in those areas that we can work most effectively for the resolution of the problems of minorities. We are citizens of local communities, states, and the nation—and through those governmental bodies we can work effectively for justice. We are a part of a church which needs to set its own house in order and then to serve as a conscience to the community—and we have immediate access to that church and a voice in it. We are employed in business, industry, government, or education—and through our work we have a means of effecting change. We are members of civic clubs and service organizations which have special interests—and we help to shape the policies of those organizations. We live in neighborhoods where we contact other people on an informal basis—and we can help shape attitudes. We have, in short, far more influence than we realize, and we can therefore do far more than we dream. The nineteenth-century poet Shelley declared that "poets are the unacknowledged legislators of the world." Today Christians must fulfill the roles of both leaven and legislator.

TEN

THE STATUS OF WOMEN

The subordination of women in our society is supported by the weight of long religious tradition. In an ancient prayer still in use, Orthodox Jewish men say, "Praised be God that he has not created me a Gentile; praised be God that he has not created me a woman; praised be God that he has not created me an ignorant man." In the traditional Christian marriage ceremony the minister asks, "Who gives this woman to be married to this man?" and the bride's father usually responds, "I do." Even when the response is "Her mother and I do," the woman is nevertheless handed over to the man. In that same ceremony the bride used to be asked to promise to "obey" her husband. Only recently have the wedding vows been modified so that the woman and the man now make the same promises of love, comfort, honor, and fidelity. Not for a long time, of course, have women really been regarded as the property of men, and not for a long time have wives really been expected to obey their husbands. Their status is not now what it once was and in the future it will surely be different from what it is now.

Although the number of females in this country is slightly larger than the number of males, the power of women is far less than that of men. We defined a minority group as "a subordinate segment of society, conscious of themselves as a part of a distinct group without their having chosen to be, and assumed to have certain physical or cultural traits by which they can be identified." In that sense, women might properly be called a minority group in this country.

WOMEN AND THE STEREOTYPE

Roles are a major factor in social interaction. We categorize people in terms of race, age, sex, marital status, occupation, and religion. We think that we know a great deal about them because we can place them in those categories. Conversely, we expect a person in one of those categories to act in a given way, and indeed we put pressure upon people to conform. We expect all southerners to act and react alike, for example. We expect Native Americans to be certain kinds of people, and blacks, Jews, Asians, and Mexican Americans to be certain other kinds of people. By the same token, we expect women to fit a specific role.

In a carefully documented study (*The Women's Movement*, Third Edition), Barbara Sinclair Deckard says that in the current stereotype women are "emotional rather than logical"; "passive and dependent"; "naturally mothers"; and "naturally subordinate to the male" (pp. 3–5). This stereotype is perpetuated in the home, in the schools, in TV programs and movies, in literature for children and adults, and even in the church. It teaches little children that girls play with dolls and boys play with guns, that girls may cry but boys may not, that girls must be pretty and boys must be strong. It instructs children on what career options are open to men and what options are open to women. It teaches them that women should be free to work outside the home if they wish, provided they can arrange for the care of their children, and that men must work to take care of their families. It sets patterns for home life which presume that house-work is a woman's province in which a man may help, and that a woman mows the lawn only if her husband is incapacitated. Observing that such stereotyping is as costly for men as for women, Deckard describes the stereotypical male as "aggressive, emotionally impassive, self-sufficient, athletic, brave in the face of danger, a natural leader, and competent at any task defined as masculine" (p. 53). Commenting on the pressure on men to succeed, she observes:

> While to many men, women are sex objects, men are frequently success objects to women. Because career success is defined as central to masculinity in our society, men often sacrifice all other values in pursuing it (pp. 53–54).

Ruth A. Wallace outlines what she considers to be our society's "underlying beliefs" about gender (*Gender in America*, pp. 43–55). First, there are "natural differences" in which men are strong, decisive, compet-itive, and not very emotional, while women are smaller, softer, prettier, emotional, and poorly equipped to deal with the fierce competition in the business world. Second, God has given to men the right to command and to women the right to be protected by men. Third, man's characteristics push him into the public sphere, while woman's characteristics require her to concentrate her attention on the private realm and limit her public activities to matters that are secondary, short-lived, and relatively unim-portant. Fourth, work for wages is the primary responsibility of men and only secondarily a responsibility of women. Fifth, romantic love is the ultimate bond between a man and a woman. To win this kind of love women must be physically attractive, while men must be strong, assertive, and successful in work. Sixth, for men, education is directly related to work, their chief role in life. For women, however, whose chief interests are marriage and the home, education aims at "a set of useful and second-ary relevancies."

WOMEN AND EMPLOYMENT

Regardless of the stereotype, a significant number of women have long worked outside the home. They have worked with their husbands on the farms. They have been employed in manufacturing plants. They have been sales and clerical workers, teachers, and nurses. For the most part, however, they have worked in order to supplement the income of their husbands. Few have had a sense of career, and few have had opportunities for advancement. Their work has been secondary to their chief role in life, and they have identified themselves primarily as wives and mothers, not as workers.

All of this is now changing as women in rapidly increasing numbers enter the labor force. In 1975, 44 percent of the married women in this country were employed, in 1980 the percentage had risen to 50, and in 1986 it was 55 percent. Today women constitute approximately 45 percent of the nation's total labor force. This increase has not been in those occupations in which women have traditionally been employed, but in fields that heretofore have been essentially closed to them. Crites and Hepperle say that "a greater proportion of women are employed than in any other peacetime period in our history, and are employed in a greater variety of occupations as a result of equal employment opportunities and affirmative action laws" (*Women, the Courts, and Equality*, p. 9). This broadening of opportunity has meant an improvement in the financial status of women. The fact that now they earn more money gives them an independence and a power that they have not had before, no matter how important they were at home and in the community.

The earning power of women, however, has not increased in pro-portion to their movement into the work force. The average annual salary of women is only 64 percent of that of men (Crites and Hepperle, p. 10). One reason for this difference is that they are still concentrated in low-paying occupations: more than half of them are secretaries, salespersons, waitresses, household workers, nurses, and public school teachers. Even equal education does not guarantee equal pay, for the median educational level of male workers and female workers is exactly the same—12.6 years. On the average, a woman with a high school education earns less than a man who has not gone beyond the eighth grade, and a woman with a college degree is paid less than a man with only a high school diploma. Among white-collar high school graduates, women earn only 56.6 percent as much as men. Women employees are not promoted equally with men. Management and supervisory positions in industry, business, and government are almost always filled with white males. Women managers and administrators with college degrees earn 59.9 percent of the salary of men on comparable jobs (Deckard, *The Women's Movement*, Third Edition, pp. 88–91).

In the higher-paying and more prestigious occupations women constitute a tiny minority. Only 4 percent of engineers in this country are women, 13 percent of lawyers, 13 percent of doctors, 4 percent of dentists, and 7 percent of architects. Only 2 percent of the partners in the nation's fifty largest law firms are women, and only 5 percent of the professors in law schools. In higher education the picture is better, but equality has not been attained. Only a third of college and university teachers are women, few of them are employed in the prestigious schools and most of them hold lower professional ranks (Deckard, p. 117). In all the professions, then, women have more restricted opportunities than men, are paid less than men, and have more difficulty in advancing in the profession.

Although for some time women had been moving into previously all-male occupations, the first federal prohibition of discrimination against them in those occupations came in 1963, when an amendment to the Fair Labor Standards Act required equal pay for women and men performing the same work. Title VII of the 1964 Civil Rights Act prohibits discrimination on the basis of race, color, religion, sex, or national origin in hiring, promoting, or discharging employees. Because early efforts to enforce the act concentrated on racial discrimination, attention was given to sexual discrimination only after concerned groups began to exert pressure on the Equal Employment Opportunity Commission. For the most part, court decisions have strengthened the case for women, although progress has been uneven.

WOMEN AND THE LAW

For two centuries the subordinate status of women in American society was clearly defined in law. "Under early common law doctrines of marital unity," says Deborah Rhode, "husband and wife were one, and, as a practical matter, the one was the husband" (Crites and Hepperle, *Women, the Courts, and Equality*, p. 13). Until late in the nineteenth century women could not make contracts, engage in licensed occupations, own, inherit, or dispose of property, or participate in political activities. While some women did find their way around certain regulations, most accepted and lived with the status assigned them. Court action in the late nineteenth and early twentieth centuries brought about some changes, and legislative action brought about others. The passage of the Civil Rights Act in 1964, however, provided the framework for enforcing for women the rights guaranteed by the Fifth and Fourteenth Amendments to the Constitution. Although the pressure had already been building to bring about changes, that legislation gave impetus to the movement. Because changes in law and in practice have been uneven throughout the country and throughout the various sectors of society, however, the present situation is not fixed but is in a state of flux.

Although the legal status of women is complicated, and although many laws are designed to protect women, on the whole women are still at a distinct disadvantage so far as the law is concerned. One of the most serious problem areas is the enforcement of the laws against rape. Far stricter standards of proof are enforced when rape is charged than are maintained in other crimes. A woman's failure to resist physically is often considered evidence that she consented; verbal protest is not deemed adequate resistance. A victim may be questioned extensively about her sex life, the assumption being that no woman who is sexually active could really be a victim of rape. Indeed, a woman who brings a charge of rape may even be accused of having provoked the assault. As a consequence, many rapes are never reported because for women the consequence of seeking justice is so painful. Since 1980 a number of states have amended their laws with the hope of making convictions on charges of rape more likely. Under the theory that a conviction is more difficult to win when the death penalty may be imposed, some states now prescribe imprisonment rather than death as the penalty. In addition, some states have made it improper to introduce the victim's prior sex activity as a factor in the case. As yet it is too early to know how effective these changes may be, but their purpose, at least, is to bring about a greater degree of certainty that rapists will be punished.

One legal advantage that a married woman has is that she is entitled to financial support from her husband. Whether she works outside the home is irrelevant, and the support is not even conditioned upon her functioning as homemaker. If a husband fails to support his wife, however, or if he provides only inadequate support, his wife actually has little recourse. In a dozen states she may get a divorce on the ground of nonsupport, but otherwise there is no way of forcing a man to meet this obligation. As a matter of fact, in cases of divorce on any ground, both alimony and child support orders have often been extremely difficult to enforce.

Property rights are determined by the laws of the state in which one lives. In most states each spouse controls both what he or she brings to the marriage and what he or she earns in the marriage. That means that a wife who does not work is totally dependent upon her husband's decisions about the expenditure of money. In some states, however, marriage is a legal partnership in which the earnings of both parties are considered community property. Several states still restrict the right of a married woman to make contracts and to engage in business on her own, and in five states a wife must get court approval to operate an independent business. A federal law passed in 1974 makes it illegal in any credit transaction to discriminate on the basis of sex or marital status. Prior to the passing of that law, lending agencies often refused to consider a wife's income in determining whether a couple were eligible for a loan, assuming that her income was uncertain.

A married woman's legal residence is determined by that of her husband. Even if for any reason the two want to maintain separate legal domiciles they may not do so. So far as legal residence is concerned, therefore, a married woman has no freedom of choice. This matter is important because it determines where she may vote, where she may be eligible for welfare benefits, where she must pay out-of-state tuition in a college or university, where she may obtain a divorce, and even where her will is probated.

Although by custom a woman assumes the name of her husband at marriage, the law does not require it. Most jurisdictions, however, assume that a wife takes her husband's name in such matters as voter registration, the issuance of drivers' licenses, and the receiving of some social service benefits. Most states allow a person to adopt any name he or she chooses and establish formal procedures for doing so. At marriage, however, a woman does not have to go through those procedures but may simply begin to use her "married name."

One of the greatest problem areas for women is that of sexual harassment. A number of court cases in the late 1970s brought this problem into the open. In 1980, the Equal Employment Opportunity Commission issued strong guidelines in which it defined sexual harassment. According to those guidelines, "unwelcome sexual advances" and "verbal or physical conduct of a sexual nature" constitute sexual harassment when:

> (1) submission to such conduct is made either explicitly or implicitly a term or condition of an individual's employment, (2) submission to or rejection of such conduct by an individual is used as the basis for employment decisions affecting such individual, or (3) such conduct has the purpose or effect of substantially interfering with an individual's work performance or creating an intimidating, hostile, or offensive working environment.

Although these guidelines seem clear, a violation of them is extremely difficult to prove. How can one convince a court that something is "implicit"? How can one deal with innuendo? How can one prove that an environment is "intimidating, hostile, or offensive"?

In 1972 Congress passed the Education Amendments, Title IX of which states, "No person in the United States shall, on the basis of sex, be excluded from participation in, be denied the benefits of or be subjected to discrimination under any education program or activity receiving Federal financial assistance." This governs both admission to schools and treatment of students after admission. Schools may not use quotas to balance the numbers of men and women, they may not restrict any programs to either sex, they may not discriminate on any financial benefits, and they must make all facilities available to all students. Although the implications of this law are still being determined in the courts, most educational institutions in this country have already been significantly affected by its provisions.

THE WOMEN'S LIBERATION MOVEMENT

> The problem lay buried, unspoken, for many years in the minds of American women. It was a strange stirring, a sense of dissatisfaction, a yearning that women suffered in the middle of the twentieth century in the United States. Each suburban wife struggled with it alone. As she made the beds, shopped for groceries, matched slipcover material, ate peanut butter sandwiches with her children, chauffeured Cub Scouts and Brownies, lay beside her husband at night—she was afraid to ask even of herself the silent question— "Is this all?" (Friedan, p. 11)

With these opening words in *The Feminine Mystique*, Betty Friedan sounded in 1963 the theme of what came to be known as the Women's Liberation movement.

The movement was not born *de novo*. More than a hundred years earlier Lucretia Mott and Elizabeth Cady Stanton had campaigned for the rights of women, and in 1848 the Women's Rights Convention which they organized issued a "Declaration of Sentiments" which concluded, "Now, in view of this entire disfranchisement of one-half the people of this country, we insist that they have immediate admission to all the rights and privileges which belong to them as citizens of the United States."

The industrialization which took women out of the home and into work in the mills did not give them those rights and privileges; it merely transferred the scene of their labors. The early development of schools and colleges for the education of women benefitted only a minority, and even for that minority it failed to open the doors to business and the professions. After a hard-fought battle women gained the franchise with the ratification of the Nineteenth Amendment to the Constitution in 1920, but the right to vote did not bring them into full and equal participation in the political arena. The most significant change in the status of women in America came during the Roaring Twenties. Freeman says of the women of the era:

> They drank, smoked, cut their hair, and engaged in the real sexual revolution of the twentieth century. Using the shortage of cloth after the war as an

excuse, they also shed their heavy, confining dresses and crippling foundation garments in a dress-reform movement that many thought did women
far more good than the vote. (Jo Freeman, *The Politics of Women's Liberation*,
19–20)

As early as 1923 the National Women's Party had managed to get an
Equal Rights Amendment (ERA) introduced in Congress. Beginning in
1940, in every presidential election both parties included the amendment
as planks in their platforms, though little attention was paid to it. In 1961
President John F. Kennedy established a Presidential Commission on the
Status of Women. That commission's report was issued in late 1963, just
before the publication of Betty Friedan's *The Feminine Mystique*. It included
recommendations that, if implemented, would have given women greater
rights in employment and in the political process. It also stated, however,
that the rights of women were adequately secured by the Fifth and the
Fourteenth Amendments and that the Equal Rights Amendment was
therefore unnecessary.

The Civil Rights Act of 1964, originally written to prohibit discrimination in employment on the basis of race, was amended in debate to
prohibit sexual discrimination as well. By this act the practices which
disadvantaged women in the marketplace became illegal. While the commission created to enforce the provisions of the act was more serious about
dealing with racial discrimination than about dealing with sexual discrimination, under pressure from a number of sources it did begin to fulfill its
obligations to women.

The National Organization of Women (NOW) was formed in 1966,
with Betty Friedan as its first president. Its purpose was "to take action to
bring women into full participation in the mainstream of American society
now, exercising all the privileges and responsibilities thereof in truly equal
partnership with men" ("NOW Statement of Purpose"). NOW set up task
forces, introduced programs of education and publicity, became involved
in sex discrimination cases in the courts, and organized demonstrations.
It began to work for the enforcement of antidiscrimination laws, for
special consideration for working mothers, for abortion rights, and particularly for the Equal Rights Amendment. The organization grew rapidly,
forming chapters in more than 150 cities and at its peak claiming a
membership of about thirty thousand. It suffered several splits, with some
women who considered NOW too radical forming more conservative
groups, and with others who considered NOW too cautious forming more
radical organizations. The vast majority of American women, however,
did not associate themselves with any group, either because they dis-
agreed with them or because they were indifferent or because they had no
opportunity. Yet the groups publicized their cause so effectively that,
according to a Harris Poll, by 1972 nearly half of American women favored
efforts to change the status of women in American society.

The impact of the Women's Liberation movement inevitably was felt in the churches. Many Christians, accepting as permanently valid the patriarchal pattern reflected in the Bible, insisted that men and women have distinctive roles and functions within the family, and that those roles and functions have priority over all other social relationships. This does not mean, they said, that one group is inferior to the other. It simply means that there is a difference of function. This concept determines relationships within the religious structures as well as in economics and in family life. Many women, however, challenged this way of thinking and began to seek full participation in the life of the church, even to the extent of ordination into the ministry or the priesthood. In spite of strong pressure, the hierarchy of the Roman Catholic church has refused to make any concession that opens the door to the possibility of the ordination of women. Some Protestant churches, on the other hand, have long ordained women and others are beginning to do so. In most denominations the number of women ministers is increasing, although women serve for the most part in subordinate positions.

As the Women's Liberation movement grew, colleges and universities began to develop Women's Studies programs. A sizeable literature was produced in the form of books and special-interest periodicals. Women moved in increasing numbers into political activity, not merely in voting but also in working within the political parties and in running for office both locally and nationally. On the whole, although at a slow pace, women are becoming a potent force in the whole formal structure of society.

In 1972 both houses of Congress overwhelmingly approved for submission to the states the ratification of the Equal Rights Amendment. That proposed amendment read, "Equality of rights under the law shall not be denied or abridged by the United States or by any State on account of sex." Both supporters of the Amendment and its opponents campaigned vigorously all over the country. Ratification required approval by thirty-eight states, but by the end of 1978 only thirty-five had approved it. Supporters persuaded Congress to extend the deadline for ratification until June 30, 1982. Even that extended time did not avail, however, and the amendment died without the necessary three-quarters of the states approving. Had it passed it would have rendered unconstitutional all federal and state laws that treat men and women unequally and would have required significant changes in the ways in which most businesses and social institutions deal with men and women. Whether it would have had all the ill effects that its opponents predicted we shall never know. Whether its passage was essential to the rights of women remains to be seen. Leaders of the women's movement consider the defeat unfortunate but not fatal to their cause. They expect to prepare carefully, to gain more power in the state legislatures, and when the time is ripe to introduce the bill again. "In the final analysis we were begging men for our rights," said Eleanor Smeal. "The task now is to make sure that next time, that will not be necessary" (Deckard, *The Women's Movement*, p. 448).

WOMEN AND THE SCRIPTURE

So much is said about women in the Bible that it is impossible in so brief a discussion to consider it all. We can, however, get a clear understanding of the biblical perspective by looking at general emphases and considering some specific illustrations.

Throughout biblical history the Hebrew family was patriarchal in form, and women were therefore subordinate to men. A man acquired a wife by presenting to her family a dowry which some have considered to be a "bride purchase" price (cf. Genesis 24, Genesis 29:15–30). At marriage a woman left her father's household and entered that of her husband. While the interpretation of the tenth commandment is subject to debate, a man's wife was included along with his servants and his animals among those objects which, according to that law, "You shall not covet" (Exodus 20:17). A man determined where his family would live, when his family would move, and what his family would do with its property. A man found wives for his sons and husbands for his daughters. While women had their influence, men had the authority.

In biblical days the roles of men and women were distinct. They represented a division of labor and of responsibility which sometimes functioned well and sometimes functioned to the disadvantage of one or the other. The woman was the childbearer and nurturer, a function of tremendous importance in the ancient world. Indeed, this was her chief reason for being. Within the economic division of labor, she was responsible for food preparation and for clothing for the family. In terms of religion, certain home rituals were her responsibility. The man was the provider of food and shelter, the protector, the religious leader, and the educator of the sons. Within those roles, individual personality played a major part in the establishment of husband-wife relationships and in the expression of those relationships. If we avoid the word *authority*, therefore, we can see that relationships were as varied then as now, and that then as now some women had more freedom and more power than others.

Although the established roles were distinct, the attitude toward women expressed in the Bible is as varied as the authors of the books. The author of Ecclesiastes disliked and distrusted women, saying, "And I found more bitter than death the woman whose heart is snares and nets, and whose hands are fetters; he who pleases God escapes her, but the sinner is taken by her." He concluded, "One man among a thousand I found, but a woman among all these I have not found" (Ecclesiastes 7:26,

28). The poetry in the Song of Solomon, on the other hand, voices appreciation for the beauty of a woman in an amazingly sensual manner. The inclusion of that book in the canon, made possible only by an allegorical interpretation, clearly indicates that such man-woman relationships were not objectionable to most people. In the book of Proverbs woman is seen as an enticement to evil (chapter 7), but in the same book wisdom is personified as a woman (chapters 8–9). The poem on "A Worthy Woman" (Proverbs 31:10–31), while it affirms the traditional roles in an idealized way, nevertheless injects praise for qualities of character that any person would do well to cultivate.

Jesus' attitude toward women does not fit any pattern established by his cultural background. Although the Gospels do not report any direct statement from him about women, they do offer a basis for our making some judgment about his attitude. The first thing to be noted is that while many rabbis of his day made harsh and derogatory statements about women, there is no record of Jesus ever having done so. Because such statements were common, their absence indicates an unusual kind of respect on his part. To that fact should be added a word about his relationships with women. Although none of the apostles was a woman, a number of women were numbered among his early followers (cf. Luke 8:1–3), and some were close friends (cf. Matthew 27:55–56; John 11:1–42). He seems to have dealt with women on the same basis as men, engaging in conversation with them and teaching them, and upon occasion performing some "mighty work" for them. In his teaching that every individual is of infinite worth in the sight of God he made no distinction between men and women (cf. Matthew 6:25–33, 12:9–14; Luke 15). We can hardly escape the conclusion, therefore, that Jesus considered men and women to be on the same level with each other.

A number of women were major figures in Hebrew history, and some occupied places of responsibility and authority. Moses' sister Miriam emerged as one of his chief advisers. Deborah, already functioning as a sort of "civil judge" for her tribe, became their military leader. Esther, thrust into an advantaged position, used her status as queen to save the Hebrews from an anti-Semitic pogrom. Judith, whose exploits are recorded in the apocryphal book that bears her name, used some rather questionable means to accomplish her purpose, but destroyed the enemy who was besieging Jerusalem. Alexandra, widow of two Maccabaean kings, herself ruled the Hebrews wisely and well for nine years. The achievements of these women were all the more remarkable because they occurred in a society in which women were not expected to function as leaders. It hardly seems possible, then, to think of Hebrew women as totally subordinate to men.

Women also played a significant role in the life of the early church. We have already observed that a number of women were disciples of

Jesus: Mary, Martha, Mary Magdalene, Salome, and countless others whose names we do not know. It is not surprising, therefore, that in the early church women were active in leadership positions. Lydia, a woman of Philippi who was operating her own business, was the first Christian convert in her city, and her home became Paul's base of operations for as long as he remained in Philippi (Acts 16:11–15). In time two other women, Euodia and Syntyche, also became church leaders there (Philippians 4:2–3). Priscilla and her husband Aquila were early missionaries (Acts 18:2ff). Phoebe was a deacon at Cenchreae (Romans 16:1). It is interesting that although the title is rendered "deaconess" even in the Revised Standard Version, in the original it is the masculine *diakonon*, which everywhere else in the Bible is translated "deacon." The important point, however, is that Phoebe was a deacon.

In addition to noting these general emphases, we must examine certain specific passages which are usually involved in a discussion of the status of women in general and in particular in the place of women in the church. The first three chapters of Genesis are often cited in support of the subordination of women. In the older creation account (Genesis 2:4b–25) man was created first and placed in the Garden of Eden. Then, when none of the other animals which God formed proved to be a fit "helper" for man, God made woman from a rib taken from man. Some people interpret this passage as teaching the subordination of woman to man because man was created first and woman was created to be his helper. Neither being second in time nor being of assistance to another person, however, necessarily implies subordination; indeed, they sometimes imply exactly the opposite. The real point of the story is seen in the climactic statement of the unity of the man and the woman.

In the second creation account (Genesis 1:1–2:4a) the concept of the unity of man and woman is even more explicit. After the creation of all else, God made man and woman simultaneously, in one creative process (v. 27). God did not create man and woman as separate beings; God created humankind as one being. There is no hint that either man or woman exists without the other, that either is a unit apart from and independent of the other. No distinction is made between them. To them God gave dominion over the rest of creation, but to neither did God give dominion over the other.

The Garden of Eden story (Genesis 3) is an affirmation of the sinfulness of humankind. In the account, the woman was enticed by the serpent to eat of the forbidden fruit, and the man was enticed by the woman to do the same thing. All of the offenders, the serpent, the man, and the woman, were punished by a disordering of the natural process: the serpent was doomed to crawl on his belly, the woman was doomed to suffer in childbirth, and the man was doomed to be burdened by his work. By a strange logic, the fact that the woman sinned before the man did and was the agent of temptation for the man has been interpreted by some people as justifying the domination of man over woman. That interpretation makes much of the fact that in the pronouncement of judgment on the woman she was told, "Yet your desire shall be for your husband, and he shall rule over you" (3:16). It is not at all clear, however, that this passage affirms a divine sanction for the subordination of woman to man. If it has any bearing at all on such subordination, it describes the situation and sees that subordination not as a part of the divine order but as a consequence of human sin.

Two of the most important passages in the New Testament, so far as the status of women is concerned, are found in Paul's first letter to the Corinthians. In chapter 7, on the basis of his belief in the imminent return of Christ, and on the basis of his conviction that marriage distracted one from service to Christ, Paul recommended that people not marry. Recognizing, however, that many Christians would not choose the way of celibacy, he discussed the marital relationship as he understood it. Everything that he said in that chapter he applied to both husband and wife. Each owes "conjugal rights" to the other (vv. 1–7), each should remain with the other even if the other is not a believer (vv. 10–16), and each will find marriage distracting from service to God (vv. 32–35). If this idea of complete equality is surprising to us, how much more so must it have been in a patriarchal society!

A bit later in the same letter (chapters 11–14) Paul discussed some matters of public worship. One of those was the conduct of women (11:2–16), and in that discussion he expressed a very paternalistic view. He said that "the head of every man is Christ, the head of a woman is her husband, and the head of Christ is God" (v. 3). He continued by arguing that men should pray and prophesy without covering their heads, but that women should pray and prophesy with their heads covered. The logic by which he supported his view was that "man was not made from woman, but woman from man," and that woman was made for man (v. 8). He recognized a weakness in his logic, however, and perhaps an inconsistency with positions he had stated elsewhere, for he acknowledged the mutual dependence of man and woman and added that "man is now born of woman" (v. 12). He tried to strengthen his argument by affirming that it is natural for women to have long hair and men short hair (vv. 14–15), an affirmation that he himself realized was weak. Consequently, he concluded his argument by an assertion of his own authority (v. 16).

In reading this passage we are usually so struck by Paul's stern affirmation that women should behave themselves properly in worship services that we overlook a crucial fact about what was happening: the women were actually "praying and prophesying" in the services. They were in leadership roles in exactly the same way that men were. Paul offered no rebuke for their participation in that way, but merely said that when they prayed and prophesied they should do so in a proper manner.

In the letter to the Ephesians there is a passage (5:21–6:4) which describes the ideal of relationships within the Christian family. We have already examined this ideal (chapter 7), but here we need to observe that it involves mutual respect, responsibility, and commitment. Here Paul (if indeed he wrote this epistle) did call the husband "the head of the wife" (5:23), but he did so within a context that called for each person to submit to the other. Furthermore, on the basis of this concept of mutual submission, he stressed the ideal of unity.

Rather than basing our understanding of Paul's view of women on these passages of Scripture alone, we need to consider also the implications of a principle which he enunciated on several occasions and which undergirded his entire ministry. He recognized that within the social order distinctions were made between groups of people. He insisted, however, that within the Christian fellowship those distinctions are totally irrelevant. "There is neither Jew nor Greek, there is neither slave nor free, there is neither male nor female; for you are all one in Christ Jesus," he said (Galatians 3:28; cf. Romans 10:12, Colossians 3:11). Although he used this phrase more frequently in speaking of the Jewish-Gentile matter, he did apply it to the male-female issue as well. We must not try to make a twentieth-century man of Paul. He probably would be quite uncomfortable with much of our women's liberation thought; he would be equally uncomfortable, however, with the exclusion of women from positions of service and leadership within the church.

Although the date of the writing of the Pastoral Epistles (1 and 2 Timothy and Titus) is much debated, they clearly reflect a time later than Paul, a time when the church had developed a more precise organizational structure. In that structure women were relegated to a subordinate status. In 1 Timothy 2:8–15 there are some directions for public worship in which it is clear that "the men" are leading in the services (v. 8). The women are directed to dress decorously (vv. 9–10) and to "learn in silence with all submissiveness" (v. 11). That direction is followed with the statement, "I permit no woman to teach or to have authority over men; she is to keep silent" (v. 12). In the next chapter the statements about the qualifications of the bishops and the deacons imply that those persons are men. The statements about "the women" may refer to a church office, but probably refer to the wives of the officers.

A CHRISTIAN APPROACH TO CURRENT ISSUES

Much of what was said about a Christian approach to minority group relationships is pertinent here also, because in both instances we are confronting the problem of dealing with people on the basis of their membership in certain groups rather than on the basis of their person-hood. Here, however, we need to restate some basic principles which are pertinent to current issues associated with the status of women: (1) Because every individual is of infinite worth in the sight of God, our individual actions must demonstrate respect for all persons, and we must seek to create a social order in which neither law nor custom sanctions any form of injustice. (2) Whatever may be the norm in the social order, within the Christian fellowship there can be no discrimination on the basis of sex. (3) All persons have the right and the responsibility to mature as persons, to develop their own potential, and to employ their talents to the fullest extent possible.

On the basis of these principles we can say a word about several current issues. The first is the question of whether additional legislation is needed to guarantee women the right to full and equal participation in the social structures. Some people who were committed to the ideal of equal opportunity for women opposed the Equal Rights Amendment on the ground that equal rights were already guaranteed by the Constitution. They thought that what was needed was not a new amendment, but the enforcement of the provisions that are already present in the Constitution. It is true that enforcement is a problem and that women have not enjoyed the full benefits of the laws as they are written. The supporters of the amendment, however, argued that it was needed because the other amendments did not specify that women were included in the guarantees. At any rate, although the amendment failed to pass for a wide variety of reasons, the campaign called the problem to the attention of the American public and in many spheres we have become more sensitive to the problem.

Do we in fact need an Equal Rights Amendment? Do we need additional legislation to correct current problems? Our review of the legal status has made two things clear. First, there is confusion as to what the legal status of women is because the laws vary so widely from one state to another. In particular there are problems with the laws dealing with sexual harassment, rape, and property rights. In addition, there is a need for protection for women in education, in employment opportunity, in advancement on the job, and in property rights. It may be that legislation will be introduced piece by piece and state by state. It may be that a revised Equal Rights Amendment will be proposed at some future date. But it does seem clear that as yet the law does not adequately safeguard the rights of women, and that this is one area in which we need to work to implement the biblical concern for justice.

We have noted that the Civil Rights Act of 1964 prohibits discrimination on the basis of sex as well as on the basis of race. We have noted that the affirmative action policies adopted during the early 1970s and pursued until the mid-1980s encountered considerable resistance. Those policies required employers doing business with the government to give evidence that in their hiring policies they did not discriminate against persons on the basis of race or sex. The form which that evidence was generally expected to take was a presence of women and of members of the minority groups among the employees proportionate to their presence in the general population. Where the number of members of these groups was disproportionately small, employers were required to show that they were trying to correct the imbalance. For a time this procedure was popularly understood to mean that a given number of women and a given number of minority group members had to be hired. In 1979 the Supreme Court ruled that such a quota system was unconstitutional. In the same ruling, however, the court upheld the validity of a more flexible plan of affirmative action. That same sort of affirmative action, it might be noted, was required for educational institutions in their admissions policies. As we have seen, in the mid-1980s the process of reversing those affirmative action policies was begun.

Is affirmative action an appropriate way to deal with discrimination against women in educational opportunities and in employment? Can the inequalities of the past be overcome by simply adopting a policy of employing the best qualified person, regardless of sex, of promoting the best qualified person, of admitting the best qualified persons to the colleges and graduate schools? How can we be sure that a person's sex is neither deliberately nor subconsciously considered a qualification? If not by affirmative action, how can we deal with the matter of giving women access to the best educational opportunities? How can we be sure that they are given equal consideration in the filling of positions? In salary increases? In job promotion? How can we be sure, not merely that we do not discriminate as individuals, but that in the educational, business, and professional worlds women have the same opportunities as men?

The leadership role of women in the church is an issue of very great importance. In the Roman Catholic church women are ineligible for ordination to the priesthood, and in spite of some strong sentiment in this country favoring their ordination, the situation is not likely to change in the near future. In most Protestant churches women can now be ordained as ministers, and increasing numbers of women are being ordained. Most women ministers, however, are not pastors but associate pastors, ministers of education, ministers of music, or chaplains. In spite of the official positions of the denominations, at the local level there is still significant resistance to the ordination of women. Some opponents interpret the Scripture as prohibiting it. Others are frankly unwilling to accept women as leaders in any area of life—politics, education, business, or religion.

We have observed that while much of the Scripture is patriarchal in outlook, the basic doctrines of the Christian faith require the acceptance of persons as persons without regard to sex. We have observed that in spite of the fact that the structure of society was patriarchal, some women did indeed serve as leaders both in Old Testament days and in the New Testament church. It would seem, therefore, that in refusing to accept the leadership of women today we are following the dictates of social custom rather than the principles of Christian faith. And we are now in the surprising situation that as conservative as the social order is, in that order women are making greater progress in gaining their rights than they are within the church. Is it not strange that a woman can be our president, senator, representative, or governor, can be superintendent of the public schools which our children attend, can own and operate businesses with which we deal, can be our doctor or lawyer, but cannot serve as our pastor? Rather than taking the lead on this basic issue of justice, the church may be the last bastion of discrimination against women!

ELEVEN
CITIZENSHIP
IN A DEMOCRACY

American citizenship is our birthright. Except for a small minority of people who have been naturalized, we are citizens by virtue of our parentage and our place of birth. We do nothing to earn our status, and whether we treasure it or ignore it we are never in jeopardy of losing it.

More than any other institution, the state determines the conditions of our life. It defines the family into which we are born, states the rights and privileges of the members of the family, and designates the responsibilities of the members to and for one another. It controls the education which we receive. It determines the conditions under which we work or operate our business. It regulates transportation and communication. It guards against the infringement of our personal rights. It protects us from criminals and defends us against foreign powers. It guarantees our individual freedom and defines the limitations on that freedom.

More than any other institution, therefore, the state is the arena within which we function. In the practical affairs of daily life we operate in families, schools, the workplace, the marketplace, and the world of entertainment. We relate not just to persons but to institutions, and through those institutions we affect the lives of other people. We have no option about working through the state. Whether by deliberate decision or by simply letting things take their course, we function as citizens. The question for Christian citizens is how to make this functioning the most effective expression of Christian concern.

AMERICAN DEMOCRATIC GOVERNMENT

The state, then, is a given within which we work. It may be defined as an organization which regulates the lives of the people of a particular geographic area and protects the integrity of that area from attack by outside forces. It is the final authority over all other institutions within its territory. It sets the limits within which they operate and exercises various kinds of power to enforce its regulations. Even though the organizational form of government varies from one nation to another, the government is always the instrument for the establishment and the maintaining of community. Even absolutist governments which reflect little or no concern for the rights of the governed nevertheless function as protectors and regulators in this sense.

The American democratic form of government assumes that the community itself is the final seat of authority. The state is the instrument of the community, its agent in the making and enforcing of laws and in providing for its citizens all of those functions which are necessary for the well-being of the community as a whole and of the individual citizens. The community itself, therefore, is involved in the governing process. This involvement is achieved through the selecting of representatives who act for the community. Since unanimity of judgment on specific issues can never be achieved, we subscribe to the idea that the judgment of the majority shall prevail. Yet we insist that even though the majority prevails, the rights of the minority must be carefully safeguarded. To make sure that the will of the majority continues to prevail, we choose representatives to serve for limited terms of office, we separate the powers of government (legislative, judicial, and executive), and we subject all officials to a wide variety of checks (regulatory agencies, special committees, recall, impeachment, and even nongovernmental watchdog organizations).

The majority does not in fact always participate in the process, however. By legal restrictions, by group pressure, by ignorance, or by indifference, the participation of many groups of people in our country historically has been restricted: women, blacks, the poor, and the uneducated. During the past three decades most of the legal restrictions have been removed, and the result has been greater involvement on the part of women and of blacks. The poor and the uneducated, however, are still rarely involved.

A basic function of our democratic government is to maintain order and ensure justice for all its citizens. While social justice cannot be defined in terms of law alone, the law is the basic instrument by which the state operates to this end. Laws which are general in scope and impartial in application provide the framework for social order and protect the rights of the whole of society. The enforcement of this law necessarily entails the exercise of power. Christians insist that the power of the state is limited, however, not absolute. They also recognize the danger that those who exercise power may try to hold on to it and to use it in their own self-interest. Christians therefore insist that their highest loyalty is to God, not to the state, and that in obedience to God they sometimes feel compelled to resist the power of the state. Thus they insist that the state holds power *under God.* A basic question, therefore, to which we shall give attention, is what Christians should do when they become convinced that the power of the state is on the side of injustice.

The concept of justice, as it is understood in our American democracy, presupposes the equality of all persons. One of the self-evident truths which our founding fathers cited was the fact that all persons are "created equal." Obviously they did not mean equality of intelligence, wealth, or power. They meant those "unalienable rights" of "life, liberty, and the pursuit of happiness." The framers of the Constitution made those rights quite specific in the first ten amendments which we call the "Bill of Rights." Those rights must be denied to no one because of race, sex, education, social status, wealth, or any other factor.

At all levels the activities of the government have become increasingly numerous and increasingly complex. We take it for granted now that the government will provide for education, transportation, postal service, police and fire protection, and protection against economic disaster. We take it for granted that the government should regulate matters of health, environment, and natural resources. While we agree that the government is properly involved in a wide variety of activities that affect the lives of its citizens, we debate many of the specific decisions about those activities. In deciding those specific issues we make value judgments about the good or the right thing to do.

BIBLICAL TEACHINGS

We have said that the state claims final authority over all other institutions within its territory. Christians, however, have a problem with this claim. For us, the final authority is God, and even the state stands under the judgment of God. While few American Christians are aware of any conflict between the claims of the state and their allegiance to God, most would say that if there were a conflict, we should obey God rather than the state. That approach is solidly based on Scripture.

The Old Testament

The Old Testament view of the government of the Hebrew people is that of a theocracy, government by God. This concept is quite different from that of American democracy. In a democracy the final seat of authority is the community; in a theocracy, the final seat of authority is God. We said that the basic function of government is to maintain order and ensure justice, and that to function in that way it makes and enforces laws; in a theocracy it is God who makes and enforces laws. Thus in the premonarchic days of the Hebrew people their religious leaders were also the political leaders. Even after the establishment of the monarchy the king did not have final authority; he was merely the instrument through whom God ruled the people. While there were good kings and poor ones, devout kings and wicked ones, the theory persisted that the king was God's servant and was accountable to God.

Within that theocratic concept, the state functioned as other states did. As with other nations, a primary responsibility of government was the ensuring of justice. The chief instrument of justice was the Law—the Law, mind you, which was not thought of as dictated by the king or legislated by the people but as given by God. Those laws which protected the person and the property of the people assumed a basic equality of men, so that the king was subject to the law to the same extent as his lowliest subject. As we have seen, while it offered some important protection to women, it did *not* assume their equality with men. Neither did it think of Gentiles as having the same rights as Jews, nor of slaves as having the same rights as their masters. That is to say that, like all other legal systems, the Hebrew laws upheld a concept of justice that was at some points flawed.

The New Testament

Because the literature of the New Testament emerged from the experience of the early church, it reflects the struggle of that church for its own identity. A major factor in that struggle was the attitude of the Jewish community, in which Christianity first appeared, toward the Roman government. While the Jews were far from united in their attitudes toward Rome, there was a strong and popular resistance movement. The Zealots, as the resisters were called, were responsible for frequent outbreaks of violence in the first century, and the movement reached a climax in the ill-fated revolution of A.D. 66–72. One of Jesus' disciples was identified as "Simon the Zealot" (Luke 6:1), and James and John, nicknamed "sons of thunder," might have been Zealots also. One interpretation of Judas Iscariot's betrayal of Jesus focuses on the possibility of his having been a Zealot disappointed in Jesus because he started no revolution. And while Jesus was not a Zealot, the charge on which he was convicted in the Roman court was insurrection. All of this is to suggest that many of Jesus' earliest followers, if not overtly hostile, were at least predisposed to be negative toward Rome.

Another factor in the background of the New Testament is the fact that Jesus was tried and executed by Roman officials. While Jesus was a religious figure rather than a political one, while the Gospels report no conflict with political leaders, and while his appearance in the Roman court was at the request of the Jewish religious leaders, the crime with which he was charged was an offense against the state. The death sentence was pronounced by the Roman procurator and the execution was carried out in compliance with Roman law. The New Testament writers do not play down the major role which the Jewish authorities played in the death of Jesus. Yet the fact that the Romans executed Jesus predisposed the writers to view Rome as unfriendly.

If Rome was not unfriendly to Christians in the time of Jesus, it certainly came to be so. In the earliest days of the church there was some local persecution of Christians, and there was one particularly severe episode in connection with the great fire which destroyed Rome in the days of Nero (A.D. 64). Widespread persecution of Christians broke out near the end of the first century and continued until well after the time of the writing of the last book of the New Testament. The fact of persecution, therefore, is reflected in what the early Christians wrote.

Another, perhaps related, factor that influenced the attitude of the New Testament writers toward the state was the belief that the "end of the age" was imminent. The eschatological hope played a part in the teaching of Jesus and was therefore a prominent part in the life of the early church. Its impact on Christian thinking about social problems in general and about the state in particular is of great significance. Because they believed that the world was soon to come to an end, the early Christians saw little value in trying to reform the institutions of the present order. Believing that the state was only a temporary and transitory structure, not one that would be a part of the new age, they accepted it and dealt with it as it was.

Jesus and the State. On only one occasion reported in the Gospels did Jesus speak directly about his disciples' responsibility toward the state. Mark 12:13–17 describes an incident in which the Pharisees and the Herodians, who differed radically from each other in their attitude toward Rome, teamed up to ask Jesus a question which they thought he could not possibly answer to the satisfaction of both groups: "Is it lawful to pay taxes to Caesar, or not?" Illustrating his answer with a coin bearing Caesar's image, Jesus replied, "Render to Caesar the things that are Caesar's, and to God the things that are God's." That answer affirms the validity of the claims of both Caesar and God upon the individual. While it says nothing about what one should do in case of conflicting claims, we can be sure that neither Jesus nor his questioners would have given priority to Caesar. What is clear from this answer is that Jesus did in fact recognize the legitimacy of the claims of Caesar. While he did not accept the state as in any sense ultimate, he did accept it as a valid social institution and rejected the implication that it was necessarily hostile to God.

There is other evidence in the Gospels that Jesus did not regard the state as having final authority. Not long before his arrest, for example, some friendly Pharisees warned him of Herod's hostility and cautioned him to change his plans for going to Jerusalem. Jesus, however, calling Herod "that fox," replied that his higher loyalty required him to carry out his plans (Luke 13:31–35). Again, in his conversation with the disciples on the eve of his arrest, Jesus contrasted the so-called "greatness" of those who exercise lordship with the greatness of those who served (Luke 22:24–27).

It is probably correct to say that Jesus did not spend a great deal of time thinking about the state. Rather he accepted it as a part of the context within which he lived and worked. When he contemplated his own mission, he considered and rejected the way of the Zealots (Matthew 4:8–10; cf. John 18:36). His mission, he insisted, was spiritual in nature and his final loyalty was to God. When the forces of the state took him into custody he refused to allow his disciples to resist, and he accepted without protest the sentence which the state pronounced upon him. We might conclude from his example that even a miscarriage of justice is not an adequate reason for destruction of the system!

Oscar Cullmann summarizes Jesus' attitude toward the state with the following words:

> Namely, that Jesus was in no sense an enemy of the State on principle, but rather a loyal citizen who offered no threat to the State's existence. Granted that on the basis of his consciousness of mission and his expectation of the Kingdom of God he did not regard the State as a final, divine institution, even where it observed its proper limits. He regarded it as a temporary institution, toward which he maintained a critical attitude. He refused obedience only to the totalitarian State which was exceeding its limits, drawing the line always at the point where the State demanded what is God's—but only at that point. (*The State in the New Testament*, p. 54)

Paul and the State.   Paul was a Roman citizen and that fact served him well. At the time of his arrest in Jerusalem it saved him from a scourging and ensured him better treatment than that usually accorded prisoners (Acts 22:29). Because of it, when his life was threatened he was taken from the Jerusalem prison to Caesarea where he pled his case before the governor. When after a time it appeared that he might be returned to Jerusalem, he exercised his right of appeal to Caesar and was taken to Rome (Acts 25:6–12). His freedom of activity in Rome as he awaited trial (Acts 28) was doubtless due to his citizenship. We are not surprised, therefore, to find that in the letters which he wrote while he was awaiting trial, and in which he referred to his impending trial, he raised no question about the justice of the system. He seemed to take it for granted that the system would operate properly.

The chief passage in which Paul discusses the state is Romans 13:1–7. That passage should not be considered in isolation, however, but in its broader context. The preceding chapter begins a discussion of the pattern of conduct which Paul recommends to his readers. Citing love as the basic obligation, he advises them about how to get along with one another and with people in the broader community. Verses 14 and following speak of living in harmony with all persons. From that point Paul goes on to talk about living under the jurisdiction of the state. He concludes his discussion of the state with a statement anticipating the end of the age, implying that the present situation is a temporary one.

Within that context Paul affirms that the state was instituted by God and is used by God to maintain order. Law-abiding citizens, he says, have nothing to fear, but God uses the state to punish evildoers. Because the state is an instrument of God, it legitimately claims three things from us: obedience to the law, payment of taxes, and respect for authority.

For Paul, the state was the Roman Empire. Doubtless he knew that there were areas of the world not subject to Rome, but he had no contact with them. The Empire was the world of his experience. When he wrote to the Romans he enjoyed the full benefits of his citizenship. Although he had had minor brushes with the authorities because of his missionary activity, he had no real basis for questioning the justice of the system. We cannot help wondering what he might have said had he written after he had heard his death sentence pronounced. We are persuaded that he would have challenged the justice of the verdict. We are also persuaded that he would not have challenged the right of the state to make a decision. He acknowledged, in other words, the need for order and saw the state as God's instrument for meeting that need.

In his first letter to the Corinthians Paul cited the lack of understanding which led "the rulers of this age" to crucify Jesus (1 Corinthians 6:2). He did not consider the crucifixion of Jesus to be the work of an illegitimate agency, but misguided judgment of a legitimate agency. In that same letter he cautioned Christians against taking other Christians into the courts to settle issues between them (6:1–8). He did not challenge the legitimacy of the state handling disputes between people; he challenged the propriety of Christians availing themselves of that service. As Cullmann says, Paul believed that "everywhere the Christian can dispense with the State without threatening its existence, he should do so" (*The State in the New Testament*, p. 61). He affirmed the state as a necessary institution but rejected any suggestion that it has final authority.

The Literature of Persecution. The Christian church expanded in a hostile world and at times was subjected to persecution. As a minority movement it was always looked down upon. When it grew the opposition became more overt. A limited persecution of Christians was conducted during the time of Nero (A.D. 54–68), and widespread persecution during the time of Domitian (A.D. 81–96). After Domitian there were sporadic periods of intense persecution for the next two hundred years. Many of the documents which were written during those periods instruct Christians on how to deal with hostility, and some of them were written for the express purpose of encouraging Christians to be faithful in the face of persecution.

First Peter is one of the documents intended to help Christians deal with persecution. Probably written during the time of Nero, it makes an important point about the Christian's relationship to the state (2:11–17). Regarding themselves as "aliens and exiles" in the world, and in spite of being the victims of persecution, they are to "maintain good conduct among the Gentiles." They are to recognize the authority of the governing officials, to conduct themselves as good citizens, and to endure without complaint what happens to them. They are even to "honor the emperor." This passage reflects a view quite similar to that expressed by Paul in Romans 13.

A second document written to deal with the fact of persecution is the book of Revelation. In this book the Empire no longer is seen as in any sense an agent of God, but rather as an instrument of Satan. Probably written at the height of the persecution under Domitian (A.D. 81–96), this book views the Empire as the very embodiment of evil. It is the "beast" which challenges the power of God (chapter 13) and seeks to destroy God's church. It has slain countless numbers of the faithful and there is no sign that things may get better. Indeed, this distress is seen as a part of that struggle of good with evil in which, though evil may have its temporary successes, the final victory of God is assured. The central theme of the book is the assurance that no matter how bad things may get in the present conflict, the ultimate victory is God's, and those who are faithful even to death will share in that victory.

The book of Revelation, then, has a radically different view of the Empire from that of the other New Testament documents. The other writers viewed the Empire as God's instrument in the maintaining of order—an instrument that makes errors of judgment, but God's instrument nevertheless. In the book of Revelation, however, it is seen as an instrument of Satan. How can we understand the difference in viewpoint? Cullman says that in the other passages "only the institution of the State as such was under discussion" (p. 71), "but that in the Revelation the State has become a Satanic power by demanding what belongs to God alone" (*The State in the New Testament*, p. 72).

THE CHRISTIAN AS CITIZEN

How do we move from an understanding of biblical teachings on the state to actual participation in the modern democratic political process? Do we go with Bible in hand and, ignoring the beliefs of those who are not

Christian, try to impose our convictions upon the governmental structures? Or do we take biblical teachings as applicable to our personal lives but as impossible for the nation? Or do we search for some common ground other than religion for our pluralistic society? Or do we look for ways in which in this pluralistic society we can live out our faith, responding to God by being good citizens of a nation that is by definition not religious?

The question with which we are dealing is not an abstraction. We are talking about making down-to-earth decisions on issues in which everyone has a stake. We are talking about educating our children and young people. We are talking about making and enforcing laws. We are talking about dealing with the problem of AIDS or the connection between cigarette smoking and lung cancer or the industrial pollution of the natural environment. We are talking about the problems of national defense and international relations. We are talking about coal and oil and nuclear reactors. We are talking about the care of the sick and about financial security for the aging. In short, we are talking about involvement in decisions that affect every citizen.

The Obligations of Citizenship

What are our responsibilities as citizens in a democratic society? All citizens have three basic obligations to the state. First, they owe respect for the law. That means that the law applies equally to all people, that individuals have no right to regard themselves as exempt from the requirements of the law, and that obedience to the law is based not on fear of being caught for violations but upon that respect. That is the idea which Paul expressed when he said, "Therefore one must be subject, not only to avoid God's wrath, but also for the sake of conscience" (Romans 13:5). The only valid basis for disobedience is an allegiance to a higher law, what Peter meant when he said to the Sanhedrin, "We must obey God rather than men" (Acts 5:29).

Second, all citizens owe intelligent, informed participation in the process of the making and the enforcing of laws and policies. Because democratic government is by nature participatory, it can succeed only to the extent that the citizens actually help in the choice of their representatives, help in the determination of policies, and accept the responsibility of running for office. The disfranchisement of any group, either by its own inertia or by exclusion from the process by a more powerful group, makes the process less than democratic. The greatest scandal of our government is not the misbehavior of any official but the failure of large numbers of people to participate in the process.

Third, all citizens are responsible for conscientious criticism of persons and policies. We need at all times to measure practice by the stated ideals of our nation, by the concepts of honesty and justice, and by the effects on all the people. This means that we must examine all proposals to understand their implications, that we must constantly reevaluate what is already being done, and that we must always be prepared to approve or disapprove.

Neither of these three responsibilities is uniquely Christian. Indeed, we cannot cite any responsibility that is exclusively the province of Christian citizens. What is distinctive about Christian citizenship is not any specific thing that we do that others do not, but our rooting of our obligation in God. For Christians, the exercise of our citizenship is one of the ways we relate to God. Paul said that "in him [Christ] we live and move and have our being." Christ, by that affirmation, is our environment, the world in which we live, the source from which we come. As our nature is shaped by Christ, our citizenship is an expression of that nature. As citizens we do the same things that other people do, but our doing of those things is an affirmation of our relationship to Christ.

The Contribution of Christians

Do Christians, then, have anything distinctive to offer in the political process? While we must be cautious about any claim to exclusive ownership of any idea or attitude, there are several important concepts which Christians bring into the political arena. First is our view of persons. We have said that a belief in the dignity and worth of every person is fundamental in the Christian view of human nature. It is also basic in the democratic state. This means that those persons whom many people regard as inferior—members of minority groups, the poor, the criminal, the victims of certain diseases—possess the same dignity and worth as those who look down on them. We Christians root this conviction in our belief in God and in God's dealings with people rather than in a faith in humankind. We affirm it in spite of the way in which both individuals and groups of people actually behave. We affirm it in spite of the complexity of social structures and of the dehumanizing effect of group relationships. We even affirm it in spite of the distinctions between people made in all social institutions, including the church. Our affirmation and our efforts to incorporate it in the social structure are a vital element in American democracy.

There is another side to the Christian view of persons, however, which is essential to the functioning of the democratic process. That is an awareness of the dark side of human nature, of what in religious terms is called *sinfulness*. It is because of this side of human nature that good people do bad things, that people do not always follow through on their promises, that graft and corruption are always with us, that people take advantage of the system and use it for their own benefit, that no system works perfectly, and that group conflict is always a possibility. It is for this reason that it is necessary for the people to impose limitations upon the power of their representatives and to provide for ways of holding those representatives accountable.

A second thing which Christians bring to the functioning of the democratic process is a stress on community. The concept of community, of course, is fundamental in the understanding of the church. The church is a community of faith, a group of people bound together by their relationship to Christ. The members do not think of that community as rooted in or sustained by their activity or their feelings of unity but in the work of Christ. It is a community in which people recognize a responsibility to and for one another, in which they care for one another, and in which they share experiences. When this concept of community is carried over into the nation it counterbalances the extreme individualism which at best ignores other people and at worst sets persons and groups over against each other. A national sense of community will ensure a concern for the rights of minorities, for the care of the helpless, for respect for the individual, as well as a concern for the common good. That is not to suggest that the unity of the nation is or should be the same as the unity of the church. The natures of the two are different and the functions are different. At the same time, however, the idea that the nation is in some sense a community affects for the good the operation of our democracy.

What is the basis for our national sense of community? Both nationalism and the philosophy of enlightened self-interest play a part. It cannot be these alone, however. Our nationalistic spirit is somewhat limited by the fact that we are such a diverse people. In addition, nationalism fosters a spirit of hostility toward other nations, a spirit alien to the democratic philosophy. Enlightened self-interest also requires our protection of the rights of others only when it is clearly to our own advantage to do so. Charles Patterson says that "a state must be based primarily upon the moral standard which most of the citizens are prepared to accept," and notes that "Christian love" is the standard most widely acknowledged in our society. He believes that fundamental to our national sense of community is our disposition to operate on the basis of an all-inclusive good will towards one another (*Moral Standards*, p. 303). He concludes:

> Christian love is a powerful leaven which attracts others by its perfection, its effectiveness cannot be measured by the number of those who consciously practice it or by its tangible results, and the liberal democracy of the last hundred years would have been impossible without the vast store of humanitarian good will which had been produced by Christianity in the past. (p. 303)

A third important contribution of Christians to our democratic society is the element of hope. The dream of a better world is a persistent theme in the Bible. We are deeply moved when we read Isaiah's words:

and they shall beat their swords into plowshares,
    and their spears into pruning hooks;
nation shall not lift up sword against nation,
    neither shall they learn war any more (2:4).

Christians think of themselves as, in a sense, already living in that context because they are members of a community that transcends race and nation and class and sex. Even though they know that as it exists now that community is flawed, they are moved by their vision to try to remove the flaws. Even though they project the full realization of that dream into the eschatological age, they live as if that age is breaking in on this one and transforming it.

The dream of an ideal social order is not exclusively Christian. The literature of philosophy is full of it, from Plato's *Republic* to Skinner's *Walden Two*. From early Utopian communities to twentieth-century communism, people have experimented with the institutionalizing of the dream. Nearly every political figure who comes into power does so by promising to lead the nation into a brighter future. That ideal age has never come, however. Old hostilities are not forgotten. New divisions are created by new circumstances. The struggle for power goes on between individuals, groups, and nations. Even the church, which sees itself as in a sense already living in that new age, is torn by conflict.

Yet Christians are committed to and drawn by an ideal of community. Knowing that it will never be fully realized on earth, they nevertheless do not project it entirely into another world. Rather they hold out to this world the constant possibility of approximating that ideal. In every political situation they hold out the hope that things can be made better.

Suggestions for Involvement

How can we effectively involve ourselves in the political arena? At the outset we need to set out deliberately and systematically to inform ourselves. On the surface that would not seem to be difficult. Between the media which try, with varying degrees of success, to report the news objectively, and the partisans who flood us with propaganda, it would seem that we have more information than we can use. The problem, however, is that of distinguishing between fact and fiction, between reporting and special pleading, and between accuracy and distortion. Our task is to sort through and evaluate all that we see and hear, and on the basis of what we learn make our decisions about persons and issues.

Once we have committed ourselves to a person or to a program, we can begin to exert our influence through our conversation with other people. Talk can be cheap, but it is not necessarily so. Whether in casual conversation or in deliberate and sustained discussion, words make an impact. They convey ideas and emotions, both of which are involved in most decisions that people make. By our words as we are on the job, in the marketplace, at the ballpark, on the street, or with friends in our living room we can help to create a climate and to shape public opinion. In addition, we can influence some people who have not as yet made up their minds how they are going to vote. In most campaigns a strikingly large number of people do not make their decisions until quite late in the season and they are often the ones who are the deciding factor in the way an election goes. They are likely to respond to the influence of people whom they know and whose judgment they respect.

In the long run, the most effective way to influence public policy is through direct involvement in the political structure. Most decisions of social significance are not made through personal interaction but through group interaction. Candidates vie with each other for the nomination of a political party, and they run for office on platforms determined by that party. The party system functions at every level of government. In any given campaign, local or national, the persons of influence are not likely to be newcomers to politics but persons who have worked faithfully within the system. The most effective criticism of a person or a policy comes from within the system, not from the outside.

The practice of politics always involves compromise. While we tend to regard compromise as undesirable, it is in fact essential for any group cooperation. No one person has either the wisdom or the power to determine all decisions. Certainly there are some things to which we cannot say yes and some things to which we cannot say no. Most political decisions, however, are not between such absolutes, but between alternatives that are a mixture of good and bad. In politics, as in other activities, we must work within restrictions and work for the best possible. If perchance we face an issue on which we cannot compromise, it is entirely possible that in going down in defeat we make an impact.

In addition to working through the continuing political parties, we may exercise influence through special interest groups. People of different political parties may be united in a concern about local issues such as street construction or recreational facilities or the issues before the school board. They may be united in a concern about national questions such as the safety of nuclear energy or the pollution of the environment or the spread of AIDS. By identifying with some such groups and working through them we can help make progress toward goals which we consider desirable. We do need to be careful, however, not to spread ourselves too thin. Because we have limited resources of time, energy, and money we will do well to choose a limited number of concerns and concentrate on them.

How are we to make that choice? We need to begin with our own ideals, and to choose groups whose objectives are consistent with them. After that, other considerations are important. Are these objectives important enough to claim my limited time, energy, and money? What are the possibilities of achieving the objectives of the group? Does the group employ methods that are consistent with my ideals? Do I have confidence in the people who are in positions of leadership?

Effective work in the political arena calls for the best possible use of all available means of influencing thought. Jesus once cautioned his disciples to be "as wise as serpents and as harmless as doves" (Matthew 10:16). Packaging is as important in the selling of ideas as it is in the selling of products. Whether we are trying to convince the group within which we are working, or whether we are trying to help our group convince the public, we need to learn the techniques of presenting what we honestly believe in ways that will compel people to listen. Honesty and sincerity and integrity are basic to our efforts; we must begin with them and they must permeate all that we do. But if we are to have an impact, we must use those techniques of communication that are known to be effective.

All of this takes money. Most of us have limited resources and feel that we cannot invest a great deal in political campaigns of any sort. Jesus said, "where your treasure is, there will your heart be also" (Matthew 6:21). That applies to politics as well as to religion. Since the conducting of a political campaign of any sort requires money, we make an impact by what we invest in the campaign.

Most of what has been said refers to the conducting of campaigns. In the periods between political campaigns, however, it is important to remain alert to issues and to express one's views to elected representatives. There is a sense in which we elect persons to do jobs and should therefore leave them free to fulfill their responsibilities. Unfortunately, however, they often need to be reminded of our expectations of them. Furthermore, as specific issues come up they are in the process of making up their minds how to act. This is true of the local school board and the local city government, and it is true of the Congress of the United States and of the President of the nation. People in office want to know what their constituency is thinking and are influenced by what they learn.

How much impact does the average person have in the political arena? Not very much—acting alone. But acting in concert with other persons and through groups the average person compounds strength. Working through social, civic, and political organizations, and through special-interest groups in which they are allied with a wide variety of people, Christians find in politics an important way of responding to their commitment to Christ.

TWELVE
PUNISHMENT FOR CRIME

We have said that a basic function of the state is to maintain order. The state therefore makes laws to regularize social relationships and enforces those laws through a police force and a court system. In our pattern of government the words *just* and *legal* are virtually synonymous. Indeed, the word *justice* comes from the Latin *jus* which means *law*. We do acknowledge that there are certain moral standards by which even the law of the land is to be evaluated, so that at times in the name of justice certain laws or the application of those laws may be challenged. If we find a law to be unjust, then we attempt to revise it; and if we find the law to be unjustly applied, we attempt to correct the miscarriage of justice.

THE CONCEPT OF PUNISHMENT

Basic in our legal system are two principles. The first is equal treatment of persons. We believe that no person should be given preferential treatment because of such matters as status in the community or personal influence or personal wealth, and that no person should be treated harshly for reason of not having such strength. This principle, of course, is not absolute, for *some* differences of circumstances are appropriately considered in the determination of a case: motives, circumstances, mental competence, for example. To the question of whether an individual actually violated a law, in other words, certain external factors are considered relevant and certain others not. Relevant factors are taken into account, but irrelevant factors must not be allowed to influence legal action.

The second principle is that in the legal process people should be punished in proportion to the seriousness of their crime. That is to say, people should get what they deserve; punishment should be neither too light nor too severe. This principle recognizes that certain crimes are more serious than others, that some crimes inflict greater distress on people than others, and that some crimes damage more people than others do. The more serious the crime, the greater should be the penalty.

This idea of punishment is integral to our system of law enforcement. Punishment is defined as causing a person to experience pain or loss or suffering because of his or her wrongdoing. The purpose of punishment is to make the offender worse off than before. Although we may sometimes make mistakes in our judgment about a person's guilt or innocence, we do not punish anyone until that person has been convicted of criminal action. If a person has not been found guilty, then the inflicting of hurt upon that person is itself a crime. The administering of punishment is a function of the state alone. No one has the right to take the law into his or her own hands. No one has the right to usurp the role of either the police or the courts. Within our system there is no place for vigilante groups and no place for a "Lone Ranger." Only those people duly commissioned by governmental authority and functioning for that authority have the right to decide guilt or innocence and to punish the guilty.

These two principles lead us to consider the question of why society punishes people. What is the purpose of punishment? The oldest and most common answer is summed up in the word *retribution*. This concept means that because someone has done something bad, something equally bad should be done to that person. This reflects the idea that crime is an offense against the moral order, that it creates a moral imbalance, and that the imbalance must be corrected. The Old Testament law seems to support this view: "...then you shall give life for life, eye for eye, tooth for tooth, hand for hand, foot for foot, burn for burn, wound for wound, stripe for stripe" (Exodus 21:23–24). Our modern legal system, however, does not assume that things can be set right by doing to an offender exactly the same thing that the offender did to someone else. The balance cannot be evened, for example, by requiring an offender to return what has been stolen; something more than that has to be done to force the offender to suffer as the victim has suffered. Consequently, the criminal must be fined or sent to prison or made to pay some other penalty over and above any attempt at restitution. The offender deserves punishment. This approach concentrates on the criminal rather than the victim, and therefore involves no compensation for any damage done to the victim of the crime. It is deeply ingrained in our system of justice, however, and may be rooted in the desire for vengeance which seems to characterize all of us.

Another answer to the question of why we punish offenders has come to play a part in modern times. That is the *utilitarian* approach of considering the consequences of punishment. Its basic question is, What do we hope to achieve by taking action against the offender? This approach, of course, acknowledges the nature of punishment as the inflicting of pain upon a criminal. But it insists that such inflicting of pain should be justified by some anticipated good impact on the offender, on the victim, or on society as a whole. Will the punishment undo any damage done to the victim? Will it improve the character of the criminal? Will it deter the criminal from committing other crimes in the future? Will it deter other people from committing criminal acts? Will it protect society from further criminal actions by the offender or by people influenced by the offender? This approach assumes that punishment cannot be justified merely by the fact that it evens up some theoretical balance, but only in terms of whether the future will be better because of the action taken against the criminal. So far as the individual offender is concerned, this means reformation so that he or she can go back into society as a normal and well-adjusted individual. So far as society is concerned, it means protection against future crime.

Both answers have serious flaws. The idea of retribution assumes a kind of moral balance which we do not really understand. We do not know how much pain is required to even the score for any offense, and thus how large a fine or how long a prison sentence is called for. The utilitarian idea, on the other hand, assumes that we have found a system that will produce good results. Yet the threat of punishment is really not very effective. While we may refrain from speeding or from parking illegally because we are afraid that we might be caught and fined, psychiatric and sociological studies show that fear of punishment doesn't prevent such serious crimes as murder, rape, or trafficking in drugs. In addition, the inflicting of suffering on some people in order to teach a lesson to others presents serious moral problems. Neither does a period of imprisonment often reform a criminal. John Hospers states this point vividly:

> We put a man in prison for two years for a theft, five years for armed robbery, and twenty years to life (or the electric chair) for homicide, assuming smugly that these penalties will lessen his tendency to repeat his crime. We assume that being behind bars with nothing to do but build up resentments or go mad will make him emerge from prison a better man, renewed and chastened, and that when he does emerge from prison after the five years or the twenty, he will be able to resume his role in a society that refuses to employ him, spiritually prepared at last to conform to the moral ideals of middle age and the middle class. (*Human Conduct*, p. 390)

Hospers proposes a "compromise view" which actually combines the two approaches of retribution and reformation by saying that punishment should meet two conditions: it should be deserved, and it should do some good to someone—to the offender, to society, or to both. In order to meet the second condition, he suggests, the penal system should not focus on punishment but on treatment (p. 387). Although he does not use the word "Christian," his suggestion is in line with basic Christian concepts. Many years ago Emil Brunner discussed the theory of punishment in terms of the biblical concept of *expiation* (*The Divine Imperative*, pp. 474–478). The idea of a moral balance being achieved by the punishment of the criminal is similar, he said, to the Christian concept of satisfaction being made for our sin. In theological terms, Christ has "expiated" our sin and thus reconciled us to God. Applied to crime (as contrasted with sin), this concept suggests that something must be done to provide satisfaction for the offense. That something is not necessarily what we are now doing, for that, as we have seen, is flawed. But within human and social nature there is that which cries out for justice. We feel that the guilty must make expiation.

The concept of expiation for crime can be saved from the spirit of vindictiveness only by society's recognition that it shares the guilt for crime. Of course all persons are responsible for the decisions which they make. One's decisions, however, are influenced by the circumstances in which one lives and functions. Some options are simply not open to some people because of their heredity, their social environment, or their history. Some pressures are so powerful that an outside observer might even be able to predict what choices one will make. In that sense, therefore, society shares in the guilt of that person's crime. This does not mean that society should therefore ignore the criminal actions of one who is poor, who comes from a broken home, whose education is limited, whose aspirations are frustrated, or who has no good role models. Society must recognize its responsibility for allowing such conditions to exist, however. Just as an individual criminal pays the price at the hands of the penal system, so must society pay the price of correcting those dangerous and destructive situations.

In an important work, *Crime and Justice in America*, L. Harold DeWolf attempts to describe from a Christian perspective a consistent, defensible philosophy to undergird our criminal justice system. As the "ethical norms of criminal justice" by which our system should be evaluated he lists (pp. 154–156):

1. Consistency and coherence with realities.
2. Benevolent good will and respect toward all persons.
3. Equal rights for all persons.
4. Presumption of innocence.
5. Special care to protect the poor, weak, and unpopular from unfair treatment.
6. Restoration of community when disrupted.
7. Responsibility of all individuals for the community.

DeWolf calls his approach to criminal justice "a philosophy of social defense and restoration" (p. 173). Thinking of crime as alienation from other people, he sees no place for retribution in a valid philosophy of criminal justice. He recognizes the necessity of incarcerating some offenders to give temporary protection to society, and he acknowledges that punishment may have some value as a deterrent. He warns, however, that such measures, "when taken against people who already feel frustrated, deprived, and outside of any real participation in the good opportunities of society, are almost certain to aggravate the problem of crime in the community" (pp. 168–169). Cut off from all meaningful family relationships, prisoners reach the point where their most meaningful social relationships are those with other prisoners.

Society does need to protect itself against criminal activity, and as yet we have found no more effective way of dealing with criminals than imprisonment. But society also needs to find some way to transform a criminal into a responsible citizen. To operate a criminal justice system with this objective in mind we need to be realistic about the persistence of evil in all persons and the consequent difficulty of effecting a change in any person. We also need to take seriously the possibility of redemption and wholeness and restoration which is at the heart of the Christian Gospel.

CAPITAL PUNISHMENT?

On January 17, 1977, convicted murderer Gary Gilmore was executed by a Utah firing squad, the first person to be executed in the United States in ten years. Five years earlier, in *Furman* v. *Georgia,* the Supreme Court had declared unconstitutional any law which left the imposition of the death sentence to the discretion of the judge or the jury. The reasoning behind that ruling was the possibility of the unequal imposition of the sentence. The court, however, did not rule for the petitioners that the death sentence itself constituted "cruel and unusual punishment" and was therefore a violation of the Eighth and Fourteenth Amendments to the Constitution. As a consequence of that ruling, thirty-six states rewrote their laws so as to require, rather than permit, the imposition of the death sentence for persons convicted of certain crimes. Gilmore's execution, the first to take place under these new laws, sparked fresh debate on the question of capital punishment. The usual questions were raised. For what crimes should it be administered? How can we be sure that it is fairly imposed? By what means should people be executed? How public should the execution be? Underlying all of these questions, however, was a more basic one: Should the penalty ever be imposed? Or is it fundamentally immoral?

In our discussion let us focus on this basic question. While we may refer to statistics, to the differences among the states as to what crimes are capital ones, to the factors other than the crime itself which apparently influence court decisions, and so on, our concern is whether the state should ever resort to this form of punishment. We need first to consider the teaching of Scripture. Because the literature of the Old Testament reflects the changing circumstances and beliefs of the Hebrew people for a period of more than a thousand years, we should not be surprised to discover that its teachings on capital punishment are not entirely uniform and consistent. Basic to all such teachings, however, is the conviction that everyone is made in the image of God and that we must therefore treat all human life with respect. We have already discussed this concept (chapter five), and at this point need only to note its importance. This belief in the worth of human life is not unique to the Jewish and Christian faiths; other peoples of the ancient world expressed a similar high regard. But the idea that the transcendent worth of human life is not due to any individual talent, effort, achievement, or merit but to a unique relationship to the divine is distinctly biblical. For Christians, that fact is basic to all dealings with other people.

The sixth commandment, "You shall not kill" (Exodus 20:13), affirms this principle of respect for human life. It is in the form of *apodictic law*, stating the obligation without specifying any penalty for violation of the law and without any consideration of circumstances. It prohibits murder and has no direct reference to any other form of killing—not to accidental killing, not to killing in war, and not to capital punishment. Yet, as an affirmation of our responsibility to respect human life, it may properly be involved in a discussion of any of these matters.

Some passages are often cited to support the idea of exact retribution. Exodus 21:23–24, for example, says "life for life, eye for eye, tooth for tooth, hand for hand, foot for foot, burn for burn, wound for wound, stripe for stripe." The larger context in which such phrases are found, however, is usually *case law*. That is to say, distinctions are drawn on the basis of the extent of the damage, whether the offense was premeditated, the circumstances under which the offense took place, and other factors. Furthermore, as in Exodus 21, provisions are often made for substituting some form of payment (money or property) for the inflicting of physical damage on the offender.

In spite of the principle of respect for human life, the Old Testament law does prescribe death as the penalty for a variety of offenses. According to the Code of the Covenant, "Whoever strikes a man so that he dies shall be put to death" (Exodus 21:12). That code continues to specify the same penalty for striking one's father or mother, for kidnapping, for cursing one's father or mother (21:13–10). To this list the next chapter adds sorcery, bestiality, and idolatry (22:18–20). The Deuteronomic Law calls for execution as the penalty for a large number of offenses: the worship of other gods (Deuteronomy 17:2–5), the refusal to accept the judgment of the priests in a case appealed to them (17:8–13), premeditated murder

(19:11–13), adultery (22:22), rape (22:25–28), and kidnapping (24:7). It even commands the execution of a son for being "stubborn and rebellious" (21:18–21). So far as the Old Testament law is concerned, therefore, the question is not whether the death penalty should be used but what offenses call for it.

Although the Old Testament prescribes execution for what strikes us as a rather large number of offenses, its regulations actually represent a restriction on the spirit of vengeance which characterizes all people. By carefully specifying the crimes for which a person was to be executed, and by describing acceptable substitutes for execution in a number of cases, the law places a limit on the human tendency to go to extremes of cruelty in retaliation for personal offenses. That this tendency toward minimizing the application of the death penalty was in operation among the Jews is evidenced by the fact that by the time of Jesus most of those crimes had come to be dealt with by the imposition of fines.

There is only one New Testament passage which has direct reference to the matter of capital punishment. John 7:53–8:11 tells about a woman taken in the act of adultery, one of the offenses for which the law specified execution. While this passage was not a part of the Gospel of John as that Gospel was written originally, it is generally regarded as an authentic story which was preserved independently by the Christian community and at some point in time inserted at this place in John. According to this story, when Jesus was asked for his judgment as to what should be done to the woman, he indicated disapproval of the imposition of the penalty. His answer, "Let him who is without sin among you be the first to throw a stone at her," and his words to the woman, "Neither do I condemn you; go, and do not sin again," were completely harmonious with everything else that he taught about the worth of every individual in the sight of God, about forgiveness, and about the possibility of reformation of character and conduct.

In considering the morality of capital punishment as it is administered in America today we need to begin with the matter of the objective which we have in mind. What are we trying to achieve by the execution of a person? We have already noted that one reason for punishing a person for an offense is to provide justice, to ensure the balance which a concern for justice requires. With such a concern, the penalty must be designed to fit the crime, so that a person receives the punishment that he or she deserves. Clearly the state should not take the life of a person for any other than the most extreme of offenses. No one, therefore, would think today that disobedience to parents, idolatry, bestiality, or adultery should be punished by execution. But are there some crimes so heinous that justice requires that the offender die? Is capital punishment a just retribution for premeditated murder? For rape? For kidnapping? How is the balance evened by the death of the criminal?

Another way of stating the concern for justice is to think in terms of what the offender deserves. The idea is that each person would receive that which is his or her due, that a person be rewarded or punished in proportion to the good or evil done. The question, therefore, is, Do some people deserve to die? Is the death penalty the only one painful enough to equal the harm done by murder, rape, or kidnapping? In considering this matter, we need to think about the question of whether all offenders against all laws should always be given penalties that balance their offenses. We need to consider further whether a decision in a particular case should be made only on the basis of the facts of that crime, or whether consideration should be given other factors such as background, previous record, mental condition, and the impact on all other persons related to both victim and offender.

Another stated objective of punishment is to prevent a criminal from committing other offenses. For other forms of punishment the expectation is that the offender will suffer enough from fine or imprisonment to make that person decide that he or she will not run the risk of having other such experiences. We cannot be sure that it works this way, for obviously there can be no statistics on crimes not committed, but we know of no better way of dealing with crime. Now murderers and rapists are obviously wicked and dangerous persons, and it is clearly possible that one who has murdered or raped once might do it a second time. We have no way of knowing that they either would or would not repeat the crime, or that they are more likely to repeat their crime than someone else is to commit a crime for the first time. By this reasoning, the only way that we can be sure that offenders do not repeat their crimes is by executing them. Is it valid to execute people because of what they might do in the future?

The concept of deterrence is closely related to that of prevention. This idea assumes that the fear of punishment is an effective deterrent to crime. If persons who are tempted to commit crimes know that punishment will be certain and severe, it is argued, they may refrain from committing those crimes. Obviously, not everyone responds to the threat of punishment. Some people are mentally incapable of making judgment, and some people are self-destructive. Most people, however, have a strong will to live and are unwilling to run unnecessary risks of death. If execution is a real possibility for conviction of a crime, then potential criminals may refrain from committing those crimes. Of course, merely having the law on the books does not serve as a deterrent; only the actual execution of persons will do it. The death of one condemned individual, with its accompanying publicity, is a warning to all that the penalty is not an empty threat but a real possibility.

This line of reasoning in support of capital punishment is challenged by many people who marshal figures to demonstrate that there is no correlation between the crime rate and the possibility of capital punishment. They make much of the evidence that the incidence of murder in states which administer capital punishment is not necessarily lower than in the states which do not. They conclude that the fact of capital punishment does not in itself affect the rate of the crimes for which it is administered. We cannot be sure at present whether the threat of capital punishment does or does not deter further criminal action. From our point of view, however, there is a more important issue at stake: Is it proper to execute one human being in order to teach a lesson to other people? Is it just to make an example of one offender in the hope that other possible offenders will decide not to take the risk?

The issue of the right to life is a serious one in this discussion of capital punishment. We have discussed the biblical and Christian concept of the worth of the individual. That means that every person is to be respected and that the personal rights of every individual are to be guarded. The most basic of those rights is the right to life. The Declaration of Independence affirms that "life, liberty, and the pursuit of happiness" are unalienable rights. If we believe that some persons should be executed, then we have concluded either that some other consideration is even more important than is the right to life or that some persons forfeit that right by some actions of their own. If we have concluded the former, then we must decide what those considerations are. Is it property? Is it the body or life of another person? Is it the well-being of society as a whole? If we conclude the latter, then we must decide whether our rights are dependent upon our behavior. Does misbehavior, particularly misbehavior of a serious nature, vitiate those rights? If we conclude that someone ought to die, then we are forced to the conclusion that one's rights are not derived from one's nature but from one's conduct.

Considerations of prevention and deterrence have a bearing not merely upon individual criminals and individual victims, but upon society at large. All crime is in a sense an attack upon the social order. Most persons assume that individuals have the right of self-defense, that when attacked they have the right to use whatever means are necessary to protect themselves. While they do not have the right to use excessive force, they do have the right to effective resistance. By the same logic, concern for justice and for the well-being of other people justifies the use of necessary force. Does that same right extend to the state? It is sometimes said that capital punishment is for the state what self-defense is for the individual. By this logic it is assumed that the state has the right to do what is necessary to protect itself (that is, not only its existence but also its proper functioning). Certain laws, such as those protecting life and property, are necessary for persons to live and work together. To violate those laws is to threaten the very existence of society, and society therefore has both the right and the responsibility to do what is necessary to protect itself. As it is true for the individual, so is it true for society, that excessive force should not be used. The question as regards capital punishment, therefore, is whether it is necessary or whether there are alternative methods for dealing with the threat to the existence of the state.

The question with which we are struggling is whether capital punishment is *ever* right. If we conclude that it is sometimes the right action, then we have certain other important issues to decide. For what crimes is it right? To what extent should the circumstances of the crime be taken into consideration? In what manner should persons be executed—that is, should the execution be as humane as possible or should the criminal be made to suffer? What steps can we take to be sure that the process of conviction on capital crimes functions fairly, without regard to race or sex or financial resources? If we conclude that it is never right, then we must find an appropriate alternative to dealing with heinous crimes. What does justice require? Is long-term, or even life imprisonment, a greater or lesser punishment than execution?

In this discussion nothing has been said about the victims of the crimes because no effective restitution can be made to a victim. In case of murder, nothing can bring the victim back to life, and nothing can ease the pain of the survivors. In case of violence to a person, nothing can undo that violence. We do need to find ways of helping victims cope with what has been done, of doing for them what no punishment of the criminal will do. That problem, however, is a different one from that of dealing with the criminal.

My own conclusion to the discussion is that capital punishment is wrong. That conclusion is influenced by the demonstrable fact that our best efforts to be impartial in the administration of the system have failed and almost certainly can never succeed. The chances of execution after conviction for a capital offense are far greater for men than for women, for blacks than for whites, for the poor than for the affluent. The conclusion is influenced by the lack of conclusive evidence that the threat of execution has any bearing upon the rate of capital crimes, and therefore that it is an effective preventive measure. It is influenced by my disposition to look to the future rather than to the past, and therefore to be more concerned with reformation and restoration than with balancing the scales of justice. But that conclusion is based primarily on my understanding of the Christian doctrine that every human being is of infinite worth in the eyes of God, and that my responsibility as a disciple of Christ is to deal with every person, no matter how unworthy, on that basis. I do not believe that any person ever ceases to be a child of God, no matter what crimes that person may commit. Although crime must be dealt with if the social order is to survive, as I believe it must, we must not deal with crime in any way that violates the fundamental element in that social order—the nature of the people who constitute it.

THIRTEEN

WAR AND THE QUEST FOR PEACE

The possibility of nuclear warfare is a continuing threat to the survival of humankind. All over the world people live with the constant fear that someone might push the button that will set off the final holocaust. All over the world people wait anxiously as their leaders negotiate for peace and arm for war. International relations are always in flux and scientific and technical developments are constantly bringing new pressures to bear on those relationships. We seem unable to find a balance in which the peoples of the world can hope to live in peace. How are Christians, motivated by love and concerned for justice, to function in a world always on the brink of war?

THE BIBLE AND WAR

Long before the advent of nuclear weaponry Christians struggled with the question of the morality of warfare. As might be expected, they have looked to the Scripture for guidance. In the Old Testament historical material, however, they have found little evidence of any moral problem with warfare. The Hebrews regarded themselves as God's chosen people, as a nation for whom God had a special purpose. The working out of that purpose involved the conquest of a land already occupied by other people, the establishment of a kingdom in that land, and the blessing or punishing of the nation on the basis of their loyalty to God. When the people were faithful, God gave them victory over their enemies. When they were not faithful, God used enemy nations to punish them. Their methods of warfare were no different from those of other people and their treatment of their enemy no more humane. We are not surprised, therefore, to find in many of their hymns (psalms) angry imprecations against their enemies.

Many of the Hebrew Prophets saw warfare as a tool of God in the historical process. Amos, Isaiah, Jeremiah and others spoke of oppression by foreign powers as God's punishment on the Hebrews for their unfaithfulness. Obadiah, on the other hand, gloated over the destruction that had come upon Edom, calling it God's vengeance on a nation whose crime was war against God's people. In the same vein, Nahum rejoiced at the anticipated destruction of Nineveh, the capital city of the Assyrian Empire that had long oppressed Judah. Yet in the Prophets there are passages in which the note of God's love for all people is sounded and the expectation of universal peace is proclaimed. Both Isaiah (2:4) and Micah (4:3) anticipated the time when all the nations "shall beat their swords into plowshares, and their spears into pruning hooks; nation shall not lift up sword against nation, neither shall they learn war anymore." And it was Isaiah who described what has been called "the peaceable kingdom":

> The wolf shall dwell with the lamb, and the leopard shall lie down with the kid, and the calf and the lion and the fatling together, and a little child shall lead them. The cow and the bear shall feed; their young shall lie down together; and the lion shall eat straw like the ox. The sucking child shall play over the hole of the asp, and the weaned child shall put his hand on the adder's den. They shall not hurt nor destroy in all my holy mountain; for the earth shall be full of the knowledge of the Lord as the waters cover the sea. (Isaiah 11:6–9)

Even in a nation which had no moral problem about war, whose God indeed was "mighty in battle," the dream of peace never died.

While the New Testament says little about war, people who oppose participation in any war find strong support in Jesus' teachings on love. They cite particularly his summary of the moral law in the words, "You shall love your neighbor as yourself" (Mark 12:31), and his exhortation to "love your enemies" (Matthew 5:43–48). They quote the Beatitude, "Blessed are the peacemakers, for they shall be called sons of God" (Matthew 5:9). They pay special attention to Jesus' teachings about nonretaliation:

> You have heard that it was said, "An eye for an eye and a tooth for a tooth." But I say to you, Do not resist one who is evil. But if any one strikes you on the right cheek, turn to him the other also; and if any one would sue you and take your coat, let him have your cloak as well; and if any one forces you to go one mile, go with him two miles. Give to him who begs from you, and do not refuse him who would borrow from you. (Matthew 5:38–42)

They find the essence of Jesus' teaching in the Golden Rule: "So whatsoever you wish that men would do to you, do so to them" (Matthew 7:12).

Acknowledging that those teachings were intended for personal relationships, they argue that the concepts are equally valid for social relationships as well. They do not build their case simply by citing specific passages, however. Rather they focus on Jesus' teachings on love and the way of the cross, on his general spirit and disposition toward other people. In that way they find him to be utterly opposed to any possibility of participation in armed conflict.

Other people find in the Gospels evidence that Jesus was not in fact a completely nonviolent person. They cite his apparent use of some force in the cleansing of the temple (Matthew 21:12–13, John 2:13–16), in his statement "Do not think that I have come to bring peace on earth; I have not come to bring peace, but a sword" (Matthew 10:34), and in his words to the disciples on the eve of his arrest, "Let him who has no sword sell his mantle and buy one" (Luke 22:36). It must be admitted that in neither of these instances, as in none of the instances cited by pacifists, was Jesus talking about war. To apply them to the question of war, therefore, is to extend them beyond Jesus' obvious intent.

Perhaps more to the point is Jesus' apparent nonjudgmental acceptance of the fact of war. He praised the faith of a Roman centurion without saying anything about the man's profession (Matthew 8:5–10). He warned his disciples not to think of "wars and rumors of war" as signs of the end of the age because those conditions persist in this present age (Mark 13). He made frequent use of military figures of speech as if the military were a normal part of life. That is not to suggest that he approved of war, but that he accepted it as inevitable.

As we have seen, Paul was a disciple and an interpreter of Jesus. His recommendations for dealing with other people sound very much like the things that Jesus said:

> Bless those who persecute you, bless and do not curse them. Rejoice with those who rejoice, weep with those who weep. Live in harmony with one another; do not be haughty, but associate with the lowly; never be conceited. Repay no one evil for evil, but take thought for what is noble in the sight of all. If possible, so far as it depends upon you, live peaceably with all. Beloved, never avenge yourselves, but leave it to the wrath of God; for it is written, "Vengeance is mine, I will repay, says the Lord." No, "if your enemy is hungry, feed him; if he is thirsty, give him drink; for by so doing you will heap burning coals upon his head." Do not be overcome by evil, but overcome evil with good. (Romans 12:14–21)

Elsewhere in the New Testament even less is said that can be interpreted as having a bearing on the problem of war. As we have seen, much of the New Testament was written at a time when Christians were being persecuted. Most of the New Testament documents anticipate the time when the end of the age will come with a great upheaval, perhaps some final conflict between the nations. Yet the New Testament simply does not deal directly with the issue of war. The overall emphasis of Scripture, however, clearly fosters the ideal of peace.

CHRISTIANITY AND TRADITIONAL WARFARE

Can we translate the biblical dream of peace into the realities of modern political relationships? Since the New Testament period the Christian church has constantly struggled with that question. For some three hundred years after the time of Christ there was a strong pacifist leaning in the church. Many early Christians took the teachings of Jesus as totally prohibiting the use of the sword and refused to serve in the Roman army. After Constantine made Christianity the state religion of the Empire in the early fourth century, and after the stability of the Roman Empire was threatened by the invasion of barbarians from the north, theologians debated for centuries the question of whether Christians should sometimes wage war. Out of that debate emerged the theory of a *just war*, developed by Augustine (354–430) and refined by Thomas Aquinas (1224–1274). According to that theory, to be just, a war must meet six conditions: (1) It must be conducted by a legitimate authority which explicitly serves notice that it intends to use military power to attain its objectives. (2) It must be intended for the advancement of good or for the avoidance of evil. (3) It must be undertaken only as a last resort. (4) The good anticipated from the war must outweigh the evil done in pursuit of the war. (5) There must be a reasonable expectation of success in the effort. (6) It must be conducted according to the internationally accepted rules of warfare, never going beyond certain agreed-upon moral constraints. By this last requirement such things as attacks on nonmilitary targets, unnecessary destruction, looting, and massacres are prohibited.

Today we can delineate three distinct positions with regard to the participation of Christians in war. First, many people see participation as a responsibility of Christian citizenship. This position draws support from Paul's exhortation, "Let every person be subject to the governing authorities" (Romans 13:1). Resistance to the state would be justified only if the state were to try to claim ultimate authority, and thus to assume the place of God. Otherwise our Christian duty is to support the state. When our nation is involved in war it is acting to protect itself against foreign power and to safeguard the well-being of all its citizens. All citizens, of course, retain the right of conscientious criticism of specific policies and actions, and even the right of refusal to participate in military service. In the last resort, however, we know that the use of force in world affairs is necessary because oppressive and tyrannical powers are at work in many places. If we do not prevent them from doing so, those powers will extend their control until they dominate the rest of the world. Decisions about the time when the exercise of that force is necessary are not individual decisions; they can be made only by the leadership of the nation.

Second, some Christians believe that their commitment to Christ and his way prohibits any involvement in armed conflict. In the 1930s some Christians in this country and in Europe adopted pacifism as a strategy; they believed that it was the way to achieve a warless world. Most contemporary pacifists, however, do not see refusal to participate as a strategy but as the way God intends people to live. They are pacifist not in order to achieve peace but in grateful obedience to the God of love. They are aware of persistent evil in the world and they work to overcome it. They are realistic about oppression and aggression and the danger that in any situation nations may resort to force to achieve their purposes, good or bad. In the face of all that, however, they believe that discipleship to Christ requires them to love rather than to hate, and that war can never be an expression of love.

Third, some Christians believe that war is sometimes the lesser of two evils. Recognizing the horrors of war, they believe that worse things may result from a failure to resist the activities of an evil government. The term currently employed to identify this view is *agonized participation*. People who take this approach believe that it is their responsibility, not to give unconditional support to the government, but to evaluate the situation for themselves and to support the government in those wars which they believe to be necessary. This, of course, is very close to the *just war* position. Writing during the Vietnam war, when our nation was divided on the rightness of our involvement, Edward LeRoy Long characterized this view in the following way:

1. "This position believes that while war can never be an act of justice it may sometimes be necessary for the prevention of a greater evil that would result from permitting morally perverse power to gain political dominance."
2. "The agonized participant insists that war must be conducted with contrition and kept free of vindictive hatred for the enemy."
3. "Military victory, while necessary, is but a negative attainment that clears the way for subsequent political and social programs designed to reestablish reasonable justice and order."
4. "Lastly, the agonized participant acknowledges the right and privilege of conscientious objection to war even though he disagrees with those Christians who consider themselves called to this witness." (*War and Conscience in America*, pp. 41–47)

CHRISTIANITY AND MODERN WARFARE

The development of nuclear weapons has introduced a new factor into the consideration of warfare. Now we have to reckon with the possibility of total destruction. In the foreword to a work by Paul Ramsey, John

Hallowell said in 1961, "Not only must we come to terms with the fact that all civilized life upon this planet may come to an end but that this is possible through human decision and action" (Paul Ramsey, *War and the Christian Conscience*, p. vii). The opening words of a book written by Joseph Nye in 1986, some twenty-five years later, were:

> The prospect of a nuclear war is horrifying. It brings us face to face not only with death, but with destruction of the civilization that makes our life meaningful. It might even destroy our species. There is no precedent for the challenge that nuclear weapons present to our physical and moral lives. (*Nuclear Ethics*, p. ix)

Traditional Christian eschatology, as Gordon Kaufman says, has thought of the consummation of history as God's climactic act which we could anticipate with hope. But now it appears that the end may be our own doing, not God's, and that it will not mean the salvation of the world but the extermination of life on earth (*Theology for a Nuclear Age*, pp. 3–4).

While our concern here is not the scientific and technological aspects of the development of nuclear weaponry, we do need to be aware of the potential. In a much discussed book, *The Fate of the Earth*, published in 1982, Jonathan Schell vividly described the effects that would result from an in-air explosion of a single bomb of the sort that is now considered "medium sized" (one megaton). He says that the initial radiation would kill immediately every unprotected human being within an area of six square miles, and in the next ten seconds the heat would cause second-degree burns in exposed persons within a radius of nine and one-half miles. The blast would flatten all buildings within a radius of four and one-half miles. A large portion of the radioactive dust created by the explosion would fall back to the earth within a day, but a large portion of the remainder would be pushed by the winds and would fall in lethal quantities over an area of a thousand square miles.

The presence of nuclear weapons in the arsenal of any nation presumes the possibility that under some circumstances that nation might use those weapons. In our country there are two main lines of thought regarding their use. The first is a concept of *Mutual Assured Destruction* (MAD) that goes back as far as the Eisenhower administration (1953–1960). This way of thinking assumes that the United States and the Soviet Union have the capability of launching massive attacks against each other. If either nation were to attack first, the other would launch a massive retaliatory strike. In such an exchange thousands of nuclear warheads would be employed and the losses on both sides would be incalculable. Because neither side could "win" such a war, no rational leader or group of people would intentionally start it. By this line of reasoning, therefore, we must keep our nuclear defenses equal to those of the Soviet Union so as to be sure that neither they nor we will resort to their use.

The second line of thought entertains the possibility of the limited use of nuclear weapons. Both the United States and the nations of Western Europe fear that the Soviet Union might invade West Germany. The Soviet Union has a large military force within quick striking distance of the West German border and could launch a sneak attack which would overrun the conventional defense of that nation. The only option open to West Germany and its allies, other than surrender, would be the use of the intermediate range nuclear weapons which are maintained throughout Europe. While the members of the North Atlantic Treaty Organization (NATO) have been committed to this policy, its weakness is that such action on the part of NATO would surely be met with retaliatory action by the Soviet Union and a full scale nuclear war would be launched. The treaty signed in 1987 by the United States and the Soviet Union represented a movement away from this line of reasoning.

The creation of nuclear weapons has been accompanied by a raft of other scientific and technological developments that make modern warfare qualitatively different from anything in the past. The most significant of those developments are in the area of chemical and biological warfare. As in the case of nuclear weaponry, the impact of such weapons cannot be limited to military targets but inevitably inflicts unnecessary suffering upon civilian personnel and irreversible damage to the ecological balance. The possibility of manufacturing and using these new weapons has altered the political decision-making process in our government, leaving to experts the determination of what and how much is needed, and the decision as to when and where to use the weapons. The result of such developments has not been a greater sense of security but a greater fear.

THE QUEST FOR PEACE

Whenever our nation has been involved in a declared war our people have been compelled to make individual decisions, and Christian convictions have led individuals to respond in different ways. Most have responded with "agonized participation" to the call of the nation into military service. Some, after great personal struggle, have chosen to follow procedures established by the government allowing them to register as Conscientious Objectors. Others, believing that their witness for peace would not be heard if they followed the established procedure, have refused even to register. Still others have taken direct and dramatic action to protest the presence of the military system. While each person must respect the decisions of the other, each must also face the issue and make individual decisions in response to the leading of the Spirit of God.

When our nation is not involved in a declared war (even though from time to time there are explosive incidents and skirmishes), all of us think about national policy and ultimately all of us can be involved in a small way at least in its formulation. This fact is particularly relevant to the question of the maintenance of nuclear weaponry. Most of our thinking is shaped by the fear of what the Soviet Union might do and by the simple conviction that we must keep ourselves stronger than they. We are conditioned to think that their objective is world domination, that they will use any means to attain their objective, and that we cannot trust them to keep their promises. By the same token we are conditioned to think of ourselves as committed to peace, that we have no objectives for interference in the affairs of other nations, and that we would never take aggressive action against another nation. All of these assumptions need examination in light of history and in light of a Christian understanding of human nature.

In our examination of any situation we must be realistic about the human condition. Specifically this means that we must acknowledge the persistence of evil in the life of the world. In our earlier discussion of human nature (chapter four) we affirmed the conviction that although humankind was created in the image of God, that image is flawed by humankind's sinful choices. If that be true, then we will always be plagued by the consequences of such choices. The problem is compounded when the choices are not those of individuals but of corporate entities such as the nations of the world. In the book of Genesis (4:17–24), the juxtaposition of a statement about the great steps forward in civilization with the bloodthirsty Song of Lamech suggests that progress in technology is not accompanied by a change in human nature. The development of more effective weapons does nothing but make us more effective in the slaughtering of people. Jesus' parable of the tares makes the same point of the persistence of evil in the world along with good (Matthew 13:24–30). As applied to the problem of war, this means that so long as history lasts war will always be a possibility. We shall not be able to create a world situation in which the outbreak of war is impossible. We can certainly hope to improve international relations. And we can certainly hope to resolve specific issues as they arise. In no crisis is war inevitable; in every crisis conflict may be averted. But the resolution of one crisis does not prevent another from arising. We shall move from problem to problem.

Having acknowledged the persistence of evil, and understanding that war therefore is always a possibility, we do have to come to grips with the fact that the creation of nuclear weapons has made a qualitative difference in war. In the past, new weapons have simply been more efficient ways of killing people, but it remained possible to control them at least to an extent. Even bombs dropped from airplanes on specific targets destroyed lives and property only in the immediate area hit by the bombs. When the bombing was over the damage had been done. It was possible to destroy one area (and one people) without damage to other areas and other peoples. The destruction wrought by nuclear weapons, however, is not completed with the initial blast. Its effect is spread by the wind to distant places and by the genes to future generations.

Our quest for peace is complicated by the fact that the difference between war and peace is not a clear-cut one. Are we at peace when our country maintains military bases in friendly nations all over the world? Are we at peace when our naval vessels sail in waters which we consider international but which other nations claim as their own? Are we at peace when our ships and planes in international airspace and waters defend themselves from attack by ships and planes of other nations? Are we at peace when we supply equipment and personnel to a nation defending itself against insurgents? When we supply equipment and personnel to insurgents in a nation which we consider unfriendly? Are we at peace when we impose an economic boycott upon a nation? This is not to suggest that in any of these situations we are right or we are wrong. It is only to point out that the distinction between war and peace is not always clear.

The world situation clearly calls for a reexamination of our assumption that greater military strength is the key to peace. Commenting on the insanity of this assumption, Robert McAfee Brown said in 1981:

> In the name of trying to be "realistic," we have lost touch with reality. We have the military capability to kill everybody in the world twelve times, so we want to increase that killing capacity to fifteen or sixteen times. We have 30,000 nuclear weapons in our stockpile, and Russia has at least half that many, and yet we accede without quibbling when military men, whose way of life depends on it, tell us that we need still more nuclear weapons. We are told that building more weapons will make our situation safer, when each weapon we build actually makes it more precarious. (*Making Peace in the Global Village*, p. 62)

Brown concludes that we operate on the basis of a logical madness which says, "the more weapons we build, the less secure we are; therefore we will build more weapons." We must respond to this madness, he says, by refusing to conform to this "recipe for disaster....We need the brashness to affirm that whatever we know, or do not know, about God's will, we know at least that it is not God's will that, having created this earth, God is now urging earth's children to destroy it and one another" (p. 64).

The greatest potential for war may not be a direct confrontation between the Soviet Union and the United States, but the desperate struggle for power on the part of the peoples of the Third World. To be sure, both the Soviet Union and the United States are involved in those areas of the world. Apparently neither they nor we have grasped the explosiveness of the situation, however. In recent years peoples who have long been colonized by the West have won their independence and established national sovereignty. Most of those nations are now torn by internal violence. Much of Asia, Africa, and Latin America is in a state of revolution. At issue in this world revolution are some beliefs which we take for granted: the belief that in free elections the majority can and will express their will, that elected officials will act in the best interest of their constituents, and that the power of the police force is on the side of justice. In some places the racial factor complicates the problems because a white minority controls most of the material goods and power and a dark-skinned minority live in poverty. In light of our own history, and in light of the present situation in the United States, we should not be surprised that most of the peoples of the Third World do not automatically regard us as friendly and benevolent.

The problem of poverty plagues many if not most of the nations of the Third World. Many have few natural resources and many lack the technology and the financial resources to develop what they have. Consequently, two-thirds of the people of the world never have enough food to satisfy their basic needs. One-fifth of the world's population controls four-fifths of the world's resources, and that one-fifth is white. So long as this radical discrepancy between the haves and the have-nots of the world continues, so long will the possibility of a violent explosion exist. It is difficult to convince deprived peoples that they must not resort to violence to correct this imbalance. That being the case, would not money spent on the effort to resolve this problem of the distribution of resources be more moral and make a greater contribution to world peace than money spent on arms?

Continued physical violence appears inevitable unless other and better means are found for dealing with the desperate needs of the Third World. The wealthy one-fifth of the world's population must move rapidly to find those other and better means. Those means will necessarily include in some way sharing our wealth with the rest of the world. That sharing may take the form of direct relief in emergencies. It may take the form of technological assistance in the development of resources. In the long run it may mean a less comfortable lifestyle for us. It will involve the surrender of power. It will involve the risk that people will not do what we wish or what we think is wise. It will mean that we do not ask other peoples to surrender the right of self-determination as the price of receiving our help.

Can we as a nation move in this direction? The democratic process to which we are committed assumes the possibility of changes in policies and procedures in response to the expressed will of the people. Our elected officials do remain sensitive to our expressions of our beliefs and wishes, and their actions in office can be influenced by the concerted effort of concerned members of their constituencies. We will not be able to achieve all that we wish in terms of a changed national emphasis, but we will be able to achieve something.

Another aspect of making peace is the cultivation of a sense of world community. A community is a group of people who live so near each other that they know each other well, who live so intimately that they feel for each other, and who are so involved with each other that what each person does affects the life of everyone else. If the world is not by this description a community it is rapidly becoming one. This identity is being forced upon us both by the fear of the consequences of a war in which the nations utilize their terrifying new weapons and by the fear of violent revolution in Third World nations. We are being made aware of this sense of world community by the news media, which make us see the hunger, anger, fear, and greed all over the world. It is being facilitated by the sharing of scientific and technological knowledge. It is being expressed by the contact of persons who travel for business or pleasure and who learn to appreciate the cultures of other people. More important than all of these things, however, for Christians at least, this sense of world community is the consequence of a commitment to God's purposes for humankind.

The cultivation of a sense of community involves practical, even materialistic concerns. It requires concentrated efforts to help the peoples of the world achieve their goals of nationhood and self-determination. It requires assistance to those peoples in coping with their problems of poverty. It requires the structuring of relationships between nations so that differences can be resolved in an orderly fashion. It requires reversing the arms race. It requires attention to basic human rights all over the world. As Brown says, peacemaking does not merely involve keeping us out of war:

> ...it also involves seeing to it that people have enough to eat; that they are not undernourished or mal-nourished; that they can go to bed at night without fear that someone will spirit them off to prison; that the society will be so planned that there is food enough to go around; that the politics of the country (and of the world) are so arranged that everybody's basic needs are met. (*Making Peace in the Global Village*, p. 14)

For the building of the concept of world community, Christians have a model in the church. In ideal terms the church is a world community, transcending nation, race, and class. To a limited extent it is that in fact as well. Not only do we proclaim a universal Gospel, but also we have a sense of unity with Christians everywhere. We regret the actual divisions which we see in the church along the lines of race and class and nation, and we are troubled that we allow differences of doctrine to separate us. But the fact that we are pained by the division testifies to our understanding that we really belong together. And in our faith we do have a common bond. A starting point for us in working to establish world peace, therefore, is to make the church conform more fully to its ideal. That is the starting point, however, not the ultimate objective. From that point we can challenge the divisiveness of the world and work for a world community that does not ignore or exclude any of its members.

Concerned to demonstrate the validity of the teachings of Christ for the kind of world in which we live, Reinhold Niebuhr used to talk of "the relevance of an impossible ideal." Perhaps the dream of a world community is unrealistic. Moved by that dream, however, there are many practical steps we can take. We can, for example:

1. Begin to think of ourselves not in terms of nationality or race or socioeconomic level but as members of the world community.
2. Work for an end to the arms race.
3. Work for the relief of disaster-stricken areas of the world.
4. Cooperate in the sharing of resources and technology for the long-term improvement of the economy of the nations of the Third World.
5. Encourage our government to establish its military posture on the basis of our domestic and foreign policies rather than allowing our military posture to dictate our domestic and foreign policies.
6. Deal with the reality of sin as a part of the social structure and not merely as an individual matter.
7. Work for changes in those structures of society which perpetuate our human problems.

These steps do not constitute a strategy for establishing a permanent peace in the world. Rather they are ways in which Christians can deal with present problems with the hope of making the future better. They are ways in which we can respond to our calling to be disciples of Christ in a world driven by a lust for power and torn by greed, injustice, inequality, and fear. And they are based on the belief that rather than leaving us alone, God works through us to accomplish justice and peace in the world.

FOURTEEN
WORK, PROPERTY, AND COMMUNITY

A person being interviewed for employment will be asked a number of questions: What are your qualifications? What experience have you had? Why did you leave your last position? What references can you give? The applicant, in turn, will ask: What will be expected of me? What salary is offered? What fringe benefits? What are the conditions under which I will have to work? What security will I have on the job? What are the opportunities for advancement? All of these questions are important, but do they have anything to do with morality?

All of us are profoundly affected by economic forces totally beyond our control. The interest rate on home mortgages fluctuates for reasons that none of us seems to understand. The price of gasoline is five cents a gallon higher in our town than in the town twenty miles away. A manufacturing plant closes in one city, and people lose their jobs for reasons totally beyond their control. A new industry opens up in another city, and new jobs are created, again without any special merit on the part of the new employees. The stock market plunges, and even people who own no stock are somehow affected. All of these developments are matters of very great concern, but are they moral issues?

What should determine the price which a customer pays for a product? Should a business or industry be concerned about anything other than making a profit for its owners or investors? On what basis should an industry make a decision about waste disposal? About the release of pollutants into the atmosphere or into the soil or into the water? What are the moral responsibilities of a corporation manufacturing and distributing products that are known to be dangerous to the health of individuals? What are the responsibilities of a person who works for such a corporation? What are the obligations of manufacturers to provide a safe and healthful work environment for employees? What recourse do endangered workers have?

In the relatively simple economy of early America the moral factor was not nearly so complicated. Most people were self-sufficient farmers and artisans whose moral responsibility was essentially that of honest labor and helping one another in times of crisis. In 1776 no one took exception to Adam Smith's *invisible hand* theory which said that if everyone worked diligently for his or her own good the result would be as if some invisible hand were working for the good of society as a whole (*An Inquiry into the Nature and Causes of the Wealth of Nations*, Book V, Chapter II). Today, however, one's employment is affected by fluctuations on the stock market, by war in the Near East, by the government of South Africa, and by Japanese investments in this country. One's security is tied in with the unemployment rate, with problems between labor and management, with industrial development, and with international politics. In these circumstances, how can we talk about moral responsibility? How can we function as responsible Christians in an essentially impersonal system?

THE CONTEXT: CAPITALISM

While the shape of our economic system is constantly changing, and while it is therefore not the same as that of eighteenth-century America, nor even of early twentieth-century America, our system is properly called *capitalism*. Capitalism may be defined as the system of private ownership of the instruments of production, distribution, and exchange, and the use of those instruments under a plan of individual initiative and open competition to earn private profit. The system rests upon four main concepts. The first is the right of the ownership of private property. *Property* includes not only material goods, such as land, tools, dwelling, and the like, but also the instruments of production and distribution. Ownership entails the right to determine what use shall be made of property, subject only to the restriction that the use must not interfere with the rights of other people. Some moral problems associated with ownership focus on the question of whether there are restrictions other than the legal ones on the acquisition and the use of property. They become more complicated when, as is often the case, great wealth, and therefore great power, is concentrated in the hands of a few individuals. They become even more complicated when ownership is not in the hands of individuals but rather is in the hands of corporations. These complications, however, do not invalidate the assumption that individuals have the right to own property; they only make the solution of the problems more difficult.

The second basic concept in capitalism is that of *free enterprise*. This is the idea that one is free to pursue one's own interests without interference by the government except where such interference is necessary to protect the rights of other people. It assumes that all persons naturally pursue their own self-interest, and that such pursuit is entirely legitimate. One should be free to make as much money as possible and to spend that money however one chooses. In its most extreme form this view holds that governmental restrictions should be kept to an absolute minimum. Few people today would agree with the dictum that "that government is best which governs least" because we want protection from crime, we want defense against foreign enemies, we believe in compulsory education, we depend upon government regulation to guarantee minimum quality in goods, and so on. Yet we assume that within the limits of social responsibility, free enterprise is foundational to our economic system.

The third fundamental idea of capitalism is that *competition is the life of trade.* Capitalism assumes that in the long run the best results for all persons involved depend upon free competition. Competition among buyers and sellers will regulate quality, set prices, establish wages, and determine what goods will be produced. In this connection it should be noted that the chief threat to competition today is not from the government but from large corporations absorbing smaller ones or forcing them out of business and thus gaining a virtual monopoly.

The fourth capitalistic principle is that the *profit motive* is the most effective incentive in the economic system. The same hope of personal gain that drives an individual to do good work impels a giant corporation to produce quality goods or services. People work hard when it is to their advantage to do so. The success of an individual or of a corporation, therefore, is to be gauged in terms of the profit earned. The commonly used phrase, *the bottom line,* suggests that while other matters may be important, the deciding factor in all economic activity is the size of the profit.

The system under which we operate in the United States, of course, is not pure capitalism. The government necessarily does certain things that are essential to our well-being: it is responsible for national defense, law enforcement, and the provision of equal educational opportunity for all people. In addition, we believe that we are better served by having the state do some things which could be done by private enterprise: building and maintaining roads, delivering the mail, and providing financial help for people who are unable to meet their own needs. We need governmental regulation of industries which are by nature monopolies, governmental enforcement of minimum standards in businesses and professions, and governmental assistance to individuals and businesses in times of crisis or disaster. We find it unwise, in other words, to leave the economic function entirely in private hands. Yet we are wary of too great a concentration of function and power in the hands of the government. We have therefore a mixed system in which on the one hand we cling to the principle of private enterprise, and on the other hand we affirm the principle of public control of functions that are genuinely public in scope. In between those two distinct areas there are many functions that are semiprivate and semipublic, some of which are performed by the government, some by private enterprise, and some by voluntary group activity.

A CHRISTIAN PERSPECTIVE ON PROPERTY

While the Bible teaches no theory of economics, it reflects a view of property which we can employ in our evaluation of our responsibilities within our contemporary economic system. At the heart of the biblical understanding of property is the recognition that ultimately all things belong to God. "The earth is the Lord's and the fulness thereof, the world and those who dwell therein," said the psalmist (24:1), voicing the conviction that underlies all statements about ownership. The appropriate conclusion about human ownership, therefore, is that property is always held in trust and that people are responsible to God for the use they make of property.

Within that perspective, the Old Testament supports the idea of the private ownership of property. The commandment, "You shall not steal" (Exodus 20:15), is the basic protection of the right to own property. The wide variety of laws providing for restitution for damage done to the property of another person, even accidental damage, supports that right. The laws of inheritance assume it. The Prophets denounced persons of wealth and even persons of the nobility, not for ownership, but for their violation of the property rights of others and their ignoring the needs of others.

Jesus forbade theft and fraud, he denounced people who practiced extortion, he condemned wealth gained by improper means, and he praised restitution of ill-gotten gain as evidence of repentance. Rather than stressing ownership, however, he talked a great deal about the responsible use of wealth. He spoke of people as "stewards" of their possessions, responsible to God for the manner in which they use them (Matthew 20:1–16, Luke 19:11–27). While he seems to have assumed that it is appropriate for us to use wealth to meet our own needs, he taught directly that we should share our possessions with the poor and the helpless (Matthew 6:3, Luke 18:22). Indeed, although the words which he quoted from Isaiah do not speak directly of wealth, they show that his sense of mission focuses on meeting the needs of other people:

> The Spirit of the Lord is upon me
>   because he has anointed me to preach good news to the poor.
> He has sent me to proclaim release to the captives
>   and recovering of sight to the blind,
> To set at liberty those who are oppressed,
>   to proclaim the acceptable year of the Lord. (Luke 4:18)

In addition, Jesus acknowledged the responsibility of supporting the government (Matthew 22:17, Mark 12:42, Luke 20:22) and the institutions of religion (Matthew 17:24, Mark 12:42, Luke 21:1–4), and the legitimacy of spending money to express one's affection (Mark 14:3–9, John 12:2–8). He recognized, in other words, that wealth is a necessary tool by which people live and work in the world, and he talked about people doing all of those things as children of God.

At the same time, Jesus warned against the dangers of wealth. He spoke of the false sense of security which wealth brings (Luke 12:19–21), of the insensitivity to the needs of others which often accompanies wealth (Luke 16:19–31), and of "the delight in riches" which chokes out the Gospel (Mark 4:19). Because the passion for wealth tends to crowd out all other considerations, he urged his disciples to lay up "treasures in heaven" rather than "treasures on earth" (Matthew 6:19–21). His most extreme statement was the warning that "it is easier for a camel to go through the eye of a needle than for a rich man to enter the kingdom of God" (Matthew 19:24).

The early church had a sense of community, of belonging together and of being responsible for each other, which expressed itself in a variety of ways. One striking incident was the sharing of wealth by the members of the congregation in Jerusalem (Acts 2:44–45, 4:32). While this way of life apparently did not last long and was not adopted by the church in other places, it did express in a profound way a sense of responsibility for the entire community of faith. Other expressions of that same sense of community are seen in the Epistles in frequent references to stewardship, in the directions for ministering to the poor, and in the collection of gifts for that purpose.

We can summarize the biblical teachings on property by making four generalizations. First, people have a right to own private property. Second, people are responsible to God and to one another for the manner in which they acquire property and the manner in which they use it. Third, the acquiring and retaining of more property than one actually needs entails great spiritual danger. Fourth, people who have property are responsible for helping people who do not.

A CHRISTIAN PERSPECTIVE ON WORK

Although nature provides basic materials, people must gather them and transform them into the things which are necessary for people to live and to live well. The Bible interprets this reality in terms of the plan of God for the created order, and for the place of humankind within that order. The older creation narrative says that "the Lord God took the man and put him in the garden of Eden to till it and keep it" (Genesis 2:15). While work is sometimes burdensome because of human sin (Genesis 3), it is never regarded as an option. Furthermore, there is a connection between work and reward. When Jesus commented to his disciples that "the laborer deserves his wages" (Luke 10:7), he was quoting a popular proverb. In stressing the responsibilities of his disciples he observed that "he who reaps receives wages" (John 4:36). In dealing with a problem that had arisen in the church at Thessalonica, Paul suggested, "If any one will not work, let him not eat" (2 Thessalonians 3:10). Even the belief that the eschaton was imminent was no justification for ceasing one's labor.

We tend to identify ourselves in terms of our work. Asked what we *do*, we usually respond with the words, "I *am* a...." We know biblical characters in the same way: We know Jesus as a carpenter, Peter as a fisherman, Matthew as a tax collector, Paul as a tent maker, Lydia as a seller of purple. We even know some characters only by their work: a shepherd, a Roman centurion, a priest, a jailer. While the Scripture is concerned about matters other than occupation, it reflects this idea that one *is* what one *does*. Many of our surnames are derived from the occupations of our ancestors: Baker, Smith, Joiner, Farmer, and so on. This close identity between doing and being is involved in the recognition that work is not merely something that one does to earn a living; it is also something that one does to develop as a full human being.

The word *career* is sometimes used to refer to one's life work, the means by which one earns a living. It comes directly from a French word which means "a road or a racing course," and indirectly from a Latin word which means "a wagon." The implication is that a career is the route which one's life takes, or the vehicle by which one carries oneself through life. An older term, now used less frequently but perhaps more appropriate from a Christian perspective, is *vocation* or *calling*. This term implies that what one does with one's life is a response to the *calling* of God. The Bible usually employs this term to refer to the calling of God into the life of faith. Paul, for example, in rebuking the Corinthian Christians for certain failures on their part, reminded them of their *call* (1 Corinthians 1:26). Because of the centrality of one's daily work in one's life, Christian tradition came to affirm that what one does to earn a living is a part of one's response to God. For some Christians this has come to mean that they choose their careers on the basis of what they believe God leads them to do. For others it has come to mean that their career is one way in which they serve God. "According to the Protestant doctrine of vocation," says George Thomas, "the dominant motive of a Christian in any vocation is to serve God by serving one's neighbors in love" (*Christian Ethics and Moral Philosophy*, p. 319).

PERSONAL ISSUES IN AN IMPERSONAL ECONOMIC ORDER

The person who wishes to live as a Christian within our economic system faces a wide variety of problems. The first has to do with a concept that is at the heart of capitalism. We have said that capitalism assumes that the profit motive is the most effective incentive for economic activity. This means that the entire system operates on the assumption that each of us is out to meet our own needs, that we do what we think will be most profitable for us, and that ultimately we are all responsible for ourselves. We operate businesses to make money, not to serve the needs of other people. While that does not mean unbridled competition, and while it does not mean that we have no responsibilities beyond our own needs and desires, it does mean that the basic appeal is to our acquisitive nature. Christians feel a tension between that appeal on the one hand and on the other the command of Christ to love our neighbor as ourselves. Taught by our faith that self-centeredness is the essence of sin, we live in a society which requires us to seek our own good first, not that of our neighbors.

A second problem is that of maintaining a sense of *vocation*. Certain occupations can easily be seen as ways of serving God because they offer direct and immediate benefit to other people—service careers such as medicine, teaching, and social work. Others are less direct and immediate, but might ultimately be construed in the same way—careers such as plumbing, road building, abstract research, and statistical analysis. Still others are even more remote: typesetting, archaeological research, and work on an assembly line. All of this suggests that some people may have a sense of vocation, a sense that in their work they are responding to God, but that many, perhaps most, people cannot see any real connection between their faith and the way they earn their living.

A third problem is the depersonalizing character of the work that large numbers of people are required to do in an industrialized society. The techniques of mass production which require people to do routine work that demands little or no skill and even less thought does not permit them to function as persons. They do not permit an individual to be creative or to function as a whole person. To use an old term, people are regarded as "hands." Even the most benevolent manufacturer who provides the best of working conditions and offers the greatest of financial benefits cannot eliminate the deadening effect of such routine labor. Yet a central consideration in Christian faith is the worth of the individual, a consideration that requires that each one be dealt with as a whole person and not as a tool or an object.

A fourth problem lies in the choice and pursuit of a career. This idea seems consistent with the Christian understanding of human beings as having free will and as therefore being capable of making choices. It is also consistent with our image of our country as a land where people may choose to be and do what they like. The fact of the matter, however, is that our opportunities are restricted. Young people with limited educational opportunities do not have a wide range of choice. People who live in certain areas of the country are limited. People making their decisions at a time when few jobs are available are limited. People making their decisions under the constraints of family responsibilities are limited. They are limited by the expectations of family and friends and by public judgments about what careers are prestigious or challenging. They are limited by stereotypes and role expectations. They are limited by the personal drive for security and by the social pressure toward success. One does not make career choices in the abstract but within a context that significantly narrows the options.

A fifth problem is the fact that many people find themselves trapped in work that they find personally deadening. That may be the result of having made ill-advised decisions at an earlier date, of having failed to prepare for a challenging career, or of having prepared for a career in which there was no real personal interest. It may be the result of changes in the work or changes in the person. It may be the frustration of not being able to accomplish what one had set out to accomplish or the sense of having reached a dead end so far as promotion or achievement is concerned. It may be the necessity of working with people with whom one is incompatible or on a job that offends one's sensibilities or clashes with one's ideals or values. For any one of a dozen reasons, then, many people have no sense of satisfaction in their work. Yet they cannot get out of the situation. They are not qualified for any other type of work. If they were to move into another situation, they would have to start at the bottom again. Because of personal or family responsibilities they cannot surrender the financial security which they have in their present work. In such a situation one has difficulty appreciating the virtues of free choice.

SOCIAL ISSUES IN AN IMPERSONAL ECONOMIC ORDER

Citizens of capitalist countries enjoy the highest living standards in the world. This is particularly true of the United States. In terms of the basics of housing, food, and clothing, and in terms of those "extras" which enhance the quality of life, as compared with people in noncapitalist countries, Americans are rich. We must not allow this comparative success, however, to blind us to the serious moral problems with which we must deal within the economic structures of our society.

The first and most obvious problem is the unfair distribution of wealth. "Unfair," of course, does not simply mean that wealth is unequally distributed. It could hardly be called unfair to reward an industrious worker more highly than a lazy one. It is appropriate to reward preparation, diligence, efficiency, and faithfulness. It is appropriate to value work that contributes significantly to the well-being of society as a whole more highly than work that makes little or no contribution. People are not equal in ability, they are not equal in preparation, they do not make

equal effort, and they do not value the same things equally. A fair distribution of wealth must take into account these various personal inequalities. Unfortunately, however, in our system people are rarely paid on the
basis of what they deserve. Many are paid on the basis of contracts that
allow for no variation. Many are paid on the basis of the number of
available workers, or of competition for the job. Many are paid on the basis
of custom. The wages of some depend upon whether they are male or
female, or upon whether they are black or white, or how old they are.
Many factors, in other words, other than job performance are involved in
the determination of pay.

The problem of unfair distribution, however, is far more complex
than simply a matter of wages. Our system permits the accumulation of
great wealth by a relatively small number of individuals and corporations. Since, in our system, wealth means power, wealthy persons often
gain control over the lives of many other people. A relatively small
number of people, for example, control the sources of energy for our
nation. A relatively small number control the media of communication.
The same is true of providing public transportation, producing automobiles, marketing food, and providing arms for the nation. The decision
to close a manufacturing plant that provides employment for a thousand
people, or the decision to move that manufacturing operation to another
community, or the decision to introduce new methods of manufacturing
that call for different skills, is made by executives whose job it is to
increase the profits of the corporation. Whether they are the most benevolent of persons or the most insensitive of persons, the system requires
them to act in the interest of the industry no matter how the lives of the
workers are affected.

Another aspect of this unjust distribution of wealth is the poverty
of a large segment of our population. Poverty, of course, is a relative
term and is difficult to define. Using the standards set by our own
government, however, we are dismayed by the enormity of our problem.
According to the U. S. Bureau of Census, in 1984 some 33 million families
in this country, representing approximately 14 percent of the total, lived
below the poverty line. More than 8 million people, representing nearly
7 percent of the labor force, were unemployed. This means that vast
numbers of persons are ill fed, ill housed, and ill clothed. Vast numbers
of others live at or just above the poverty level. Our concern here is not
to discuss the causes of these high rates, but to point out the fact that in
spite of the great wealth of our nation, we have not learned how to deal
adequately with the problem of poverty.

A second and related moral issue is the contrast between our affluence as a nation and the poverty of much of the rest of the world. By the
most conservative estimates, 400 million people in the world do not get

the daily food necessary for a normal healthy life. Consequently, not only are they constantly hungry, but they also suffer from diseases and infections which they would be able to resist if they were on a better diet. Children are the most seriously affected, and every year more than 15 million children under the age of five die from malnutrition. The problem, however, is not that the world cannot produce enough food for its people. While an unchecked growth in the world's population may bring us to that point, we have not reached it yet. The problem is one of distribution. Our methods of consumption in this country are unbelievably wasteful. When we feed grain to animals and then convert it into meat, milk, and eggs, we waste up to 95 percent of its food value. "If we stopped feeding animals on grains, soybeans and fishmeal," says Peter Singer, "the amount of food saved would—if distributed to those who need it—be more than enough to end hunger throughout the world" (John Arthur, editor, *Morality and Moral Controversies*, p. 272).

We have not been totally indifferent to this problem. With varying degrees of success, some groups have made some effort to deal with emergency situations. Some affluent nations have made some effort to assist developing nations. Many of those efforts have been a part of an ideological struggle and have thus been seen as a form of imperialism. Yet no well-to-do nation of the world has made a major effort to deal with the problem. No effort has been free of problems of administration, and no approach has been found that could be considered the "correct" answer to any nation's economic problems.

The issue here is not whether affluence in itself is immoral, nor even whether waste in itself is immoral. Rather it is the fact that one part of the world wastes what another part of the world desperately needs. Christians generally acknowledge their responsibility for helping people who are in need. They are moved by Jesus' words in the parable of the last judgment, "As you did it to one of the least of these my brethren, you did it to me" (Matthew 25: 40). What they have not generally acknowledged is the necessity of extending this kind of ministry beyond the range of personal relationships. It is difficult to avoid the conclusion, however, that the most effective way of feeding the poor, particularly those vast numbers of poor in distant places in the world, requires an alteration of our patterns of consumption and a devising of some techniques of assisting the nations of the world in meeting the basic needs of their own people.

Once we acknowledge our responsibility to help, our task then becomes one of finding the most appropriate ways of achieving that goal. Those ways may include helping the poor nations of the world raise the living standards of their people. They may involve the encouragement of land reform measures in those nations, the sharing of technology, assistance in the improvement of education, and help in the liberation of women from a purely childbearing role. All such assistance will have to be recognized as just that—assistance to a people dealing with their problems, and not the imposition of an alien culture upon those people.

A third moral issue is the wanton exploitation of our natural resources. We have had a long history of such exploitation. For decades our forests were stripped from the land without concern for replacement and without attention to problems of flooding and of soil erosion. Minerals were extracted from the earth without considering the impact of the mining methods upon the surrounding area. Oil was produced and used as if the supply were inexhaustible. Even farmland was used in ways that in a few seasons made it worthless. Only recently have we begun to give attention to conservation and renewal, and then only because we have become aware that we were about to deplete those resources.

Even so, neither self-interest nor governmental regulation has resolved the problem. By continued exploitation we are still destroying our three basic natural resources: the water, the atmosphere, and the land. We empty vast amounts of urban sewage and industrial waste into our rivers, so that they are rapidly becoming open sewers. Many are now so polluted that fish taken from them cannot be eaten and food grown near them cannot be used. The rivers, in turn, pollute the lakes into which they empty and ultimately the ocean which is their final destination.

> Millions of tons of pollutants consisting of hundreds of different substances annually reach the seas. Sewage, industrial wastes, oil spills, garbage refuse, and chemical runoff from the land threaten the oxygen-producing plants and animals of the sea, without which man cannot survive. (Henlee H. Barnette, *The Church and the Ecological Crisis*, p. 16)

The atmosphere has become a receptacle for other kinds of waste—pollutants from our homes and factories and automobiles. To breathe the air in almost any large city in the land is as hard on one's lungs as smoking a pack and a half of cigarettes. A permanent smog which blots out the sun hangs over many areas affecting human and plant life. Aerosol sprays that destroy the ozone layer of the atmosphere are sold indiscriminately and used by millions for nonessential purposes. The land is poisoned by pesticides and herbicides which are considered necessary in agricultural production, and all birds, animals, marine life, and ultimately human beings are endangered.

But why is this exploitation of natural resources considered a problem within the economic order? Is it not a matter of science and technology rather than one of economics? Much of the research and experiment that has been conducted has been financed by private industry, and private industry has used the knowledge gained to produce materials and goods for general consumption. The ultimate goal of industry is to earn a profit, and the attainment of that goal requires the production of the goods at the lowest possible cost. Cleaner ways of producing energy are more costly than their alternatives. Efficient disposal of waste is also more costly. The production of nonessential goods requires equally as much energy and produces equally as much waste as does the production of essential goods. With profit as the motive, however, we expect business and industry to do what is necessary to earn that profit.

That we must take steps to deal with this problem is self-evident. Is the problem, however, a *moral* one? What in the Christian faith has a bearing on the issue? Several theological convictions seem relevant:

1. Nature has an intrinsic value. In biblical terms, the entire natural order is good because God created it. "And God saw everything that he had made," said the Yahwist, "and behold, it was very good" (Genesis 1:31). Nature itself praises its creator (Psalms 19, 89, etc.), nature reflects the glory of its creator (Psalm 8), and nature will take part in the final fulfillment of God's purposes (Romans 8:19ff).

2. Human beings are a part of the natural order. In biblical terms, the creation of humankind was a part of a total creative process (Genesis 1 and 2). "You are dust, and to dust you shall return," said God to the offending Adam (Genesis 3:19). As a part of that order, humanity is interdependent with the rest of it.

3. Human beings have a responsibility for the natural order. That responsibility is not that of owner but of trustee. In the older account of creation God placed humankind in the Garden of Eden with the command "to till it and to keep it" (Genesis 2:15). In the later account of creation God is said to have given humankind "dominion" over the rest of creation (Genesis 1:14).

Within the framework of these convictions, humankind is seen to be unique in the natural order. While we are a part of that order, we occupy a unique place within it. Gustafson (Ethics from a Theocentric Perspective) may be right in his insistence that we not assume that the world was created for our benefit. Yet we cannot ignore the biblical affirmation of the uniqueness of that creature which alone is said to be "in the image of God." We cannot avoid the implication that as the crown of creation humankind has a unique and distinctive place of responsibility. That responsibility permits (even requires) the use of the natural order ("to till it and keep it," to "have dominion" over it), but not its exploitation and destruction.

At one time in history it may have been possible to think of this responsibility for the earth in individual terms. In an age of industrialization and urbanization, however, that is impossible. We do not function merely as individuals; we function as a human society. Individual efforts to conserve energy or to reduce the use of certain chemicals or to discourage the production of nonessential goods may have some impact, but only a little. The individual's greatest contribution is in helping make other people aware of the problems. The most effective approach is through group activity, and the larger the group the more powerful it may be.

When the group power is great enough, industry and/or government may be compelled to take steps.

What steps need to be taken to deal with these problems? Ian Barbour (*Earth Might Be Fair*, pp. 11–12), suggests four. First, he says that we need legislation to set up enforceable standards for auto emissions, for air and water effluents, for pesticides and detergents, for radiation and thermal pollution, for solid waste disposal, and the like. Second, he says that we need to exercise restraint in consumption. Third, we must redirect technology so as to give priority to the abolition of hunger, poverty, and pollution at home and abroad. And fourth, because the resources of the earth are finite and limited, we must take steps to limit the growth of the world's population.

In *The Church and the Ecological Crisis* (pp. 53–60), Henlee Barnette suggests six "strategies for survival." First, he recommends the practice of "personal ecotactics." By this he means such things as avoiding the purchase of nonbiodegradable goods, using car pools and other methods of cutting back on auto pollution, engaging in a personal antilitter campaign, and so on. Second, he encourages the recycling of materials. Third, citing the automobile as a major source of pollution, he calls for the development of adequate rapid mass transportation systems. Fourth, he recommends the exercise of political pressure to secure adequate legislation and effective law enforcement. Fifth, he calls for a massive educational campaign. And sixth, without endorsing any particular approach, he says that we must effectively limit population growth.

A fourth moral issue is the relationship between capital and labor in establishing the conditions under which work is to be done. Does an employer, whether an individual or a corporation, have the exclusive right to set wages and benefits and working conditions? Is an employer free to exercise complete control over the business? Or do the employees have the right to bargain with the employer? If the employees have the right to bargain, must it be done individually or can it be done collectively? If it is done individually, then the employer has a distinct advantage because the loss of one worker is unlikely to cripple an operation. A worker who has no job, however, may have difficulty finding other employment. If it is done in concert with other employees, that is, through a union, then the workers have an advantage because they can in fact cripple an entire operation.

Although the first labor unions in the United States appeared about the time of the Revolutionary War, the major development of national unions came only with the industrialization that followed the Civil War. The movement has always been a controversial one. In the year that Congress made Labor Day a legal holiday, 1894, President Cleveland called out federal troops to keep order during the Pullman strike in

Chicago! Today the unions are strong in certain sections of the country and weak in others, strong in certain industries and virtually nonexistent in others. At present, nearly 20 percent of all workers in this country are members of labor unions. Transportation workers and public utilities employees are the most highly organized, with more than 38 percent of such workers being members of unions.

Beyond the general requirements of love and consideration for all persons, are there religious considerations which might have a bearing on the question of the relationship between capital and labor? The ideal of respect for the rights of others is relevant. We have affirmed that individuals have the right to private property, and it seems appropriate to extend that concept. Property held by corporations, therefore, merits the same respect as property held by individuals. By the same token the labor of the worker is a valuable asset, property if you will, which merits the same respect. Negotiations between management and labor should be conducted in such a manner as to safeguard those rights.

The matter of justice, or *fairness*, is also pertinent. We have observed that power is concentrated in the hands of management when negotiations are on an individual basis. When management negotiates with representatives of a larger group of employees, however, both sides have significant power. Of course power can be abused by either group. It does seem more fair, however, for each side to negotiate from strength than for one side to be strong and the other weak.

Related to this consideration is the conviction that all persons should be free to make significant choices. No one ought to be at the mercy of another, no one should be victimized by another. That is to say, each person should have a voice in determining what happens to him or her. It is not quite adequate to say that one is never forced to accept or to keep a job. There really is no choice if the options are either having this job or not having one at all. Neither is there any choice if the job is available only on unacceptable terms. Real freedom is the ability to be involved in decisions affecting what one does and how one does it.

Also related to this idea of fairness is the concept of honesty. Christians have long been taught that they should give "an honest day's labor for an honest day's pay." The reverse is also true: they should be given an honest day's pay for an honest day's labor. Granted that the determination of what is "an honest day's labor" and what is "an honest day's pay" is difficult. How intensely can one be expected to work, for example, on an assembly line or in an office? How much time does one need for a coffee break or for lunch or for going to the rest room? What determines the value of the work which an individual does? The intensity of the work? The skill required? The number of people in the labor pool? The market value of the finished product? As difficult as these questions are, the generalization holds true. The worker and the employer have mutual responsibilities. If there is disagreement as to what those responsibilities are, that disagreement should be dealt with on the basis of mutual respect and concern. Andrew Cecil says:

> The basic questions in labor relations are: Are the persons in industrial organizations, from top to bottom, directed in their economic motivations by respect for personal dignity and the eternal worth of every human being? Do the persons engaged in economic institutions meet the needs of others in a spirit of compassion? (*The Third Way*, p. 73)

We have noted that people have a strong tendency to identify themselves in terms of what they do. We have noted also that a Christian understanding of the concept of vocation or calling incorporates one's work in the idea that one's life is to be an expression of one's faith. Today, however, employees of large enterprises, particularly those employees whose work is of a routine nature, understandably have some difficulty in thinking of their work in this way. The difference, however, may not be so much the nature of the work they are doing as their lack of a sense of ownership. In earlier days, the person who took raw materials and from them made a chair could take pride in the skill and craftsmanship that went into it, and no matter who purchased it the worker could say, "That is one of *my* chairs." Can modern assembly line workers who place one part on each of hundreds of chairs each day, think in the same way? They may be able to do so if they are involved in some way in the decision-making processes, if they have a sense of security with the company for which they are working, and if there are ways in which their workmanship is recognized. While this approach is good business, it is more than that; it is the recognition of employees as persons who express themselves in their work. "One of the responsibilities of labor and management," says Cecil, "is to protect the uniqueness of the special endowment of the individuality of each worker" (p. 84).

IDEALS AND ECONOMICS

When Jesus said, "You shall love your neighbor as yourself," he did not command us to love ourselves. Rather he recognized the depths of our self-love and proposed it as the standard by which we are to measure our love for our neighbor. He understood that we naturally seek our own good, and he did not say that we should not do so. He did say that we should seek our neighbor's good, and he gave us some dramatic examples of how we can do that through our use of our material possessions. He did so in a nation in which there was competition for power and possessions, in which there was a wide difference between the haves and the have-nots, in which there were widows and orphans, in which there were social outcasts, in which there was corruption in business and government, in which some people invested wisely and some foolishly, in which many people had misplaced values. He said it in a world in which nations went to war against each other, in which the powerful nations exploited the weak ones, in which natural disasters wrought death and destruction. His teachings, therefore, were not intended for people living in a perfect society. They were intended for people living in a world beset by human weakness and human sinfulness—a world like the one in which we live. They were intended for people who are by nature grasping, self-centered, indifferent, hostile, jealous, afraid, and materialistic. In that context Jesus said, let the way you seek your own good be the standard by which you seek the good of other people.

Two facts determine the parameters within which we function in the economic realm. First, we live in a capitalistic society. We find certain aspects of the system of capitalism to be quite in harmony with our Christian faith, and certain aspects to be at odds with it. It is a cohesive system, however, and we must live with all parts of it. All of our getting and our spending will be done within that context. Second, we live in a world that is in upheaval, a world in which rival economic systems clash as peoples who are desperately poor struggle for the physical necessities for survival. While we feel a strong impulse to respond to the needs of the world, we do not know what is the best thing to do and we are not sure how much we are willing to sacrifice to do it.

We have said that the basic element in the Christian understanding of our relationship to the material world is that of stewardship. If we regard God as the owner of all things, and ourselves as entrusted with the management of certain goods, we may be guided by several considerations. First, the economic factor is elemental in human existence. Perhaps the founding fathers of modern communism overstated their case when they said that economic forces determine all our attitudes and shape all our social institutions. The way things actually operate in our world, however, demonstrates that the economic factor, if not determinative, is at least highly influential. On the one hand, we find it impossible to operate without money, we find it impossible to have money without working for it, and we demonstrate what we think is important by the way we spend our money. On the other hand, forces quite beyond our control set rather precise limits on what we can earn and how we can earn it.

Second, we are interested in people, not systems. What Jesus said about the Sabbath can be applied to any economic system: the system was made for people, and not people for the system. We are not therefore primarily interested in defending capitalism. We are interested in making the system within which we live and work operate effectively to meet the needs of people. We are not primarily interested in attacking any other system; we are interested in holding up all systems to the test of how well they serve the people who live within them.

Third, economic activity is a major area in which we can implement Christian love. That statement is quite general, of course. It does not tell us how to earn our money or how to spend it. It does not tell us how to take care of the poor in our own country or anywhere else in the world. It does not tell us how to deal with the threat of environmental pollution or industrial disputes. It does not guarantee success in any of our efforts to meet human need. It does say that as disciples of Christ we must be actively concerned about the distress of the world around us.

Finally, we must deal with specific issues. This statement, of course, is an extension of the third. Many of us are like Stephen Leacock's character who "flung himself upon his horse and rode madly off in all directions." Troubled about many things, we are effective in dealing with none of them. We implement Christian love most effectively by choosing specific problems and doing everything we can to deal with them. That choice may be dictated by a crisis: a natural disaster in some distant land or an industrial dispute in our own city. It may be the result of a gradually developing awareness of the needs of the Third World nations or of the powerless and the impoverished in our own society. It may be the result of the study of such current problems as environmental pollution or occupational health hazards. In any event, we do well to choose our targets and concentrate on them rather than fragmenting our efforts.

No one of us can do everything, but all of us can do something. No system works properly, and even the best one can be ruined by the activities of self-centered, dishonest, uncaring people. Our system can be made to work better to the extent that we heed the command, "You shall love your neighbor as yourself."

BIBLIOGRAPHY

ABELSON, RAZIEL, and MARIE-LOUISE FRIQUEGNON, *Ethics for Modern Life*. New York: St. Martin's Press, 1982.

ARTHUR, JOHN, editor, *Morality and Moral Controversies*, second edition. New York: Prentice Hall, 1986

ASHLEY, PAUL P., *Oh Promise Me But Put It in Writing*. New York: McGraw-Hill, 1978.

ATKINSON, DAVID, *Homosexuals in the Christian Fellowship*. Grand Rapids: Eerdmans, 1979.

BACH, JULIE S., editor, *Biomedical Ethics*. St. Louis: Greenhaven, 1987.

BAHR, HOWARD M., BRUCE A. CHADWICK, and JOSEPH S. STAUSS, *American Ethnicity*. Lexington, Massachusetts: D. C. Heath, 1979.

BARBOUR, IAN G., *Earth Might Be Fair*. Englewood Cliffs: Prentice Hall, 1972.

BARNETTE, HENLEE H., *Introduction to Communism*. Grand Rapids: Baker, 1964.

BARNETTE, HENLEE H., *The Church and the Ecological Crisis*. Grand Rapids: Eerdmans, 1972.

BARRY, VINCENT, *Moral Aspects of Health Care*. Belmont, California: Wadsworth, 1982.

BATCHELOR, EDWARD, JR., editor, *Abortion: The Moral Issues*. New York: Pilgrim Press, 1982.

BATCHELOR, EDWARD, JR., *Homosexuality and Ethics*. New York: Pilgrim Press, 1980.

BAYLES, MICHAEL D., editor, *Reproductive Ethics*. Englewood Cliffs: Prentice Hall, 1984.

BEAUCHAMP, TOM L., and JAMES F. CHILDRESS, *Principles of Biomedical Ethics*. New York: Oxford, 1979.

BENNE, ROBERT, *The Ethic of Democratic Capitalism*. Philadelphia: Fortress, 1981.

BENNETT, JOHN C., *Christians and the State*. New York: Scribner's, 1958.

BONEPARTH, ELLEN, editor, *Women, Power and Policy*. New York: Pergamon, 1982.

BORNKAMM, GUNTHER, *Jesus of Nazareth*. New York: Harper and Row, 1960.

BROWN, ROBERT MCAFEE, *Making Peace in the Global Village*. Philadelphia: Westminster, 1981.

BROWN, ROBERT MCAFEE, *Religion and Violence*, second edition. Philadelphia: Westminster, 1987.

BRUNNER, EMIL, *The Divine Imperative*. Philadelphia: Westminster, 1947.

CARY, EVE, and KATHLEEN WILLERT PERATIS, *Woman and the Law*. Skokie, Illinois: National Textbook Company, 1977.

CECIL, ANDREW R., *The Third Way*. Dallas: The University of Texas at Dallas, 1980.

CRITES, LAURA L., and WINIFRED L. HEPPERLE, *Women, the Courts, and Equality*. Newbury Park, California: Sage, 1987.

CULLMANN, OSCAR, *The State in the New Testament*. New York: Scribner's, 1956.

CUTLER, DONALD R., editor, *Updating Life and Death*. Boston: Beacon, 1969.

DAILEY, ROBERT H., *Introduction to Moral Theology*. New York: Bruce, 1971.

DECKARD, BARBARA SINCLAIR, *The Women's Movement*, third edition. New York, 1975.

Defining Death: A Report on the Medical, Legal, and Ethical Issues in Determination of Death. Washington: United States Government Printing Office, 1981.

DEWOLF, L. HAROLD, *Crime and Justice in America*. New York: Harper and Row, 1971.

FLETCHER, JOSEPH, *Morals and Medicine*. Boston: Beacon, 1960.

FLETCHER, JOSEPH, *Situation Ethics*. Philadelphia: Westminster, 1966.

FREEMAN, JO, *The Politics of Women's Liberation*. New York: McKay, 1975.

FRIEDAN, BETTY, *The Feminine Mystique*. New York: Dell, 1963.

FROMER, MARGOT JOAN, *Ethical Issues in Sexuality and Reproduction*. St. Louis: C. V. Mosby, 1983.

GARDNER, E. CLINTON, *Biblical Faith and Social Ethics*. New York: Harper and Row, 1960.

GUSTAFSON, JAMES M., *Ethics from a Theocentric Perspective*, Volume One: Theology and Ethics. Chicago: University of Chicago Press, 1981.

GUSTAFSON, JAMES M., *Ethics from a Theocentric Perspective*, Volume Two: Ethics and Theology. Chicago: University of Chicago Press, 1984.

HARING, BERNARD, *Toward a Christian Moral Theology*. Notre Dame: University of Notre Dame Press, 1966.

HARRON, FRANK M., editor, *Biomedical-Ethical* Issues. Binghamton: Vaill-Ballou Press, 1983.

HASELDEN, KYLE, *The Racial Problem in Christian Perspective*. New York: Harper, 1959.

HEALEY, EDWIN F., *Moral Guidance*. Chicago: Loyola, 1943.

HETTLINGER, RICHARD F., *Living with Sex*. New York: Seabury, 1966.

HEWLETT, SYLVIA ANN, *A Lesser Life*. New York: Morrow, 1986.

HIDALGO, HILDA, TRAVIS PETERSON, and NATALIE JANE WOODMAN, editors, *Lesbian and Gay Issues*. Silver Spring, Maryland: National Association of Social Workers, 1985.

HOLLIS, HARRY N., JR. et al., *Christian Freedom for WOMEN* and Other Human Beings*. Nashville: Broadman, 1975.

HOSPERS, JOHN, *Human Conduct*. New York: Harcourt Brace Jovanovich, 1972.

HUNT, MORTON, *Gay*. New York: Pocket Books, 1977.

JONES, H. KIMBALL, *Toward a Christian Understanding of the Homosexual*. New York: Association, 1966.

KAUFMAN, GORDON D., *Theology for a Nuclear Age*. Philadelphia: Westminster, 1985.

KING, MARTIN LUTHER, JR., *Letter from Birmingham Jail*. Philadelphia: American Friends Service Committee, n.d.

KURTZ, PAUL, *In Defense of Secular Humanism*. Buffalo: Prometheus Books, 1983.

LEHMANN, PAUL, *Ethics in a Christian Context*. New York: Harper and Row, 1963.

LEONE, BRUNO, and M. TERESA ONEILL, editors, *Male/Female Roles*. St. Paul: Greenhaven, 1983.

LESTER, ANDREW D., *Sex is More than a Word*. Nashville: Broadman, 1973.

LEVINE, MARTIN P., editor, *Gay Men*. New York: Harper & Row, 1979.

LICATA, SALVATORE, and ROBERT P. PETERSEN, *Historical Perspectives on Homosexuality*. New York: Hayworth, 1981.

LOESCH, JUDI, "Unmarried Couples Shouldn't Live Together." *U. S. Catholic*, July, 1985, pp. 16–17.

LONG, EDWARD LEROY, JR. *War and Conscience in America*. Philadelphia: Westminster, 1968.

MCCORMICK, RICHARD A., "Abortion." *America*, June 19, 1965, p. 898.

MCLEMORE, S. DALE, *Racial and Ethnic Relations in America*. Boston: Allyn and Bacon, 1980.

MALLOY, EDWARD A., *Homosexuality and the Christian Way of Life*. Washington: University Press of America, 1981.

MARDEN, CHARLES F., and GLADYS MEYER, *Minorities in American Society*, fifth edition. New York: D. Van Nostrand, 1978.

MARMOR, JUDD, *Homosexual Behavior*. New York: Basic Books, 1980.

MARX, KARL, *Capital*. New York: Modern Library, 1936.

MITCHELSON, MARVIN, *Living Together*. New York: Simon and Schuster, 1980.

National Conference of Catholic Bishops, *Economic Justice for All*. Washington: National Conference of Catholic Bishops, 1986.

NELSON, JAMES B., *Human Medicine*. Minneapolis: Augsburg, 1973.

NYE, JOSEPH S., JR., *Nuclear Ethics*. New York: The Free Press, 1986.

O'CONNELL, TIMOTHY E., *Principles for a Catholic Morality*. New York: Seabury, 1978.

O'NEILL, NENA and GEORGE, *Open Marriage*, New York: Avon, 1972.

PAGE, ALLEN F., *Life After Death: What the Bible Says*. Nashville: Abingdon, 1987.

PATTERSON, CHARLES M., *Moral Standards*. New York: Ronald, 1949.

PETERSON, GEOFFREY, *Conscience and Caring*. Philadelphia: Fortress, 1982.

PIERCE, RUTH A., *Single and Pregnant*. Boston: Beacon, 1970.

RAMSEY, PAUL, *Basic Christian Ethics*. New York: Scribner's, 1950.

RAMSEY, PAUL, *Fabricated Man*. New Haven: Yale University Press, 1970.

RAMSEY, PAUL, *War and the Christian Conscience*. Durham, N. C.: Duke University Press, 1961.

RAND, AYN, *Capitalism: The Unknown Ideal*. New York: Penguin, 1967.

RAND, AYN, *For the New Intellectual*. New York: Random, 1961.

RAND, AYN, *The Virtue of Selfishness*. New York: American Library, 1964.

REGAN, TOM, editor, *Matters of Life and Death*. Philadelphia: Temple University Press, 1980.

ROWE, DOROTHY, *Living with the Bomb*. London: Routledge and Kegan Paul, 1985.

SCANZONI, LETHA, and VIRGINIA RAMEY MOLLENKOTT, *Is the Homosexual My Neighbor?* New York: Harper, 1978.

SCHELL, JONATHAN, *The Fate of the Earth*. New York: Knopf, 1982.

SHANNON, THOMAS A., editor, *Bioethics*, revised edition. Ramsey, New Jersey: Paulist, 1981.

SIMMONS, PAUL D., *Birth and Death: Bioethical Decision-Making*. Philadelphia: Westminster, 1983.

SIMPSON, GEORGE E., and J. MILTON YINGER, *Racial and Cultural Minorities*, fifth edition. New York: Plenum, 1985.

SKINNER, B. F., *About Behaviorism*. New York: Knopf, 1974.

SKINNER, B. F., *Beyond Freedom and Dignity*. New York: Knopf, 1971.

SMEDES, LEWIS B., *Mere Morality*. Grand Rapids: Eerdmans, 1983.

SMITH, HARMON L., *Ethics and the New Medicine*. Nashville: Abingdon, 1971.

SMITH, RACHEL R., "Abortion, Right and Wrong," *Newsweek*, March 15, 1985.

STORER, MORRIS B., editor, *Humanistic Ethics*. New York: Prometheus Books, 1980.

SUZUMSKI, BONNIE, editor, *Abortion*. St. Paul: Greenhaven, 1986.

SWITZER, DAVID K. and SHIRLEY, *The Parents of the Homosexual*. Philadelphia: Westminster, 1980.

THIELICKE, HELMUT, *The Ethics of Sex*. New York: Harper and Row, 1964.

THOMAS, GEORGE F., *Christian Ethics and Moral Philosophy*. New York: Scribner's, 1955.

THURMAN, HOWARD, *The Luminous Darkness*. New York: Harper and Row, 1965.

TITUS, HAROLD H. and MORRIS KEETON, *Ethics for Today*, fifth edition. New York: Van Nostrand, 1973.

TRUEBLOOD, D. ELTON, *Foundations for Reconstruction*. New York: Harper, 1946.

TWISS, HAROLD L., editor, *Homosexuality and the Christian Faith*. Valley Forge: Judson, 1978.

VAN DEN HAAG, ERNEST, "In Defense of Capital Punishment," in Abelson, Raziel and Marie-Louise Friquegnon, *Ethics for Modern Life*. New York: St. Martin's Press, 1982.

VANDER ZANDEN, JAMES W., *American Minority Relations*, fourth edition. New York: Knopf, 1983.

VARGA, ANDREW C., *The Main Issues in Bioethics*. New York: Paulist, 1984.

WALLACE, JIM, editor, *Peace Makers*. New York: Harper and Row, 1983.

WALLACE, RUTH A., *Gender in America*. Englewood Cliffs: Prentice Hall, 1985.

WELLMAN, CARL, *Morals and Ethics*, second edition. Englewood Cliffs: Prentice Hall, 1988.

WHITE, JAMES E., *Contemporary Moral Problems*. St. Paul; West, 1985.

WHITE, R. E. O., *Biblical Ethics*. Atlanta: John Knox, 1979.

INDEX